McCALL'S
BIG BOOK
of
BAZAAR CRAFTS

McCALL'S BIG BOOK *of* BAZAAR CRAFTS

The Editors of
McCall's Needlework and Crafts Magazine

Chilton Book Company • Radnor, Pennsylvania

Manufactured in the United States of America

Library of Congress Cataloging in Publication Data
Main entry under title:
McCall's big book of bazaar crafts.
    Includes index.
    1. Handicraft. 2. Needlework. 3. Bazaars,
Charitable. I. McCall's needlework & crafts
magazine.
TT157.M35 1984   745.5   83-45386
ISBN 0-8019-7440-2 (pbk.)

1 2 3 4 5 6 7 8 9 0   3 2 1 0 9 8 7 6 5 4

PREFACE

All of us at one time or another have helped put on a bazaar or fair to raise money for a local project, such as a community center. This kind of activity brings people together with a unity of purpose, widens their acquaintances, and all have the pleasure of feeling that they are doing something worthwhile.

Here we give the ''how-to's'' of putting on a bazaar or fair— large or small. Not all of the information will apply to the event you are planning, but please read the entire section to glean from it the suggestions and hints that meet your needs. When you come upon something pertinent, underline it for quick reference or copy it into your bazaar notebook.

There are many small bazaars put on by church groups who have had years of experience; but, they too may find ideas, such as how to set up easy, inexpensive displays to give their bazaar a ''new look'' and heighten the interest of prospective customers.

For all bazaars, large or small, we offer a selection of items to make, keeping in mind that the cost of materials is a big factor and that most of the items made for a bazaar should be from scraps or low-cost materials, if the sale of the items is to obtain the greatest profit.

What sells well in one locality may not be as popular in another area. Before making a large quantity of any one item, find out what sells best at local bazaars; if, for example, pot holders sell well, make a large supply, cutting down on quantity, but not variety, of other merchandise—have something for everyone!

CONTENTS

Terrific Things for Terrific Kids

Gifts: Something for Everyone

General Directions

ORGANIZING A BAZAAR

Officers and Committees

General Chairman

Duties

1. Form a Master Committee by appointing department chairmen in each of the following areas:

    Merchandise
    Theme and Decoration
    Properties and Supplies
    Entertainment and Prizes
    Dining Room, Food
    Publicity
    Clean-Up

2. Organize a meeting several months before the event to present the overall plans and an outline of the program to the Master Committees.

3. Request a weekly report from all chairmen in order to keep advised of progress of committees.

Master Committee

Duties

1. Make major decisions, such as time, place, and theme of bazaar.

2. Approve all large expenditures, such as rentals, catering, decorating, and budget for each committee.

3. Each chairman sets a schedule for her workers, assigns their duties, calls committee meetings, and files weekly progress reports with General Chairman.

4. Each chairman has a bazaar note book in which to keep all records, plus any helpful hints.

Merchandise Chairman

Duties

1. Appoint an individual to take charge of each booth.

2. Coordinate their activities by taking overall responsibility for the merchandise of the bazaar—arrangement, pricing, and promotion of specialties.

Theme/Decorating Chairman

Duties

1. Plan decorations and make them well in advance of the day of the event. (We offer some ideas on pages 29–32.)

2. Using a scale model of the room or rooms available, plan position of all booths well in advance of the event.

3. A day or two before the bazaar, begin constructing booths. Final decorating is done the day before.

Property/Supplies Chairman

Duties

1. Supply the decoration committee with all materials necessary for the con-

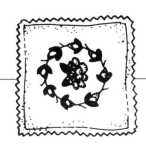

struction of the booths and for any decorations planned.

2. Obtain any other props required and see that necessary chairs, tables, etc., are on hand.

Entertainment/Prizes Chairman
Duties

1. Decide upon and set up entertainment for the bazaar-goers—including children's playroom or game room, babysitting service, Polaroid photographer, portrait artist, or musician.

2. Organize raffles, door prizes, or auctions—especially if one or more large items has been donated to the bazaar.

Dining Room/Concession Chairman
Duties

1. Decide what kind of food service will be offered to the fairgoer—light snacks or a large dinner.

2. Appoint a committee responsible for providing and serving the food.

Publicity Chairman
Duties

1. Contact newspapers, radio and television stations, and local store owners (for possible advertising space in their windows) as soon as the date, time, and place of the bazaar have been decided.

2. Order fliers and bumper stickers (if the bazaar is to be a large one); plan signs that will be posted near the site of the bazaar; distribute postcard "invitations" for organization members to send to their friends, and plan souvenir program (if desired).

Clean-Up Chairman
Duties

Make up a schedule for all members of the committee for keeping the bazaar clean during working hours and for cleaning up completely when bazaar closes.

Choosing a Theme

A theme is not a must when planning a bazaar, but it does have advantages worth considering: it provides a focus for advance publicity, and the job of decorating and arranging booths is also easier. There are several themes that have proven workable as a unifying element for bazaars. One, the "Old-Time Town," can be especially charming, with all the booths decorated to look like shops along a small-town street. (See our diagram of a floor plan on page 13.) This nostalgic theme can be altered slightly for a "Country Store." Each booth would be a different "counter" in an old store—including a post office in which grab bag gifts would be collected. Other successful themes are the "Home," in which each booth represents a room in the home (especially good for small bazaars); a "Holiday Fair" where, for example, the pastry booth represents Washington's Birthday, the gardening booth, Easter, and, of course, the Christmas Booth offers gifts. Some other possibilities: Mardi Gras, The Good Old Summertime, The Big Top, and The Old West. Classic or currently popular songs may also supply a theme. Before deciding on a theme, however, take stock of what you are planning to offer at your bazaar and decide which theme would lend itself best.

Deciding which booths to have is the job of the General Chairman and the Master Committee. It is better to have a large number of small, attractive booths displaying items that are closely related, than to have a few large booths with a clutter of things for sale. The following is a list of workable booth ideas that can be expanded or condensed as needed for the size of your bazaar.

The Stitchery Booth should comprise a general collection of members' handwork—sewing and embroidery as well as knit and crochet. This is a good booth for a small bazaar; in a larger bazaar, the items would probably be distributed to other booths—housewares, tots' booth, an apron booth, etc.

The Apron Booth, from all reports, is the runaway best seller at almost every bazaar. The aprons for sale should show a variety of types—pretty aprons (both long and short) for entertaining—sturdy ones for no-nonsense cooking, including men's barbecue aprons. Other best sellers—mother-daughter combinations and aprons with matching pot holders.

The Candy Booth will be most popular with the children, so be sure to have inexpensive penny candy on hand to please them. But remember that everyone loves candy, so be well stocked with homemade candies, too.

The Kitchen Booth is always a favorite spot at any bazaar. Have plenty of place mats, pot holders, aprons, and kitchen organizers.

Pantry Booths are best if they can be set up in individual units; have one booth for baked goods and another for jams, jellies, pickles, fancy preserves, and home-grown herbs. To assure proper packaging, have plenty of paper bags on hand, and, at the baked goods counter, paper plates and clear plastic wrap are a must. If you are planning to serve some refreshments at the bazaar, a "coffee shop" could be set up near the baked goods counter—customers can choose their cake and eat it on the spot (with a cup of steaming coffee).

The Tiny Tots Boutique features a selection of toys, beanbags, dolls, quick-knit sweaters—plus bootees, bibs, mobiles, crib toys and other huggables for baby—and maybe a soft coverlet or a special photo album.

The Ladies Boutique should display a variety of jewelry and pretty little items, such as eyeglass cases, bags, belts, and handkerchiefs. If someone in your group makes jewelry and is willing to demonstrate her craft, a special booth is in order.

A Candle Corner might create a great deal of excitement with a display of candles in a variety of interesting forms—from floating flowers to sturdy mushrooms.

Or try a "Nothing to Make" Booth for added bazaar fun.

"Attic Treasures" will be sure to attract everyone. Ask for donations that are in good condition or newly repaired. Keeping in mind that this is a booth for browsers, locate it in a quiet corner of the bazaar, where the shoppers can take their time to look over all the "treasures." A variation on this booth could be the "Fix-It" booth. In this case, all items for sale would be in need of minor repairs. But, in all fairness to the shopper, be sure to have the booth attendant point out the flaw of each item.

The "5 and 10" or Dollar Booth is the place to display small, low-cost items such as bookmarks and felt book covers—anything that costs under one dollar. This, too, is a popular booth for children, whose buying power is limited!

Grab Bags are both popular and fun. But to avoid any disappointments, have a committee wrap and label each item—it's best to have separate grab bags for men, women, and children. For the really little tots, devise a fish pond, where each tot can "go fishing" for his very own prize.

Books are another best-selling item. However, books should be arranged in some order—have a special section for children's books, and arrange the others according to fiction and non-fiction to make it easier for the shoppers to find books that will really interest them.

The Garden Booth adds color and freshness as well as revenue to your bazaar. To get plants for sale, contact your local florist; he might be willing to arrange special prices for bulk purchases. Other bright floral ideas include cut flowers (especially if your members have gardens), seed packets, or even pretty corsages!

"Special Order" Booth can be most profitable, but only if your members are willing to keep on working for the bazaar for the rest of the year. Special-order items, such as simple clothing, kitchen accents (aprons, pot holders, etc.) can be offered for delivery at any time throughout the year. If you plan such a booth, display made-up items being offered, along with fabric samples for the buyers' choice. Remember to record all orders carefully and to have the customer reread and initial the order as

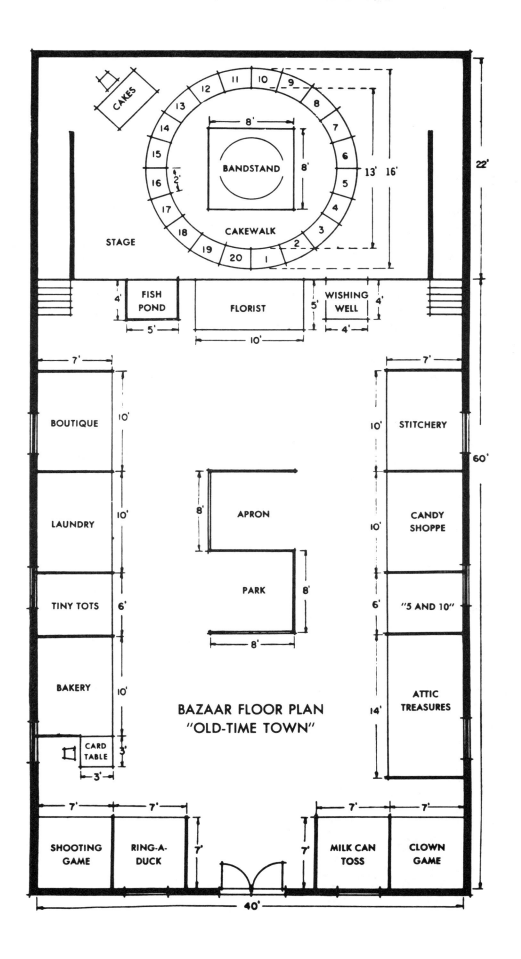

BAZAAR FLOOR PLAN
"OLD-TIME TOWN"

it appears in the order book, to avoid mistakes in sizes, colors, or monograms.

A Wishing Well will entice the penny tossers. Build a square of bricks or trim a barrel with ivy—fill the bottom with water.

A Cake Walk is both money-making and entertaining. Build a "bandstand" in the center of a platform. Enclose the bandstand within two concentric circles that form a continuous "walk"; divide the walk into 20 numbered sections. Both the walk and numbers can be indicated with masking tape. Twenty people walk in a circle for a minute or two while the music (live or recorded) plays from the bandstand; they stop when the music does. A number is drawn and read aloud; the person standing on that lucky number wins a cake. At 25¢ a turn, each donated cake will net $5.00. For drawing of a Cake Walk, see floor plan for "Old-Time Town."

Construction

Planning

The actual construction of the booths and decorating of the hall are usually not done until a day or so before the bazaar. But planning should start as soon as your bazaar's theme has been chosen. Measure the room and make a scale diagram on graph paper; include all doors, windows, balconies, and side rooms. Divide the space according to the number of booths needed and the relative requirements of each booth. Allow for wide aisles behind and between booths. In assigning space to specific booths, try to visualize traffic patterns and avoid bottlenecks.

Booths

Display units can be as elaborate or as simple as you like, depending on the size of your bazaar and your budget. The booths illustrated would each require a fair amount of construction. If your resources are limited, set up simple counters by placing a board over sawhorses; both can be rented from a party supplier. Use crepe paper to cover the board and to make a skirt for hiding stored merchandise. Decorate cardboard boxes with paper or water-based paint and stack them on the counter—in a pyramid for same-size boxes, in random fashion for assorted-size boxes. Place some of the boxes with open ends to the back, for storage; place others open-end-to-front for use as shadow boxes; pin small items to sides.

To give your counter more of a "booth" look, make upright poles by clamping or nailing 1″ × 2″ stripping to the board. A single pole at center back

Boxes are stands or frames for toys; flat articles are pinned to side.

could hold a cardboard sign. Or print your sign on shelving paper and stretch between two poles attached to the sides or the back corners. Or wrap crepe paper around four corner poles. Add swags, streamers, balloons!

Backdrops can be purely decorative or used to display items for sale. A wooden framework can be built behind the table and covered with cardboard, paper, or cloth. A simpler device is to set up a solid-panel folding screen, to be hung with small articles for sale. Ordinary cardboard cartons can be decorated and stacked behind the table in a number of ingenious ways. Packing cartons for refrigerators are especially strong and make excellent units for displaying large articles (cut a window out of one side, tuck in a quilt).

Display trees, made of laths or dowels, are particularly apt for Christmas bazaars, especially when trimmed with tiny lights. Those illustrated on page 29 are about three or four feet high and can be adapted to stand on a counter or floor or to hang on a wall. Rose trellises can be used in the same way. Or set out your merchandise on stairsteps, decorating large and small ladders for the occasion.

If your bazaar is being given out of doors, make use of your natural surroundings; the day before the bazaar, hose down small trees in a garden to remove dust; on the day of the bazaar, drape them with aprons and quilts or hang baby clothes on ribboned hangers from the lower branches.

Decorating

In a large hall full of people, only the big, bold effects will be noticed. Do not get bogged down in expensive, elaborately detailed decorating that may be all but invisible on the day of the bazaar. Remember, too, that your decor's primary purpose is to set off your merchandise, the real star of the show. Determine how much time will be actually available to you in the hall to construct and decorate before bazaar day, and plan accordingly. For theme-oriented decorating ideas, see pages 29–32.

Before you plan paper decorations, check out local fire laws with your fire department. Use only fire-proof crepe paper. Crepe paper can be draped, stretched, crushed, fringed, fluted, and ruffled to lavish effect. You can use it to make flowers, twisted ropes, fishnet, lanterns, tassels, pennants and banners. It comes packaged in large, folded sheets or in narrow strips called streamers.

To make your own streamers, cut two-inch strips with heavy shears or a paper cutter before unfolding package. You will find streamers especially useful for wrapping around uprights, in a single color or in multicolor combinations. When draping streamers across a ceil-

ing, cut them shorter then you actually want, as they have a tendency to sag in humid weather. To cover booths with ruffled skirts, gather crepe paper on the sewing machine.

Brown or white wrapping paper is useful for covering large, flat areas or for making tailored skirts for booths. Decorate with glued-on paper cutouts or designs painted directly on the paper. Do not make drawings too detailed; strive instead for a stylized, even primitive effect, concentrating on the most distinctive features.

Where it is unfeasible to tack paper to walls, use double-faced masking tape; the same effect can be achieved with ordinary masking tape by folding pieces into thirds.

Keep the Property and Supplies Committee informed of your needs; then, a week or so before decorating, gather all your equipment together. A suggested list: large, sharp shears, hammers, saws, C-clamps, two-inch tacks, small nails, thumbtacks, straight pins, wire staples and stapler, picture wire, spool wire, strong twine, masking tape, cellophane tape, yardsticks, tape measure, rulers, wire cutters, screw eyes, small turnbuckles, paste or glue, extra pieces of $1'' \times 1''$ or $1'' \times 2''$ pine and several stepladders. Be sure to have everything in sufficient quantity so that your available time will be spent in decorating rather than in exasperating searches for the equipment. If possible, assemble a separate working kit for each member of the committee.

Merchandising

Some of the knottiest problems that arise when planning a bazaar are not major policy decisions, but such matters as the soliciting, pricing, and selling of merchandise.

Soliciting of Articles

The chairman of the Merchandise Committee will have an up-to-date list of the entire membership of the organization and all those interested in helping the bazaar. She will divide her list among her various booth chairmen, who will in turn assign names to their workers to do the actual soliciting. Thus each member will be contacted once. It is important that the chairmen and solicitors keep careful records—as a means to avoiding oversolicitation, as a check list for promised goods, and as a useful guide for next year. The actual date for soliciting will of course vary with the type of article—six months in advance for needlework items; one month for baked goods, perhaps, with reminders sent out the week before the bazaar.

The solicitor is responsible for seeing that the items are delivered on time; she should be specific about delivery dates, to avoid confusion.

Use diplomacy in all your dealings with contributors; people like donating their handwork but like also to feel that their efforts are appreciated. Let people make what they enjoy making. You may still find it necessary to use tactful persuasion to obtain a balanced variety of goods. Thirty-five aprons and two pot holders, for example, would present an obvious picture of poor planning. Discuss in advance your specific needs for the most popular items, and suggest these to contributors. Plan on having most of your merchandise in the low-price range; this means you will want many more bootees and mittens in your knitwear booth than sweaters, for example.

Never turn down anyone's donated handcraft, no matter how unsuitable or poorly made it may be. There are ways to handle these items on bazaar day (see Selling). And your careful record-keeping will pay off the following year, when you may try to channel some of your members' energies in other directions.

Pricing

You will find that overpriced merchandise simply will not sell. On the other hand, underpricing goods will only incur the wrath of those who spent long hours making them. Here are a few guidelines:

Do not ask contributing members to set the price for their own items. Pricing is definitely a function of the committee.

The price you set should take into account the cost of materials and labor (even though both were donated), the quality of the workmanship, and the demand for the particular item. One rule of thumb for pricing time-consuming knitted and crocheted articles is to triple the cost of materials—a scarf costing $1.00 sells for $3.00

Attach large, clear tags to each item as soon as you have decided its price. Do not depend on the memory of salespeople on bazaar day, but cater instead to the browsing instinct of your patrons, who will want to see prices for themselves. Use ingenuity: ''three for a quarter'' rather than ''ten cents each.''

Selling

A good part of successful selling depends on packaging. Candy, for example, if packaged in small, attractive boxes, will sell more quickly than when displayed in quantity, and at a higher price, too. Tiny, low-priced toys can be grouped together in net bags and tied with a ribbon. Small, potted plants take on style when wrapped in colored foil. Display knitwear in shallow boxes with transparent wrap stretched over the top.

Arrange your items in a way that makes sense, practically and artistically. Each booth should display only articles that have some relation to its theme. Group similar items together within each booth; elaborate party aprons would be separated from sturdy work aprons, for example, with another corner set aside to display aprons for men. Avoid overcrowding a counter; keep some items back, replenishing your stock as needed. A few items, well arranged, will move more quickly than a jumble of unrelated articles.

What to do with the less appealing merchandise you were forced to accept? Tie two or three things together, perhaps in a net bag, and sell them as a package at a bargain price. Or keep them under the counter until late in the day, when the better merchandise has been sold. Gather all the leftovers together at the end of the fair and auction them off.

Feeding the Fair

Fair-goers get hungry, and some arrangement must be set up to feed them. These preparations can be simple or elaborate, depending on your goals. You must first decide whether you are offering food as a profit-making venture or simply as a service to your patrons.

Remember that in serving food you will not earn as much money per square foot of space used as you will in your regular booths. Remember, too, that a great deal of work will be required if all the food is donated by members; you may want to consider turning part or all of the food operation over to an outside concessionaire. If you do plan on showing a profit, add 20% to the price of any food you buy.

The elaborate sit-down dinner once traditional with bazaars has lost much of its popularity. The space, time, and effort involved in producing such a spread do not seem worth the slim financial rewards. You may decide, however, that a dinner fits in so well with the scope of your fair—a Harvest Festival, for example—that you want to have one anyway. You must, of course, have the available space—a large, separate room most likely—and enough tables and chairs. A buffet service would probably be easiest. As the amount of food must be planned in advance (a gallon of coffee to serve 21 people), it is a good idea to sell dinner tickets in advance, too. Then increase your food estimate 10% over the ticket sales; there are sure to be some unexpected diners. Do plan a simple and inexpensive menu (goulash instead of roast beef, perhaps), as people will not expect to pay much for their meal.

A less ambitious way to feed your patrons is to set up a cafeteria or coffee shop. As service will be constant, people will not all be eating at once, and a small room or balcony may be sufficient. Have soup, sandwiches, cakes, cookies, milk, coffee, and tea. One committee member might act as hostess, assigning tables, overseeing service, and making the customers feel at home.

Perhaps the best way to handle the food problem is to set up booths on the floor of the bazaar, away from the most crowded areas. Each booth will sell some simple food, such as hot dogs, soup, or ice cream.

An even easier system is to have vendors wearing trays with shoulder straps circulate through the crowd, selling easy-to-handle wares. Food vendors are recommended only for outdoor bazaars, however.

In planning your food needs, do not neglect the hard-working people who will spend the day before the bazaar setting up their booths. They will much appreciate being served a light refreshment during a break in their labors.

Consult a lawyer regarding local, state, and federal tax laws governing the sale of food. These laws may well affect the setting of your prices and your choice of menu. Sometimes one kind of food serving will be taxed, but another will be tax free.

Entertainment

Games

Games of skill and games of chance are always popular. You can set up these booths yourselves or rent them from carnival supply houses, who will furnish booths, backdrops, equipment, and prizes and will make suggestions for suitable games, as well as actually set up and take down the booths.

Tossing Games, easy to stage, can have an infinite variety of form; choose one that fits your general theme:

Goldfish Bowl—ping-pong balls are thrown into goldfish bowls full of water; winners are awarded goldfish in plastic bags.

Clown Game—darts are thrown at balloons thumbtacked to a large plywood clown.

Penny Pitch—pennies are pitched at small aluminum plates floating in a large tub of water.

Prizes: There are several ways to handle game prizes. You might offer a particular type of prize for each game, so that patrons could choose their game according to the kind of prize that interests them—toys, kitchen gadgets, groceries. Or keep the players moving by jumbling the prizes among all the booths. Or group all the prizes for all games of skill and chance together in a central booth; winners are awarded tickets of different colors, signifying different values, to "cash in" at the prize booth.

Special Features

Shows and other added attractions are well worth considering; give them sufficient advance publicity to draw in the crowds, who, hopefully, will stay to browse among the booths. Your show can be an elaborate one requiring a large cast and months of preparation or a simple audience-participation event arranged by a single committee member. Plan according to your available space and talent and your financial goals. If you are going to charge admission to the bazaar, you should offer enough entertainment to make the charge worthwhile. On the other hand, you may decide on free general admission with a charge for each separate entertainment. This plan requires facilities with separate rooms adjacent to the main hall. At the very least, plan to have some kind of background music.

Selecting a "Queen of the Fair": This contest will probably appeal most to the teen-age crowd. It offers excellent possibilities for publicity, particularly if it becomes a yearly custom, and adds much excitement and suspense to the fair itself.

Fortune-Teller: The fortune-teller needs only an exotic costume, a keen imagination, and a little help from a library book on her subject. She may decide to read palms, a crystal ball, a deck of cards—or the stars. Because many people take fortune-telling seriously, it should be emphasized that it is all in fun and that any predictions made are not to be taken literally.

Artist: Caricaturists, silhouettists, or quick-sketch artists are good money-makers and offer entertainment for the crowd as well.

Raffles, Auctions, Awards

There are several ways of keeping interest high until the very end of the bazaar:

1. Gather up all the unsold goods in one spot and auction them off (keeping this final-sale auction a secret until just before it happens); get a professional auctioneer or at least a good salesman who can hold the attention of the crowd and a cashier to help him.

2. Have an appropriate prize from each booth or one grand prize, such as a color television, to be raffled off, announcing the winners with great ceremony just before the close.

3. Give a prize to the customer who comes closest to guessing the correct number of beans in a jar.

These special prizes may be donated by merchants, who will, of course, be given the proper credit.

Publicity

Publicity may be the single most important factor in the success or failure of your bazaar. No matter how perfectly planned the bazaar itself may be, it will not succeed unless people have been told, over and over, when and where it is to be and why you are having it, and are convinced they want to attend. The committee's job is to draw the people; it will be up to others to please them after they arrive.

The chairman should be selected at the very outset, as work should begin immediately. She will keep in close touch with the General Chairman, following the week-by-week progress of the bazaar. Hopefully, the chairman will have had some training in advertising or promotion; she should have a flair for spotting the dramatic possibilities in ordinary events. In order to employ as many publicity techniques as will work in your locality, the committee must be chosen carefully, looking for experience in every phase of publicity.

"Decorative" Committee Members: The job of your Publicity Chairman will be easier if there is a prominent name or two to display—as a member of a committee or even as Honorary Chairman. Several important people can be utilized by creating a Board of Patrons. Be sure, however, that any emphasis on these "decorative" names does not overshadow appreciation for the efforts of the real workers; you cannot afford hurt feelings.

Newspapers

Your local newspapers are perhaps your best outlet for publicity. Two to six months before your bazaar, depending on its size, arrange an interview with the publisher or a staff member and sell him on its newsworthy aspects. Take along a release that describes the theme and the cause it aims to promote. As in all your releases, be sure to mention the time and the place. Write each release around a different news point of view; one might feature a prominent person involved in the project; another might show special items to be sold at the bazaar. Type your releases on $8\frac{1}{2}'' \times 11''$ paper, double spaced, with several carbons; keep a copy for your files. Include a glossy photograph if you can, with a suggested caption attached to the bottom of the picture, its edge glued to the back of the photo.

Radio and Television

Seek out any opportunities for free publicity from your local station; perhaps there is one in your locality connected with a college or university. Try to arrange interviews with your more prominent workers or promote panel discussions. As bazaar time approaches, send newsy announcements to disk jockeys and commentators, with a request for some kind of plug. Television interviews could be supplemented with a display of typical merchandise or with a teasing short of the entertainment in store for the fair-goers. You may even decide to invest money in spot announcements during the final week of preparations.

Display

Posters

Talk to store owners and persuade as many as you can to display your posters in their windows. This calls for considerable tact on the part of a mature member who can convince them of the reliable, worthwhile nature of your project. You can use a few of the younger members to do the actual legwork of distributing posters.

There are two ways to handle posters. One way is to have them done professionally by a printer. In this case you will show a dummy poster to the storekeepers before placing your print order. Be sure to ask for a proof of the poster before final printing, to check details and spelling. Do not be hesitant about asking for a reduced rate; the printer may be willing to donate his services in return for credit on the posters and in the souvenir program. Or he may do the posters free in exchange for the job of printing the souvenir program.

Another way is to stage a poster contest in the schools. You might offer a prize for the best poster from each age group. Display the posters together, about two weeks before the bazaar, and invite a panel of experts (art teachers, commercial artists, art buyers for department stores) in to judge. Of course, you will exploit the publicity value of your contest by inviting a newspaper reporter and photographer as well. After the contest, either keep the posters on prominent display, in an art store window, for example, or distribute them to your cooperating storekeepers.

Fliers and Bumper Stickers

These are two inexpensive ways to reach a large audience. Make them colorful, even a little gaudy, using at least two colors for fliers, and perhaps glow-colors for the bumper stickers. Remember that printing costs go down sharply as the number printed increases, so these methods are really practical only if you can make use of a large quantity.

Signs

Large signs should be posted a day or two before the bazaar, pointing the way. Tack these on trees, posts, or buildings, after obtaining permission from property owners, of course. And remember to take them down after the bazaar.

Younger members will enjoy parading through the busiest part of town wearing sandwich-board signs. Construct these of light wood or heavy cardboard, with straps of rug-binding tape; glue on your poster, front and back.

Mail

Send letters and postcards to the secretaries of local organizations, to be read at their meetings, and to churches for inclusion in their weekly bulletins. If your organization is large, keep in touch with your own membership this way, particularly with those not actively involved in the fair. A small organization might give ten postcard announcements to each member, who will mail them to ten friends, thus issuing a personal invitation to attend your bazaar.

Parade

A good parade is sure to capture everyone's attention. It can take a variety of forms, from a marching parade with the high-school band to a motorcade of decorated cars and floats, with a sound truck to broadcast music and frequent repetitions of the time, place, and purpose of your fair. Whatever sort of parade you choose, don't neglect the music. Remember, too, to obtain a parade permit from the proper authorities and to investigate your local noise ordinances.

Souvenir Program

This can be a complicated but very rewarding effort. Programs may vary from simple four-page folders printed on stock paper to elaborate, slick-paper books. In any case, the program should carry enough advertising to pay for itself. Talk to a printer first, getting comparative prices for paper, type styles, and bindings. Then make an estimate of how much advertising you can expect. Prepare a dummy and a rate card, listing costs for whole-, half-, quarter-page and even inch ads; set a higher rate for the inside front, inside back, and back covers. Search your membership for someone with professional (even high school or college yearbook) experience to do the layout. Separate editorial content (all non-advertising matter) into an even number of pages, so that four-page folios of ads can be added to the front and back of the book. Souvenir programs are usually distributed free of charge to patrons of the fair, thus giving advertisers the maximum audience for their messages and fairgoers an attractive memento.

Long-Range Goals

If your bazaar is an annual event, you will want to keep careful records of publicity releases and of the merchants who participated. Take the trouble to write thank-you notes to all workers and contributors. Even a little post-bazaar publicity in the newspapers or on the radio will help pave the way for an even more successful bazaar next year.

Day of the Bazaar

Transportation and Deliveries

How will people get to your bazaar? If you have chosen a hall or site any distance from town, you may find it necessary to set up a special system of transportation. For a large fair, buses may be chartered, to leave from central points at regular intervals. A small bazaar could manage with private cars, also running on a schedule. Either way, you should make your arrangements well enough in advance to include them in your publicity, particularly during the last week or so before the bazaar.

Deliveries from the manufacturers or caterers must also be carefully scheduled so they do not all arrive at the same time. The Properties and Supplies Chairman will appoint someone to be at the hall to receive and inspect these goods as they arrive.

Special Services

There are several services that you should try to offer your patrons that will add to their comfort and make them feel welcome. A checkroom or booth for coats and packages is most important. Have it near the entrance, issue large-size checking tickets, and charge a small fee or set out a plate for tips. A station for checking small children is also a good idea. It must be staffed with competent attendants, equipped with a good supply of borrowed toys, plus cookies, milk, and fruit juices for snacks. An information booth may be needed for a large bazaar; this service could include a corps of ushers with identifying armbands, who will circulate through the crowd, greeting customers and answering questions.

Police

Call your police department beforehand and ask for their help in rerouting traffic, posting no-parking signs, and closing off streets, if necessary. You may need someone to help with crowd control and to deal with any unusual disturbance. If you are having exhibits of any great value, you may also need the services of a plainclothesman.

Clearing Aisles

You will have arranged your booths so that the crowds can move freely about the hall. While the bazaar is in progress, you must keep the aisles clear of all refuse that might obstruct the flow of traffic. Appoint a squad of youngsters in armbands who will patrol the premises, pick up soda pop bottles, papers, boxes, and crates, and deposit them in trash barrels. The final clean-up job, at night or the following day, will also be much easier.

Booth Schedules, Procedures

The chairman of each booth will set up a careful schedule for the booth attendants, arranging their time in shifts. It is important that these shifts be not too long to maintain a fresh and enthusiastic sales force. By not overtiring your workers, you will build up a loyal crew ready to volunteer their services year after year for the same booth. Make sure that each worker knows a day ahead exactly when her hours will be. To avoid sudden emergencies, have a few standbys on call to replace absentees. If a booth chairman does not have enough workers on a committee to maintain a day's schedule, she should get in touch with the General Chairman beforehand, who will find other workers.

Each booth chairman should prepare a work sheet that shows how the booth will be manned listing names and hours; give one copy to the General Chairman, post another copy in the booth, and keep one for the bazaar's records.

Handling Money

The mechanics of making change, collecting cash, and keeping accounts can be tricky and should be handled with foresight. Usually, each booth will have its own cash box and keep its own records. The Treasurer will go to the bank on the morning of the bazaar and draw out enough cash in change to supply a box for each booth. Only one person at a time should handle the cash box at each booth. In a large bazaar, it is advisable to have a cashier at each booth,

someone apart from the salesperson, to make change. The cashiers can work in shifts, also; at the end of a shift, each will hand the money that has accumulated over the original amount of change to a collector for a receipt, entering in a record how much was earned during the shift. The money collectors, coming around to each booth at regular intervals, should carry change with them to exchange for larger denominations, in case any booth runs short. They should also carry identification, if the bazaar is a large one, and cashiers should be warned against turning over their money to anyone not properly identified. If your bazaar is really large, you might have bank tellers on hand to count the money as the collectors turn it in. As soon as your doors are closed, the Treasurer will probably want to count your receipts then and there and take the money directly to the bank for a night deposit (in the company of a policeman, perhaps).

Planning for the Future

After the bazaar, the Treasurer will study the figures, determining which booths or activities were the most profitable, which merely broke even, and which, if any, operated at a loss. Were too many prizes awarded at the game booths, for example, thus diminishing the profits? He or she will then make a report to the entire membership. This kind of study will result in more careful

planning for the following year. If your bazaar is an annual event, such planning can only mean better and more profitable bazaars each year.

Services to Contact

Supply Rental

Look in the Yellow Pages under "Rental Services" and telephone to have a price list mailed to you. You should visit the store to see the merchandise before renting it.

Caterer

Ask chairpersons of other organizations who have hired caterers to recommend their favorite. You can look in the Yellow Pages as well. Telephone for an appointment to meet the caterer and discuss menus, costs, and necessary equipment.

Garbage Removal

A large bazaar may require pick-up service. Check first with the management of the building in which you will hold your bazaar to find out the scheduled sanitation company, then telephone the company to see if additional pick-ups are required.

Fire Department

Regulations vary from area to area, so it is wise to telephone your local fire station a few weeks before the bazaar. Find out if there are any precautions necessary or if safety equipment or personnel are required. You should make certain that no regulations are violated, even if you see no obvious fire hazard.

Nurse

If your bazaar is large, it makes sense to hire a nurse to administer to minor injuries that may occur. Telephone your local hospital for a list of nurses, then discuss your needs with each before making your choice.

Radio and TV

You may be able to schedule a live broadcast at your bazaar. Contact local station managers at least three weeks in advance; tell them all the details and offer the opportunity of an interview or news feature during the bazaar. Suggest specific people to interview or an angle from which to present the bazaar.

The Mayor

Inviting your Mayor to the bazaar is good for community relations and publicity; the media may pay more attention to your bazaar and the aims of your organization if the Mayor decides to attend. The bazaar chairperson should mail a formal letter at least three weeks before the bazaar, describing your organization and the bazaar and inviting him or her to attend. Address the invitation to City Hall. You may wish to telephone the Mayor's secretary one week before the bazaar to politely inquire whether he or she will attend.

Suppliers

Any neighborhood lumberyard and stationery store should be able to provide you with the supplies necessary for constructing and decorating booths. If you have difficulty finding materials for craft projects, the following companies will accept mail order sales:

Acrylic Paints

Arthur Brown & Bro., Inc., 2 West 46th St., New York, NY 10036

Connoisseur Studio, Inc., Box 7187, Louisville, KY 40207

J. L. Hammett Co., Box 545, Hammett Pl., Braintree, MA 02184

Beads

Home-Sew Inc., Bethlehem, PA 18018

Lee Wards, 1200 St. Charles St., Elgin, IL 60120

Northeast Bead Trading Co., 12 Depot St., Kennebunk, ME 04043

Hazel Pearson Handicrafts, 16017 E. Valley Blvd., City of Industry, CA 91744

Embroidery Hoops

Herrschners, Inc., Hoover Rd., Stevens Point, WI 54481

Lee Wards, 1200 St. Charles St., Elgin, IL 60120

Mary Maxim, Inc., 2001 Holland Ave., Port Huron, MI 48060

The Needlecraft Shop, P.O. Box 2147, Canoga Park, CA 91306

The Stitchery, Wellesley Hills, MA 02181

Embroidery Yarns and Floss

Belding Lily Co., Box 88, Shelby, NC 28150

Herrschners, Inc., Hoover Rd., Stevens Point, WI 54481

Mary Maxim, Inc., 2001 Holland Ave., Port Huron, MI 48060

Needlecraft House, West Towsend, MA 01474

The Needlecraft Shop, P.O. Box 2147, Canoga Park, CA 91306

Fabric-Burlap

Belding Lily Co., Box 88, Shelby, NC 28150

Herrschners, Inc., Hoover Rd., Stevens Point, WI 54481

Holiday Handicrafts, Inc., Winsted, CT 06098

Lee Wards, 1200 St. Charles St., Elgin, IL 60120

Mary Maxim, Inc., 2001 Holland Ave., Port Huron, MI 48060

Needlecraft House, West Townsend, MA 01474

Fabric-Calico

Ginger Snap Station, Box 81086, Atlanta, GA 30341

Hearthside Mail Order, Box 24, Milton, VT 05468

North Shore Farmhouse, Greenhurst, NY 14742

Quilts & Other Comforts, Box 394, Wheatridge, CO 80033

Fabric-Linen and/or Other

Herrschners, Inc., Hoover Rd., Stevens Point, WI 54481

Lee Wards, 1200 St. Charles St., Elgin, IL 60120

Mary Maxim, Inc., 2001 Holland Ave., Port Huron, MI 48060

Needlecraft House, West Townsend, MA 01474

The Needlecraft Shop, P.O. Box 2147, Canoga Park, CA 91306

Felt

Herrschners, Inc., Hoover Rd., Stevens Point, WI 54481

Lee Wards, 1200 St. Charles St., Elgin, IL 60120

Newark Dressmaker Supply, 4616 Park Dr., Bath, PA 18014

Hazel Pearson Handicrafts, 16017 E. Valley Blvd., City of Industry, CA 91744

Knitting and Crochet Accessories

Herrschners, Inc., Hoover Rd., Stevens Point, WI 54481

Lee Wards, 1200 St. Charles St., Elgin, IL 60120

Mary Maxim, Inc., 2001 Holland Ave., Port Huron, MI 48060

Needlecraft House, West Townsend, MA 01474

Yarns Unlimited, 1434 Santa Monica Mall, Santa Monica, CA 90406

Knitting and/or Crochet Yarns

Belding Lily Co., Box 88, Shelby, NC 28150

Herrschners, Inc., Hoover Rd., Stevens Point, WI 54481

Mary Maxim, Inc., 2001 Holland Ave., Port Huron, MI 48060

Newark Dressmaker Supply Co., 4616 Park Dr., Bath, PA 18014

Yarns Unlimited, 1434 Santa Monica Mall, Santa Monica, CA 90406

Displays

There are numerous ways to display merchandise, depending on available space, budget, and merchandise size and weight. A creative display will draw more browsers and sell more merchandise. A few ideas are mentioned on page 14; more are listed below:

Chicken wire or fishnet can be tacked to a board, a back wall, or to wooden supports. Lightweight items can be taped on or attached with paper clips in pleasing groups. Many small items can be shown this way. Fishnet comes in a variety of colors; pick one to match your decor or to set off the merchandise.

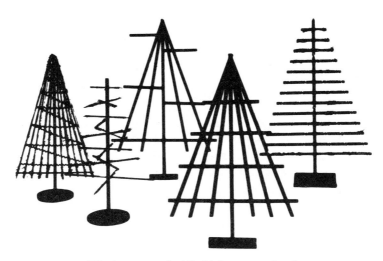

Display trees, 3–4 ft. high, are made of laths or dowels; adapt them to suit your needs (see page 15).

Pegboard can display heavier items than chicken wire or fishnet. Many types of hooks are available for hanging items. Long hooks are good for storing merchandise; hang ten matching pot holders on one hook, then keep selling the front one. You'll be able to watch your inventory this way.

A board covered with fabric is ideal for a jewelry display. Choose a dainty print or a bold graphic. Tack fabric edges to back of board, then hang jewelry on front using safety pins. A small board can sit on the counter, or a larger one can hang or lean against a wall.

Shelves are good for displaying knick knacks or folded clothing. Build shelves using boards supported by bricks at each end and in the center, or stack milk crates or wooden boxes. Nail crates or boxes together for stability, place shelves behind booth or use as booth sides.

If your budget is large, you may want to rent clothing racks, bookshelves, or other display equipment. Check with your local supplier to learn what is available.

Theme Decorations

Patriotic Theme

The key to a patriotic bazaar theme is simple—just remember Red, White and Blue. Cover tables with red, white or blue crepe paper, hang up bunting, streamers, and balloons using those colors, and have booth operators dress in one or more of the colors. In addition, you can:

Cut out white paper stars and glue or tape randomly on booths and walls.

Hang large and small flags from the walls and ceiling or from trees if outdoors. If you can obtain copies of older flags (Stars and Bars, etc.) or state flags, they would provide an interesting contrast.

Decorate each booth using a different color combination. For example, a red booth, one that's red-and-white striped, one red with white stars, one blue with white stars, etc.

Design booth signs to resemble flags. Prepare a striped or solid-color background, then paint or glue on solid-color or striped letters. Perhaps place "THE" in the upper left corner on a blue rectangle to resemble a flag's field, or place blue letters across a red-and-white striped background (see illustration below). Hang signs on wooden posts with round finials on one end to resemble flagpoles, securing upper right corner of sign with string hanging from the ceiling if necessary.

Create "stovepipe" hats for booth operators. They are fun to make: Cut and tape a wide tube of thin cardboard to fit head, cut a 4″-wide hat brim with

an inner diameter the same as the tube, tape tube to brim, then cover with crepe paper (red, white and blue, of course) or paint. Glue a ring of white stars around bottom of "stovepipe" for hat band.

Hang up copies of old war posters. Most large stationery stores sell the famous "Uncle Sam Wants You!" poster, and others are usually available as well.

Seasonal Theme

A seasonal bazaar theme will work two ways. You can concentrate on a single season or utilize all four when planning decorations. Suggestions below are divided into seasons; use them all or choose only those ideas which fit the season you select.

Plan each corner of the room to be one season and decorate booths according to their placement in the room. Colors play an important part of a seasonal theme. Our suggestions: Spring—light green with pale pink and white accents. Summer—sky-blue with yellow and bright green accents. Autumn—orange and yellow with brown accents. Winter—white with green and red accents.

Tape or tack each month of a large twelve-month calendar high on the walls to correspond with the "seasons."

Spring

Cut out simple flower shapes and attach to booth sides and table. Operators

30

can wear paper or real flowers in their hair or pinned to their collars. Large paper flowers can hang from the ceiling. Signs should include spring colors and flowers; underline words with simple painted vines or dot any *i*'s with daisies.

Summer

A large yellow paper sun can be suspended, with yellow streamers for rays. Decorate booths with red checkered tablecloths and paper seashells, beach toys, picnic baskets, kites, or large sunglasses. Operators should pick one motif to wear as a paper pin. For signs, paint a simple seashore with tan sand and blue water, then paint bright letters bobbing in the waves.

Autumn

Cut out large paper leaves in autumn colors to decorate booths and walls. Smaller paper leaves can be worn by booth operators as name tags. Simple bird shapes can be cut from brown paper and taped high on a wall in "V" formation. Paint a border of autumn leaves around each sign.

Winter

Green paper holly leaves with red paper berries can decorate white booths while white snowflakes (fold paper squares in eighths and cut designs) will spruce up green or red decor. Booth operators can wear real or paper holly sprigs or paper snowflakes. Paper snowmen and icicles can hang on walls. Signs should be decorated with winter motifs. Why not paint the letters with caps of snow on them!

Circus Theme

What could be more fun that a bazaar with a circus theme? The atmosphere can be developed very simply—a few balloons and colored streamers—or you can present an "extravaganza." Some suggestions:

Rent a helium tank to inflate balloons, then tie them together in groups of three or more and anchor them to the walls. Someone can stand near the tank and fill balloons to sell to children throughout the day.

Hang circus posters around the room. Any large stationery store should stock a variety of classic posters.

Drape bunting and streamers around booths, walls, and doorways. Bright colors such as red, yellow, blue, orange, and green will work best.

Attach streamers to upper edges and corners of each booth, bring ends together and tie high above booth center, then attach to ceiling with string for a tent effect (see page 15).

Paint or cover each booth in the bright colors mentioned above. White polka-dots can be painted or taped to booth sides and tables. For variation, plan a few white booths with colored polka-dots.

Booth operators should dress in bright colors; polka-dot or red-and-white striped shirts will work best.

Paint each operator with a clown face before the bazaar opens, if a make-up booth is planned. This will focus attention on the make-up booth, attracting more customers.

Hire professional clowns to mingle with the crowd and entertain all day, if you have a large budget. If you are limited, perhaps you can find volunteer clowns in your organization. Clowns can make balloon creatures or do tricks, pantomime skits, or comic routines.

Paint booth signs with lots of red, yellow, blue, and white. A simple cluster of balloons can be painted next to the words, or circus animals (such as a seal balancing a ball, an elephant, or a dressed-up chimpanzee) can be used.

Tropical treasures in hand-painted fabric add zest to your decorating and shopping, and they are so easy to create with acrylic paints. Purchased canvas tote bag makes a sunny market-day bag when painted with a woven wicker and flower pattern. Add sunshine to your decorating with brilliant accent pillows. Cut cotton duck squares, paint, and stitch together with plump welting at edges. Designs by Sarah Hilton. Tote Bag and Pillow directions begin on page 41.

Bright colors team with white to give a bold, new look to traditional quilting patterns. We call it white and bright quilting—and you'll call it terrific for every room in your home. We've used traditional log cabin designs with variations to create the cross and "zigzag" patterns. Make large and small pillows, place mats, or a runner (30″ × 56″) to decorate table or wall. Designed by Margaret Pennington. Directions for White and Bright Quilting are on page 43.

A traditional house in patchwork shines anew with bright and pretty fabrics; child's face shows at window for an amusing variation. Designed by Carolyn Mack.

Cathedral window design, so popular for quilts, works as easily for a pillow—in two or many colors.

Directions for Star-Fold and House Pillows begin on page 48; Cathedral Pillow, page 52.

Stars radiating from center of round pillow are created with an easy novelty technique: square patches, folded into triangles, are arranged in over-lapping circles. Designed by Johanna Close.

Bold geometrics pattern four pillows.
All were painted with acrylics, then
quilted. If you prefer, adapt patterns
to patchwork or applique. Designed by
Nina Pellegrini. Directions for
Painted Pillows begin on page 46.

Open-air embroidery in the pulled-thread
technique creates lovely pillows, using
white matte cotton on large-mesh canvas.
Directions for Pulled-Thread Pillows
begin on page 49.

Dynamic contemporary wall
accessories provide spectacular
settings for your thriving plants
or dried-flower arrangements.

The two-tiered holder can also
serve as a room divider, while
the bowed ceiling hanger can be
suspended dramatically by your
window. Both are worked in white
cord with accents of ceramic or
wooden beads. Directions for
Plant Hangers begin on page 61.

Now, more than ever, plants are the most noticed accents. Planters can coordinate the look of an entire room. We've woven and wrapped burlap strips to echo the look of ever-popular natural baskets and fibers. Directions for Burlap Planters begin on page 62.

Fabric Painting

Shown on pages 33 and 93

SIZES: Pillows, 14″ square; Large Apron, 28″ × 34½″; Small Apron, 20¾″ × 23½″; Tote Bag, desired size.

EQUIPMENT: Sharp pencil. Ruler. Paper. Tracing paper. Automatic clothes dryer. Iron and press cloth. Flat acrylic paintbrushes, ⅛″, ⅜″, and ¾″ wide. Plastic coffee-can lids or coated paper plates, etc., for palettes. *For Tote Bag:* 1″-diameter button. *For Pillows and Aprons:* Scissors. Sewing machine. Straight pins. Sewing needle. Staple gun and staples. Stretcher frame pieces in the following lengths: Pillows, four 20″ pieces; Large Apron, two 34″ pieces, two 42″ pieces; Small Apron, two 28″ pieces, two 30″ pieces. *For Aprons:* Colored pencil. Paper for patterns. Dressmaker's tracing (carbon) paper. Tracing wheel. Masking tape, ¾″ wide. *For Pillows:* Can, 3″ diameter.

MATERIALS: Liquitex Acrylic Artists' Color Paint, one tube each in the following colors: Cerulean Blue, Light Emerald Green, Vivid Red, Orange. *For Tote Bag:* Additional tube of Liquitex paint in Chromium Oxide Green. Purchased unbleached canvas tote bag in desired size. Large scrap of unbleached canvas or white duck for practice painting. *For Each Pillow:* Unbleached lightweight canvas or white duck, 45″ wide, one yard. Welting cord, ¼″ wide, 59″ long. Fiberfill. Off-white thread. *For Aprons:* Unbleached lightweight canvas or white duck, 45″ wide, 1½ yards for Large Apron, 1 yard for Small Apron, plus large scrap. Double-fold bias tape, 3½ yards for Large Apron, 2¼ yards for Small Apron. Thread, off-white and green.

GENERAL DIRECTIONS; Cut and prepare canvas and any patterns needed, following individual directions; work out those designs without patterns on paper, following individual directions and using photograph as a guide. Lightly pencil-sketch design on canvas, transferring pattern lines as indicated. Practice painting on canvas scrap, then paint design as follows: Squeeze a small amount of paint onto palette; thin with a little water. To paint broad lines and large flowers, use the widest brush; for thin lines, small rings, squares, etc., use finest brush. Paint all lines in a smooth, continuous movement. For dots, daub canvas with paintbrush. Shapes do not need to be perfect; variations in size and form enhance the design. Clean brushes with water when changing colors. When paint has dried, seal it by putting piece into a hot clothes dryer for several minutes (or pressing with a hot dry iron and press cloth).

Pillows

For Each: Cut canvas piece 20″ square for pillow front. Draw a 14″ square in center of canvas, leaving a 3″ margin all around. Assemble stretcher frame according to manufacturer's directions. Staple canvas tautly to frame, keeping grain straight. Following General Directions, paint each design within 14″ square.

For Floral Pillow: Trace actual-size flower pattern (not leaves); cut out. Lightly trace flower outlines on pillow front, in a random arrangement; see photograph. Paint flowers orange; fill in background with large and small orange dots, medium green dots, medium blue rings; paint flower centers blue.

For Ringed Pillow: In center of pillow, lightly draw three circles, evenly spaced, using a 3″-diameter can as a pattern. Inside each circle, paint a ½″-wide orange ring; connect rings and pillow edges with ½″-wide diagonal bands (see photograph). Inside each orange ring, paint a thin blue ring; paint ¾″-diameter blue circle in ring centers; paint a thin green ring around blue circles. For upper half of design, paint a ¾″-wide wavy green stripe 3¼″ above rings. Paint a thin wavy blue stripe, then slightly wider orange stripe, on both sides of green stripe. Just above circles, paint wavy stripes in this order: thin blue, thin green, wider blue. Turn canvas 180° and repeat stripe painting for lower half.

For Stripes and Squares Pillow: Paint a 1¾″-wide blue stripe across center of pillow; paint a ¼″-wide orange stripe and a ¼″-wide blue stripe on either side as shown. Paint lower half of design as follows: Mark a section below blue stripe, 2¼″ wide. Paint six evenly spaced 1″ blue boxes across center of section; paint slightly smaller solid green squares inside each. Paint seven ⅝″ green boxes slightly above and in between blue boxes. Repeat below blue boxes. Dot centers of green boxes with blue. Dot background with orange. Next, paint a thin blue stripe, a ½″-wide orange stripe, and another thin blue stripe as shown. Fill in remaining area with blue, orange

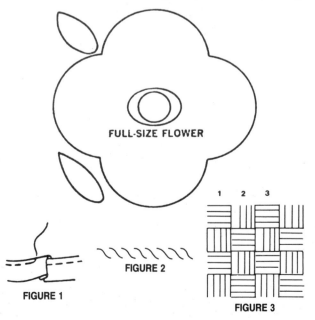

FULL-SIZE FLOWER

FIGURE 1

FIGURE 2

FIGURE 3

and green small dots. Turn canvas 180° and repeat, for upper half. Finally, paint a thin green stripe across wide blue center band.

Finishing Pillows: When design is completed, let dry; remove from stretcher and seal, following General Directions. Press on wrong side to remove wrinkles from dryer, if necessary. Cut out pillow front ½″ beyond marked square all around. From blank canvas, cut pillow back same size. To make welting, cut 1½″-wide bias strips of canvas, piecing strips to obtain 59″ length. Center welting cord along bias strip on the wrong side; fold strip over cord so that edges are aligned. Using zipper foot attachment, machine-stitch along strip with needle as close to cord as possible.

To attach welting to pillow front, begin in the middle of one side; pin welting to right side of front so that raw edges of welting and pillow front are even; overlap ends 1″. Starting 2″ from beginning of welting, stitch all around to 2″ from end of welting. Snip out 1″ of cord from overlapping end. Turn under ½″ of extra fabric and, butting ends of cord, fit it over the start of welting (see Figure 1). Finish stitching welting to pillow front.

With right sides facing, stitch front and back together, making ½″ seams; leave opening in center of one side. Clip corners of canvas diagonally; turn pillow right side out. Stuff with fiberfill until firm; slip-stitch opening closed.

Aprons

Using sharp pencil, draw lines across pattern, connecting grid lines. (Outline for small apron is indicated by dot-dash line, except for common solid line at bib top; large flower on bib front is for both aprons.) Enlarge patterns by copying on paper ruled in 2″ squares. Complete half-pattern indicated by dash lines. For each apron, assemble stretcher frame according to manufacturer's directions; cut canvas to fit. Using dressmaker's carbon and tracing wheel, transfer apron to center of canvas. Mask straight side edges with tape, covering ¾″ area within outline. Staple canvas tautly to frame, keeping grain straight.

For Large Apron: Trace large flower on apron bib; use as a pattern to transfer a second flower to apron skirt at center right, as shown in photograph, and at bottom left (not shown). Following General Directions, paint large flowers orange with blue circles in centers; paint small flowers blue, dotting centers with orange; paint wavy stripes, one in each color, as shown. Paint large and small orange dots, medium green dots, and medium blue rings to fill in apron background above stripes. Fill in area below stripes with small blue and orange dots, and medium green dots.

For Small Apron: Paint as for large apron, omitting large orange flower on skirt, small blue flowers and dots below stripes, and adding small blue dots to background above stripes.

Finishing Aprons: When paint dries, remove tape and canvas from stretcher. *(Note:* Measurements given are for large apron; for small apron, use measurements in parentheses.) Cut out apron, adding 1¼″ (¾″) to straight side and bottom edges. Turn side edges under ¼″ (¼″), then 1″ (½″); press; hem-stitch with off-white thread. Turn bottom edge under and finish in same manner. Cut 9½″ (8″) of tape; sandwich apron top edge (from A to A) in tape; stitch. Pin remaining tape to curved raw edges of apron as follows: Leaving 30″ (18″) of tape free at one end for tie, sandwich one curved raw edge (B to A) in tape; leaving 20″ (17″) of tape free for neck strap, sandwich second curved raw edge (A to B) in tape; remaining tape is for second tie. Starting at one end of tape, topstitch across, making ties and neck strap and

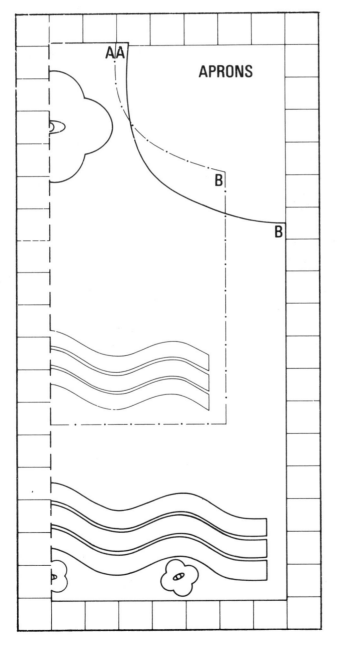

enclosing raw edges. Paint visible sides of bias tape green, and let dry.

Tote Bag

Read General Directions. If strap ends at upper edge of bag, draw mock straps on bag by continuing strap outlines down bag sides. Paint one side of bag as follows: Lightly draw a line across side 2½″ down and parallel to bag top, skipping over straps. Trace actual-size flower and leaves separately; cut out patterns. Working above line, use flower pattern to draw flowers at random, overlapping line and straps slightly at times; trace one or two flowers below line (see photograph). Use 1″ button to draw round flowers in the same manner. Using leaf patterns, fill in around flowers, as shown. Paint straps as follows: Paint thin blue stripes down each edge and center of strap, skipping over flowers. Fill in area between blue stripes with Light Emerald Green, in same manner. Paint large flowers orange with blue-dot centers. For round flowers, use ⅜″ brush to paint blue rings within circles; dot centers. Paint some leaves with Light Emerald Green and some with Chromium Oxide Green. Make a few small freehand leaves in either color to fill in spaces.

Lightly draw a line ½″ below first line. Within this band, use ⅛″ brush to paint a rope effect (Figure 2); do not paint over flowers or straps. With sharp pencil and ruler, lightly rule remainder of bag in 1″ squares, skipping over painted designs. Using Figure 3 as a guide, paint "basket weaving" as follows: Begin with top left square (Square 1); with ⅛″ brush, paint five horizontal lines in square, using top of square as first line. Move right one square (Square 2); paint five vertical lines, using left side of square as first line. Move right one square; paint as for Square 1. Continue across row, alternating horizontal and vertical lines. Paint the row just under top row in same manner, but beginning with a square of vertical lines. Paint third row, beginning with horizontal lines, and so on, until all rows are painted. Let paint dry.

Turn bag over; repeat painting on other side. Seal, following General Directions. ◇

Whites and Brights
Shown on pages 34–35

EQUIPMENT: Pencil. Ruler. Graph paper. Thin, stiff cardboard. Glue. Straight pins. Sewing needle. Sewing machine.

MATERIALS: Unbleached muslin 45″ wide: see individual directions for amounts. Polished cotton, red, blue, purple, yellow, green, olive: small amounts for each project. Batting. Fiberfill for stuffing. Sewing thread to match muslin. White twill tape ¼″ wide, for Pillows C and D.

GENERAL DIRECTIONS: The patchwork for each item is a variation of the "log cabin" pattern. Patchwork and quilting are done simultaneously in one or several blocks for each item, using the same general method throughout.

Read General Directions for Quilting (see Contents). Make patterns for patch pieces: For each item, see diagram (following page), which represents one block. Following dimensions shown, mark actual-size outline of block on graph paper, using ruler and sharp pencil. Beginning at outer edge of block with longest strip and working towards center, mark strips and squares as shown on diagram, making each strip 1¼″ wide. When all are marked, label shaded parts with letter shown. Glue graph paper design to cardboard; let dry. Cut on marked lines for individual patterns.

Cut out patch pieces; press fabrics smooth. Place patterns with the grain, on wrong side of fabric, leaving at least ½″ between pieces; mark around pattern with sharp pencil held at an outward angle. Place lettered patterns on polished cotton, following color key; place unlettered patterns on muslin. Cut out each piece ¼″ beyond marked lines, for seam allowance.

Block: For each block, cut two pieces of muslin and one of batting, all ½″ wider and longer than dimensions given on diagram. On one muslin piece, mark two corner-to-corner diagonal lines, crossing in center, unless otherwise directed. Place batting between muslin pieces, with marked side facing up, and baste layers together.

Sew strips and squares to prepared block, starting in center and working in circular fashion out to edges. Place center square, right side up, on marked muslin, matching corners of square to marked lines; do not turn under seam allowance. Baste in place ¼″ from edges. Place smallest adjacent piece right side down over center piece, matching raw edges on adjacent side. On this side, machine-stitch through all thicknesses on marked seamline of second piece. Turn second piece to right side and press lightly in place. Place another adjacent piece (same size or next largest) right side down over first two pieces, matching raw edges on adjacent side; stitch, turn and press as before. Continue adding pieces in this manner, always overlapping one piece with another, until all are used and muslin block is covered; raw edges of outer pieces and block should match. To finish block, machine-baste all around ⅛″ from edges. Complete item as directed.

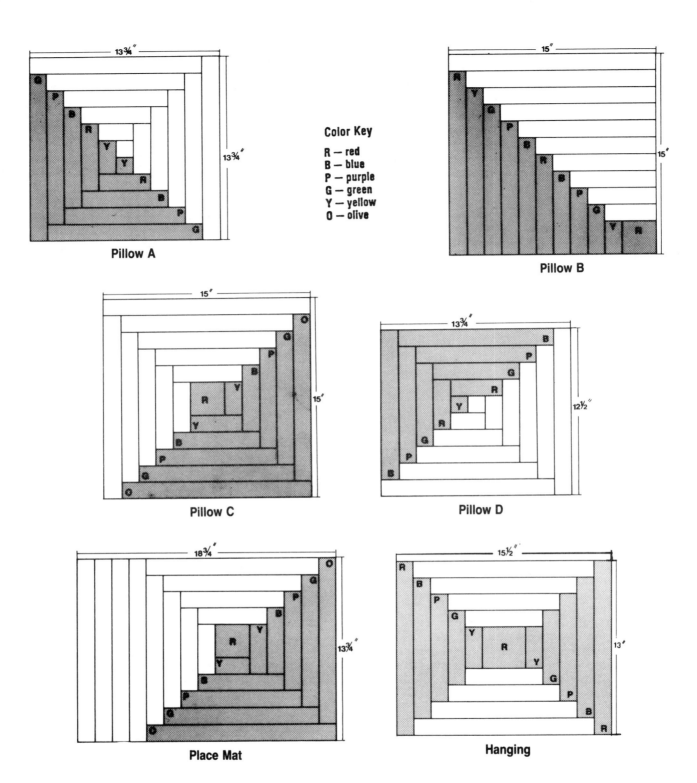

Color Key

R — red
B — blue
P — purple
G — green
Y — yellow
O — olive

Pillow A

Pillow B

Pillow C

Pillow D

Place Mat

Hanging

Pillow A

(Pillow in chair, right). **Size:** 13¾″ square. Muslin, ½ yard. Read General Directions. Make patterns and cut patch pieces for one block, as directed. Prepare muslin block (14¼″ square), then sew on pieces: Begin in center with muslin square; add Y square, then Y strip; continue around in clockwise direction until all pieces are added. Finish edges for pillow top.

To assemble pillow, cut piece from muslin same size as pillow top, for backing. Place pillow top and backing together, right sides facing. Stitch around edges with ¼″ seams, leaving opening in one side for stuffing. Turn pillow to right side, stuff firmly, then turn in edges at opening and slip-stitch closed.

Pillow B

(Pillow in chair, left). **Size:** 15″ square. Muslin, 1 yard. Make patterns and cut patch pieces for one block, as directed. Prepare muslin block ($15\frac{1}{2}''$ square), omitting guidelines, and sew on pieces: Baste R square in lower right corner of block, matching outer raw edges. Add short Y strip, then short muslin strip, then short G strip, etc., always matching outer raw edges with block. Continue towards upper left corner until all pieces are added. Finish edges, for pillow top. Assemble pillow as for Pillow A.

Pillow C

(Floor pillow). **Size:** 30″ square. Muslin, $2\frac{5}{8}$ yards. Read General Directions. Make patterns for one block, then cut patch pieces for four identical blocks, as directed. Prepare four muslin blocks (each $15\frac{1}{2}''$ square), and sew on pieces: For each, begin in center with R square; add short Y strip, then long Y strip, then shortest muslin strip; continue around in clockwise direction until all pieces are added. Finish edges on the four blocks.

For pillow top, join the four blocks as shown in color illustration, making $\frac{1}{4}''$ seams. Assemble pillow as for Pillow A; to strengthen seams, place twill tape over seamline as you stitch.

Pillow D

(Floor pillow). **Size:** $26\frac{1}{4}'' \times 28\frac{3}{4}''$. Muslin, $3\frac{1}{4}$ yards. Read General Directions. Make patterns for one block, then cut patch pieces for four identical blocks, as directed. Prepare four muslin blocks (each $14\frac{1}{4}''$ wide × 13″ deep), omitting diagonal guidelines; mark vertical and horizontal lines, crossing in center, as guides. Sew on pieces: For each block, begin just above center with muslin square, aligning bottom seamline (not raw edge) of piece with horizontal guideline and centering piece widthwise. Add Y square, then shortest horizontal muslin strip, then shortest vertical muslin strip. Continue around in counterclockwise direction until all pieces are added. Finish edges on the four blocks.

For pillow top, lay out the blocks as shown in color illustration on page 34; do not sew together. Cut joining strips from yellow fabric, two $1\frac{3}{4}'' \times 14\frac{1}{4}''$ and one $1\frac{3}{4}'' \times 26\frac{3}{4}''$ (measurements include seam allowance). Sew a short strip between blocks in each vertical row, then sew long strip between vertical rows, making $\frac{1}{4}''$ seams. Pillow top should measure $26\frac{3}{4}'' \times 29\frac{1}{4}''$.

To Assemble Pillow, cut piece from muslin same size as pillow top, for backing. Cut piece $5\frac{1}{2}'' \times 115''$ for boxing strip. Right sides facing and making $\frac{1}{4}''$ seam, stitch strip around edge of pillow top, starting in center of one side; to strengthen seam, place twill tape over seamline as you stitch. When you have returned to starting point, cut off excess beyond 1″, fold under end $\frac{1}{2}''$ and stitch folded end over raw end. Stitch other edge of strip to backing in same manner, and complete pillow as for Pillow A.

Place Mat

Size: $19\frac{1}{4}'' \times 14\frac{1}{4}''$. Muslin, $\frac{1}{2}$ yard. Read General Directions. Make patterns and cut patch pieces for one block, as directed. Prepare muslin block ($19\frac{1}{4}'' \times 14\frac{1}{4}''$), marking guidelines as follows: Mark a $14\frac{1}{4}''$ square on muslin piece, measuring from right edge and leaving 5″ beyond square on left side. Mark corner-to-corner diagonal lines within marked square. Sew pieces to block within square: To begin, press under seam allowance on one long edge of both Y strips; place pressed edge of Y strips over seam allowance of R square as shown and pin to hold, creating the center "square" of design. Place R-Y square on muslin, matching corners of entire square with diagonal lines; pin R piece in place, then remove Y pieces. Proceed as in General Directions, basting R square, then adding smaller Y strip, larger Y strip, smallest muslin strip, next largest muslin strip, etc., continuing around in clockwise direction until marked square of block is covered. Fill out block with four muslin strips on left side. Finish edges.

To complete mat, cut two 1″-wide strips on straight of fabric, one 40″ long from muslin, one 32″ long from olive. Sew strips together at one end with $\frac{1}{4}''$ seam; press seam flat. Press one long edge of combined strip $\frac{1}{4}''$ to wrong side. Right sides facing and raw edges even, pin strip all around edge of mat, matching colors and mitering corners. Stitch around with $\frac{1}{4}''$ seam. Fold strip to back of mat; slip-stitch folded edge in place.

Hanging

Size: $55\frac{3}{4}'' \times 29\frac{3}{4}''$. Muslin, 3 yards. Read General Directions. Make patterns for one block, then cut patch pieces for eight blocks, omitting one R strip from four blocks. Prepare eight muslin blocks (16″ × $13\frac{1}{2}''$), then sew on pieces: Begin in center with R square, then add Y strips, shortest muslin strips, G strips, next muslin strips, etc., until all pieces are added; on four blocks, there will be an empty "strip" on one side, instead of an R strip. Finish edges.

Join each incomplete block to a complete block, placing them with right sides facing and stitching outer seamline of a red strip in complete block to outer seamline of blue strip in incomplete block. Turn blocks to right side, press lightly on joining seam and slip-stitch overlapped edge of empty strip in place on wrong side.

Place the four pairs of blocks one under the other in horizontal rows, as shown in color illustration on page 34. To join rows, cut six strips from muslin $1\frac{3}{4}'' \times 30\frac{1}{4}''$. Baste together three pairs of strips with batting between. Sew long edges of padded strips to rows, right sides facing and making $\frac{1}{4}''$ seams. Turn under outside seam allowance of hanging $\frac{1}{4}''$ to wrong side; slip-stitch in place. For lining, cut piece $56\frac{1}{4}'' \times 30\frac{1}{4}''$ from muslin; turn in edges $\frac{1}{4}''$ and press. Place lining and hanging together, wrong sides facing, and slip-stitch all around edges. ◇

Painted Pillows

Shown on page 37

SIZE: Each, 17″ square.

EQUIPMENT: Pencil. Ruler. Scissors. Compass. Paper for patterns. Tracing paper. Dressmaker's tracing (carbon) paper. Tracing wheel or dry ballpoint pen. Wooden working surface. Scrap fabric and newspapers to cover surface. Pushpins. Masking tape. Small and medium-sized bristle brushes. Saucer. Straight pins. Sewing needle. Sewing machine.

MATERIALS: *(For Each Pillow):* For pillow front and backing for quilting, cotton muslin, 36″ wide, ½ yd. For pillow back, blue cotton, 18″ square. Polyester stuffing, 1½-1¾ lbs. Black sewing thread. One tube acrylic paint for each color; see illustration. (One tube will do all four pillows). Batting.

DIRECTIONS: *Patterns:* Enlarge the four complete patterns on this page by copying on paper ruled in 1″ squares. To aid in drawing patterns, trace actual-size patterns given for heart, wave, and star; complete half-patterns of heart and star indicated by dash lines and repeat wave as shown. Use compass for drawing circles (4″ diameter for first and third pillows; 5″ for fourth pillow).

Wash muslin to remove sizing; press smooth when dry. For each pillow, cut one 18″ square for pillow front; reserve remainder. Place pillow front on wooden surface; secure smoothly with pushpins and tape. Using dressmaker's carbon and tracing wheel, trace pattern onto pillow front, leaving ½″ margins all around.

Painting: Remove pillow front from wooden surface. Cover surface with several sheets of newspaper, taping them down smoothly. Cover newspaper with fabric scrap, taping it smoothly. Place pillow front next, marked side up; secure all around as before.

Following illustration for colors, paint pillow front; white areas of designs remain unpainted. To paint, squeeze a small amount of one color into a saucer; squeeze more as you need it. Dampen brush, choosing a size appropriate for each area. Dip brush into paint, then wipe off excess. Carefully paint all areas of one color, keeping within the outlines. Cover area thoroughly, but not thickly; only one coat may be necessary. Let each color dry before painting the next area. Wash brushes with warm water and soap; do not let paint dry on brush. When painting is completed and pillow front thoroughly dry, remove from working surface.

Quilting: For backing, use remaining 18″ muslin square; cut batting same size. Following General Directions for Quilting (see Contents), pin and baste backing, batting, and pillow front together, avoiding unpainted areas as much as possible. Using black thread and fine stitch, machine-quilt around each motif; begin quilting in center of piece and work outward.

Assembling: When quilting is completed, place pillow front and blue back together with right sides

facing. Using ½″ seam allowance, stitch around three sides and both ends of fourth side, rounding corners. Clip into seam allowance at corners. Turn pillow right side out. Stuff firmly. Turn raw edges inside and slip-stitch closed. ◇

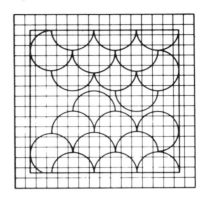

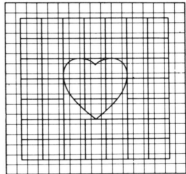

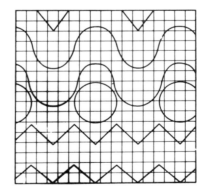

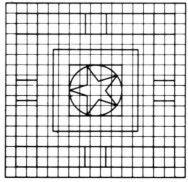

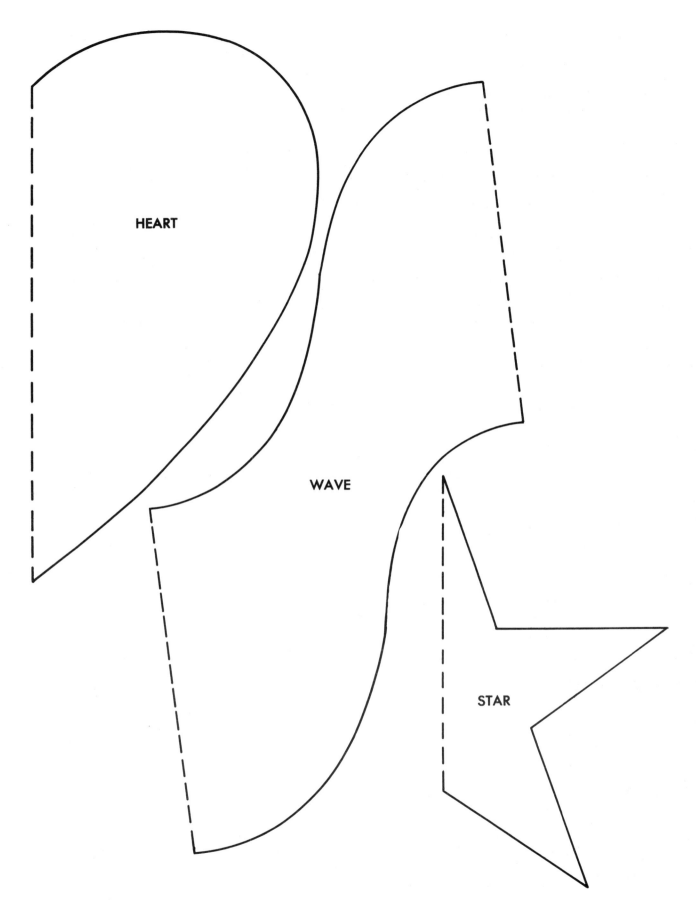

HEART

WAVE

STAR

Star-Fold Pillow

Shown on page 36

SIZE: 17″ in diameter.

EQUIPMENT: Light and dark colored pencils. Scissors. Ruler. Straight pins. Sewing needle. Thin, stiff cardboard. Thumbtack. String.

MATERIALS: For star design, seven print and solid-color fabrics in compatible colors, 36″ wide, $\frac{1}{4}$-$\frac{1}{2}$ yd. each; see directions below. For lining, muslin 18″ square. For pillow border and backing, two pieces of red fabric 18″ square. Matching sewing threads. Fiberfill for stuffing.

DIRECTIONS: Pillow is constructed with 76 square patches folded to form a star design.

Patches: For pattern, cut several 5″ squares from cardboard; discard when edges begin to fray. For patches, place pattern on fabric, mark around with pencil, and cut out; there is no seam allowance. Before cutting patches, plan arrangement of colors, working from the center of star design outward in circular fashion. For center, cut four patches (in our pillow, red-and-white print); for first, second, and third circles, cut eight patches each (red print, solid blue, solid white); for fourth, fifth, and sixth circles, cut 16 patches each (blue, red, blue prints).

Star Design: On muslin square, draw diagonal lines between opposite corners to find center of square. Patches will be folded and sewn to muslin for star design.

Place a red-and-white print center patch on a flat surface, wrong side up. Fold patch in half horizontally. Fold the top corners down to meet at center of bottom edge, forming a triangle; pin to keep folds in place. Make three more center triangles in same manner. Place the four triangles on muslin, with folded points all meeting in center of piece; pin in place. With thread doubled in needle, tack down each triangle at folded point and along outer edge opposite folded point.

For first circle, fold eight red-print patches into triangles as before. On each red-and-white center triangle, mark a point on center fold $\frac{3}{4}$″ from folded point of triangle; mark points where sides of adjacent triangles meet, $\frac{3}{4}$″ from folded points. There are now eight points marked, evenly spaced in a circle. Place the eight red triangles in a circle on muslin, overlapping the red-and-white triangles and each other; place folded points on points marked. Tack down as before.

For second circle, fold blue squares into triangles and add to star design as before, with points $\frac{3}{4}$″ from folded points of red triangles; place blue triangles in center folds only of red triangles. Make third circle in same manner. Make fourth circle as for first circle. Make fifth and sixth circles as for second circle.

Pillow: Tie a pencil to one end of string, a thumbtack to other end, with $8\frac{3}{4}$″ length of string in between. Place tack in center of an 18″ red piece and, with pencil held upright, draw around for a circle $17\frac{1}{2}$″ in diameter; cut out circle. On second red piece, cut another circle the same size. In center of one circle, draw another circle $11\frac{1}{2}$″ in diameter, using $5\frac{3}{4}$″ length of string; cut out second circle, leaving the red border piece.

In center of muslin backing of star design, draw a circle $17\frac{1}{2}$″ in diameter. Place border piece over muslin, wrong side of border on right side of muslin and matching raw edges. Stitch pieces together, $\frac{3}{16}$″ from edge. On border, turn in edge of inner circle $\frac{1}{4}$″ (or enough to just cover outer edges of star design); clip curve, press, and slipstitch folded edge to star design, completing front of pillow.

Sew front of pillow to remaining red circle, right sides together and with $\frac{1}{4}$″ seams; leave 7″ opening. Turn pillow cover to right side, stuff with fiberfill; slip-stitch opening closed. ◇

House Pillow

Shown on page 36

SIZE: 13″ × 14″.

EQUIPMENT: Pencil. Scissors. Ruler. Thin, stiff cardboard. Dressmaker's tracing (carbon) paper. Tracing wheel or dry ball-point pen. Sewing and quilting needles. Quilting frame (optional). Glue.

MATERIALS: Small amounts of closely woven cotton fabric in black, blue, red, red gingham, yellow, and green print. Special print for girl's face in window. Print fabric and muslin $14\frac{1}{2}$″ × $13\frac{1}{2}$″. Red yarn for tassels. Black, white, and yellow sewing thread. Batting.

DIRECTIONS: Read General Directions for Quilting (see Contents). Pillow top is a pieced block, set in a plain border.

Pieced Block: To make pillow front, enlarge pattern by copying on paper ruled in 1″ squares. Dash lines indicate quilting lines. Glue pattern to cardboard; cut on marked lines for separate appliqué patterns. Marking patterns on wrong side of fabric and adding $\frac{1}{4}$″ seam allowance all around, cut 17 patch pieces in colors desired or following color illustration. Assemble patch pieces for a block measuring $11\frac{1}{2}$″ × $12\frac{1}{2}$″, including outside seam allowance.

Borders: From black fabric, cut two pieces $1\frac{1}{2}$″ × $12\frac{1}{2}$″ and two $1\frac{1}{2}$″ × $13\frac{1}{2}$″. Stitch two shorter pieces to top and bottom of pillow block, then two longer pieces to sides, right sides together and making $\frac{1}{4}$″ seams. Piece should measure $13\frac{1}{2}$″ × $14\frac{1}{2}$″.

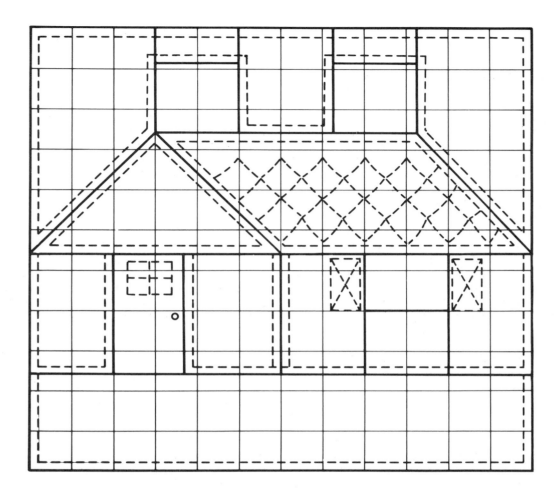

Quilting: Using dressmaker's carbon and tracing wheel or dry ball-point pen, transfer dash lines of pattern to pillow front. Cut batting and muslin $13\frac{1}{2}''$ × $14\frac{1}{2}''$. Following General Directions, pin and baste pillow front, batting, and muslin together. Quilt around marked lines, starting in center and working around and outward; use thread in contrasting colors.

Lining: Cut print lining fabric $13\frac{1}{2}''$ × $14\frac{1}{2}''$. Place pillow front and lining right sides together; machine-stitch around with $\frac{1}{4}''$ seams, leaving several inches unstitched in center of one long side. Turn right side out. Stuff pillow fully, packing corners. Slip-stitch opening closed.

Tassels: Cut cardboard to size of tassel desired. Wind red yarn around cardboard about 30 times. Tie a strand tightly around yarn on top edge of cardboard; remove cardboard, clipping opposite ends of yarn. Tie a second piece of yarn $\frac{3}{4}''$ below first tie. Trim ends of tassel evenly. Make three more in same manner. Stitch to corners. ◇

Pulled-Thread Pillows

Shown on page 38

SIZE: Approximately 17″ square.

EQUIPMENT: Masking tape. Ruler. Pencil. Scissors. Sewing and tapestry needles. Straight pins. Sewing machine. Artist's canvas stretcher frame, 21″ square (inside dimension about $18\frac{1}{2}''$ square). **For Blocking:** Softwood surface. Brown wrapping paper. Rustproof thumbtacks.

MATERIALS: *For Two Pillows:* Cream-colored rug canvas, 6 mesh-to-the-inch, 40″ wide, $\frac{3}{4}$ yard. Lily Sugar-'N-Cream cotton yarn in 125-yard balls, 4 balls white. Aqua linen-like fabric for pillow covers, 36″ wide, $1\frac{1}{2}$ yards. Muslin for inner pillows, 45″ wide, $1\frac{1}{4}$ yards. Polyester fiberfill, about 3 lbs. for two pillows. Cable cord $\frac{1}{4}''$ thick, 4 yards for pillow cording. Sewing thread to match fabric.

DIRECTIONS: For two pillows, cut two canvas pieces 20″ square, including one selvage edge for each. Tape raw edges to prevent raveling. Wash pieces by hand in cold water to remove sizing. Mark center of each side of the canvas. Staple or tack canvas to stretcher frame so that it is taut.

To work pillows, refer to charts, Stitch Details, and directions for each pillow. Both designs are worked over 104 threads in each direction, including the border.

Cut cotton yarn in 44" lengths and use doubled in needle. To start, leave 1" of cotton at back of canvas and cover as work proceeds. Fasten ends of strands by weaving through a few stitches on back of work, as invisibly as possible. Avoid long jumps across back of work.

In the charts and stitch diagrams, each line represents a thread of the canvas and each square the space between the threads. Horizontal and vertical stitches are taken between two parallel threads and over a specified number of perpendicular threads. Diagonal stitches are taken over a specified number of thread-crossings or by counting a number of threads across, then up or down.

In working some stitches, the canvas threads are pulled toward each other by the yarn. We have used asterisks in the following descriptions of stitches to indicate the degree of tension needed for each stitch.

*indicates a normal tension (as for needlepoint).

**indicates a medium tension, with enough pressure to compress and distort the threads of the canvas.

***indicates a really tight tension, with the thread pulled as hard as possible.

Border: The border pattern is the same for both pillows. It consists of an outside row of Straight Satin Stitch, a middle row of Overlapping Star Eyelets, and an inside row of Straight Satin Stitch.

Measuring from the inside of the frame, find the center of the canvas. From center point, count 50 threads down toward frame, then 50 threads to the left; mark this thread with a pin. Following chart, begin border in lower left corner, working eyelet row first: Referring to Stitch Details, begin first eyelet over marked thread. Continue working overlapped eyelets until you have 15. Work one Con-

densed Eyelet between two full eyelets and continue the row, working full eyelets, until you have 33 overlapped eyelets. The 33rd eyelet at the end of row is counted as the first eyelet of the adjacent row. Each row covers 100 threads. Give canvas a quarter turn and work next side in same manner, working one Condensed Eyelet in the center of side. Continue until border is complete around four sides.

Following chart work one row of Straight Satin Stitch outside the eyelet row, pulling the stitches toward the mounting frame; work corners as shown. Work one row of Straight Satin Stitch inside the eyelet row, pulling the stitches toward the center.

Satin-Bar Pillow

Following chart and starting inside upper left corner, work alternating Straight Satin Bars across row, completing 14 bars. Reverse direction of canvas and work second row above first row from left to right, beginning again with a horizontal bar. Repeat until you have completed 14 alternating rows.

Eyelet Pillow

Following chart, start inside upper left corner and work Diagonal Satin Bars in zigzag pattern across row, completing 14 bars. Continue working rows across, alternating the zigzag pattern, until you have completed 14 rows. Next, work a Diamond Eyelet in the middle of each diamond space created by the bars. Work partial eyelets at the border edges, as shown on chart.

When embroidery is complete, block, if necessary, face up.

To Assemble Pillows: After embroidery is blocked, trim canvas margins to ½". Cut two pieces of aqua fabric the same size as trimmed canvas. Pin the wrong side of the embroidery to the right side of one piece of fabric and topstitch all around close to stitching, for pillow front. Reserve other fabric piece for backing.

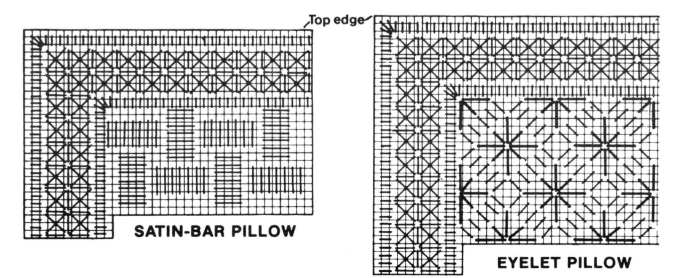

Top edge

SATIN-BAR PILLOW

EYELET PILLOW

To Make Fabric Cording: Cut 1½″-wide bias strips from remaining fabric. Join to make one strip long enough to fit perimeter of pillow plus ½″ overlap. Lay ¼″-thick cable cord along center length of strip on wrong side of fabric. Fold strip over cord and stitch along length of strip close to cord. With raw edges of cording facing out, baste cording to right side of canvas, keeping cording seam along edges of embroidery and rounding corners slightly. Overlap cording ends ½″; trim off any excess. To fit ends together, cut off one end of cord ½″ inside fabric casing; turn in casing ¼″. Insert other end and slipstitch fabric of both ends together. Stitch cording to pillow front.

With right sides facing, stitch backing and pillow front together, making ½″ seams; leave opening at center of one side; turn right side out.

To Make Inner Pillow: Cut two pieces of muslin 2″ wider and longer than pillow. With right sides facing, sew edges together with ½″ seams, leaving an opening at center of one side. Clip into seams at corners. Turn. Stuff fully. Turn in raw edges of opening; slip-stitch closed.

Insert inner pillow through opening of pillow. Add stuffing in corners if necessary. Turn in raw edges; slip-stitch closed.

Stitch Details

Straight Satin Stitch: Work a row of stitches from left to right, stitching over 2 horizontal threads of canvas and going into each hole across the row (***).

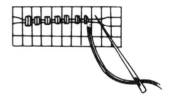

Straight Satin Bars: Work blocks of 7 stitches over 4 threads (**). Work blocks in opposing directions and in alternating rows from left to right.

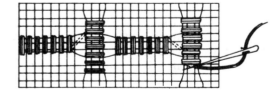

Diagonal Satin Bars: Work blocks of 5 stitches over two thread-crossings (*). Work in zigzag lines and in alternating rows.

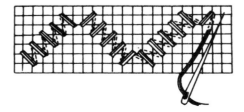

Eyelets: All stitches of an eyelet converge on a common center hole. Work stitches up from the outer edge and down through the center, pulling the center outward.

Diamond Eyelet: Consists of 8 stitches (each worked twice) within a square of 8 threads. Take 1 double stitch from each side of the square over 4 threads, then 1 double stitch from each diagonal over 2 thread-crossings (**).

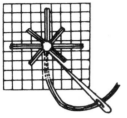

Star Eyelet: Consists of 8 stitches worked within a square of 6 threads. Work 1 stitch from each corner of the square over 3 thread-crossings, and 1 stitch from the center of each side of the square over 3 threads (**). Work each eyelet clockwise, starting in the lower left-hand corner; see stitches numbered 1 through 8 in the figure.

Overlapping Star Eyelets: Work a star eyelet as shown below. Begin second eyelet in same hole as stitch 8 of the first eyelet, crossing stitch 7 to the new eyelet center. Continue around clockwise so that stitch 2 of second eyelet completely overlaps stitch 6 of the previous eyelet and stitch 3 crosses stitch 5. Finish as for first eyelet. The left side of each succeeding eyelet will overlap the right side of preceding eyelet.

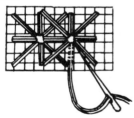

Condensed Star Eyelet. A condensed star eyelet covers 4 threads widthwise, instead of 6, and appears as a link between two regular eyelets. Work first eyelet, covering 3 threads on the left but only 2 on the right; work the condensed eyelet, covering 2 threads on both sides; work the third eyelet, covering 2 threads on the left and 3 on the right. ◇

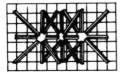

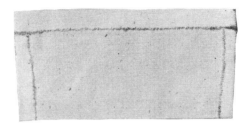

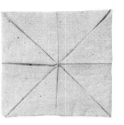

Cathedral Pillow

Shown on page 36

SIZE: 19″ square.

EQUIPMENT: Ruler. Scissors. Pencil. Straight pins. Sewing needle. Thin, stiff cardboard.

MATERIALS: Cotton fabric 45″ wide: blue, $\frac{2}{3}$ yd.; orange, $\frac{1}{4}$ yd.; white unbleached muslin, $\frac{1}{2}$ yd. Matching sewing threads. Loose filler for stuffing. Orange double-fold bias binding tape, $\frac{1}{4}$″ wide, $2\frac{1}{4}$ yds.

DIRECTIONS: *Window Design:* For pillow, no sheet batting is required, as there is no actual quilting stitch. For design, squares of muslin are folded into a multithickness and then joined together. Wash fabrics to be used, to preshrink, then press. Cut nine pieces of muslin, each 9″ square.

On one square, fold over one edge $\frac{1}{2}$″ and press down; fold over opposite edge, then remaining edges in same manner. (To facilitate folding edges, cut an 8″ square from cardboard). Fold squares in half with folded edges on outside; see first detail. Sew edges together from the open corners at top down sides for $1\frac{1}{2}$″; use close overcasting stitch, catching just the edges of the fabric. Turn piece inside out and refold flat into a square, with seams meeting in center (see second detail); press. Sew the open edges together from center out, $1\frac{1}{2}$″ on both sides; use slip-stitch and do not sew through bottom fabric. Piece is $5\frac{3}{4}$″ square. Turn piece over so plain side is on top. Fold corners in so they meet at center; press and pin (see third detail). Tack corners together securely at center, then tack to square, going through all thicknesses in center. Piece is 4″ square. Make eight more pieces in same manner.

Join two 4″ squares as follows: Hold pieces with open-fold sides together; overcast along one edge; open out and press. (Open-fold sides will be right

side of design; seamed sides will be underneath.) Join a third square to make a strip of three squares. Make three more strips in same manner. Join strips, overcasting edges, for a piece 9″ square.

For colored "window" patches, cut a $2\frac{3}{4}$″ square from cardboard. Cut 20 patches from orange fabric and four patches from blue fabric. Place muslin piece with open-fold side up. Window patches are placed over the diamond shapes formed by two adjacent squares (see fourth detail). Pin a window patch in place, trimming edges a little if necessary. Fold one edge of diamond shape in a curve over onto window patch and slip-stitch in place, leaving both ends of curved edge unstitched for $\frac{1}{4}$″. Repeat with an adjacent edge of diamond shape, then tack the adjacent ends together. Continue around diamond shape in same manner. When four window patches have been added to a block of four squares, the touching points form four petals in the center. Continue adding window patches until all squares have been covered, placing the four blue patches in center and the orange patches all around. Fold back the excess orange fabric around edges of piece and sew to underside.

Pillow: From blue fabric cut two pieces $19\frac{1}{2}$″ square. Place window design in center of one blue piece and slip-stitch in place. Place both blue pieces with wrong sides together and stitch with $\frac{1}{4}$″ seams around three sides and beginning and end of fourth side; seam allowance will be on right side of pillow. Stuff pillow firmly and stitch opening closed. Enclose seam allowance with orange double-fold bias binding tape $\frac{1}{4}$″ wide. Stitch through all thickness with one seam, close to folded edge of tape. ◇

A pair of birds embroidered in
soft crewel yarns decorates
matching pincushion and needle
book. Book is about 4″ tall.
Directions for Songbird Set
begin on page 64.

Modern patchworks star
on two colorful pillows
that go as a pair or
stand alone.
By Constance Spates.
Directions for Geometric
Pillows begin on page 65.

Drunkard's Path patchwork, traditional for calicos, becomes exotic made in vivid Japanese silks. The same little pieced squares can be arranged in many ways to make a variety of pillows. Directions begin on page 66.

Pretty towel edging is a great way to dress up your bathroom inexpensively. Directions are on page 67. Pillow cases, opposite, are decorative assets, embellished with machine embroidery. Designed by Verna Holt. Directions begin on page 68.

Don't throw away empty bottles and jars. With wrapping cord and a few knots, each can be transformed into a handsome vase or pencil holder. Designs range from fairly easy to intricate. Start by wrapping the mounted cords around the neck of bottle and work your way down. Bottles designed by Lynn Thurston; mustard jar by Jackie Dynan. For directions, see page 71.

This mirror takes a special view, revealing the lovely insides of a variety of seashells. Designed by Mr. & Mrs. Robert T. Worman. Directions for the Shell Mirror are on page 81.

Complete seashells can be glued together to form countless useful and decorative objects. Shown here, a bouquet of "flowers" and a soap dish. For other fun shapes, see pages 190 and 191; for directions see page 235.

Ceiling Plant Hanger

Shown on page 39

SIZE: 56″ long.

EQUIPMENT: See General Directions for Macrame (refer to Contents). Crochet hook.

MATERIALS: Cotton cable cord, 3-ply, ¼″ diameter, 74 yds. Four ceramic or wooden beads, 1½″ diameter, with hole large enough for 3 cords.

DIRECTIONS: Read General Directions for Macrame.

Cut 8 cords 9 yds. each, and 2 cords 1 yd. each for wrapping.

Fold 9-yd cords in half and wrap them 3″ down from fold (top), leaving loop for hanging. To wrap, take one wrapping cord and make a loop longer than the wrap will be; place along cords to be wrapped (Detail 1). Start wrapping with the long end of the wrap cord from the bottom of the loop towards the top. When this wrap is long enough (about 6 times around), put end of cord through loop at bottom; pull short end so loop and long end are pulled inside the wrap (Detail 2). Hang from hook above to continue with knotting.

Divide cords into 4 groups of 4 cords each. * Start 4″ down from bottom of wrap. Using 2 outer cords to knot around 2 inner cords, tie a half square knot (Fig. 2A-B) from left to right. Tie 7 additional half square knots in same manner to make a sennit twisting to the right.

If the long cords are unmanageable, make butterfly bobbins as in Detail 12.

Skip down 2″ and tie a square knot (Fig. 2A-D), using the same knotting cords as above.

Slip a bead on the two center cords and slip bead up to knot. Tie another square knot directly below bead to hold it in place.

Skip down 2″ and tie another half square knot twisting sennit of 8 knots.

Skip down 6″ and tie an overhand knot (Fig. 4) with all 4 cords.*

Repeat from * to * with each of the remaining 3 groups.

Skip down 6″ and tie cords together in groups to form a basket: Mark groups #1 to #4. Take 2 cords from #1 and 2 cords from #2 and tie these together with overhand knot. Now take 2 cords from #2 and 2 cords from #3 and tie together with an overhand knot. Continue in this way with 2 cords from #3 and 2 cords from #4; then 2 cords from #4, 2 cords from #1.

Skip down 4″ and wrap all cords with remaining wrapping cord as for above.

+ To make bow, divide cords into 5 groups of 3 cords each. Leave one cord in center unknotted; it will be wrapped later with the others. Leaving ½″ space below the wrap, take one group and tie 9 square knots (2 knotting cords around one filler cord) to form a flat sennit. With crochet hook, bring the cords up, then down through the space below the wrap; tie a half square knot to hold the top half of the bow in place.

Leaving a ½″ space below the first loop in the bow, tie another sennit of 10 square knots. Bring these cords up and down through the space with crochet hook and secure with a half square knot below the loop. +

Repeat from + to + with each group of cords.

To finish, wrap all cords directly below the loop as above. For fringe, cut cords varying in length from 10″ to 13½″ from wrap. Tie an overhand knot at the end of each cord. ◊

Double Wall Planter

Shown on page 39

SIZE: 18″ × 65″.

EQUIPMENT: See General Directions for Macrame (refer to Contents).

MATERIALS: White cotton cable cord, ¼″ diameter, 158 yds. Four wooden dowels, ½″ diameter, 18″ each. Eight tapered, tubular beads, 1″ wide, 3″ long.

DIRECTIONS: Read General Directions for Macrame. All square knots start with cord on right. Cut cords as follows: four, 12 yds.; twelve, 9 yds.; two, 1 yd.

Fold all but the 1-yd. cords in half. Double half hitch (Fig. 5B) each cord onto 1st dowel, placing the 2 12-yd. cords at each end. You have a total of 32 cords.

1st Section: Divide cords into 5 groups: 4, 4, 16, 4, 4. With the group of 16, you will make the diamond center. Make a square knot (Fig. 2A-D) with 4 center cords (of the group of 16). Make 3 rows of alternate square knots, picking up 2 more cords at each end for each row until the 3rd row uses all the cords. Make 3 more rows of alternate square knots, dropping 2 more cords at each end for each row, ending with one square knot at center. With each remaining group of 4, make a twisted sennit of 18 half square knots. Double half hitch each cord to 2nd dowel.*

2nd Section: **Divide cords into 5 groups again: 4, 4, 16, 4, 4. With the center 16 center cords, make 4 square knots. Make 3 more rows of alternate square knots, decreasing number of square knots by one each row by dropping 2 more cords on each row.

With the same center cords, make a row of 4 square knots across, 7″ below 2nd dowel. Leaving 2 outer cords on each side unknotted, redivide the cords to make a row of 3 square knots, 3″ below last row. Bring the 4 outer cords together and make a square knot (use the 2 outer cords as center), leaving 4″ between this knot and last square knot of these cords. To form basket, wrap all the center cords with one 1-yd. cord for 1½″ following directions for Ceiling Plant Hanger (3rd paragraph) and details 1 and 2.**

With each outer group of 4 cords, make a twisting sennit of 45 half square knots. With each remaining group of 4 cords, make a square knot 2″ below 2nd dowel; thread a bead on center cords; make a square knot; make another square knot 3″ below last knot; thread bead on center cords; make square knot. Double half hitch cords to 3rd dowel.

3rd Section: Repeat from * to *, adding 4th dowel.

4th Section: Repeat from ** to **, making each twisted sennit of 50 half knots.

Finishing: Make a square knot by tying the 4 cords from each sennit over all the other cords. Make another square knot below. For tassel, cut cords to 12″ long. Make overhand knot (Fig. 4) at each end. ◊

Burlap Basket Planter

Shown on page 40

SIZE: 5″ square at base; approximately 4″ deep.

EQUIPMENT: Ruler. Tape measure. Iron. Ironing board. Scissors. Pencil. Sewing needles. Sewing machine with zigzag attachment. Straight pins.

MATERIALS: Natural-colored burlap, 36″ wide, one yard. Sewing thread to match. One package fusible nylon web, 18″ wide.

DIRECTIONS: Cut four rectangles of burlap, each 12¾″ long, 5″ wide, on crosswise grain of fabric. Cut one strip of burlap 24″ long, 2¼″ wide, on lengthwise grain of fabric for binding.

Fuse two burlap rectangles together with nylon web, according to package directions. Repeat with remaining two rectangles. Center one piece over the other to form a 5″ square for base of planter (see diagram). Using a medium-width zigzag stitch, stitch around the four sides of square (see dash lines on diagram). With pencil, lightly draw two diagonal lines from corner to corner within square (see dotted lines on diagram). Zigzag stitch over pencil lines to make a firm base. Fold sides up; press to form a crease at base of each side.

Turn under ½″ of one long side of binding strip; baste. Match other long side of strip to outside raw edges of planter box; pin. Stitch ½″ in from raw edges.

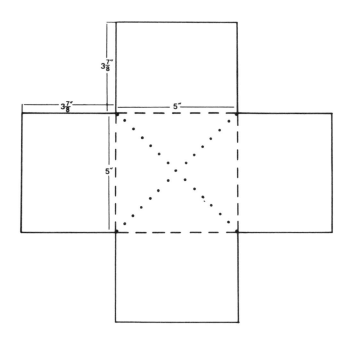

Do not trim seam. Fold binding strip in half lengthwise, towards inside, encasing raw edges; pin. Slip-stitch to inside of planter. Neatly tack ends of binding strip together. ◊

Braided Planters

Shown on page 40

EQUIPMENT: Ruler. Tape measure. Pencil. Scissors. Tapestry and sewing needles. Sewing machine with zigzag attachment. Iron. Ironing board. T-pins or stapler. Brown paper. Cardboard. Heavy cord for turning strips, 5 yards.

MATERIALS: Natural burlap, 36″ wide (approximately 1¼ yards for each planter). Sewing thread to match. Polished jute (parcel-post twine), 60 yards (1 ball) for sewing burlap. Spool.

DIRECTIONS: ***To Make Strips for Braiding:*** Using 1¾ yards of burlap for each planter, fold on the true bias grain of fabric, following Figs. 1A-1C. Dash lines indicate fold lines; the first fold is made over the front of the fabric; the second and third folds are made toward the back of the fabric. Mark the folded fabric into 3″ strips with ruler; baste on marked lines to hold (Fig. 1D). Slowly cut layers of fabric along basted lines, being careful not to let fabric shift. First strip cut will be double; cut along fold line to separate. Unfold other strips into their separate pieces. Stitch strips together at short ends to form one long, continuous strip, making ¼″ seams. Press seams flat.

Thread cord through an empty spool and tie one end around spool; knot other end of cord. Fold one long edge of strip to within ¾″ of other long edge. Insert cord in folded strip, placing knotted end at top. Set zigzag stitch for 2″ width and sew across top of strip, under knot and only where fabric is doubled; repeat stitching (to prevent knot from being pulled through) and continue stitching down length of fabric for five yards (Fig. 2). Keeping fabric in sewing machine, grip spool firmly and push sewn fabric up under knot. Continue stitching strip, pushing up each section as it is completed. When entire strip is sewn, pull cord through to turn strip to right side. Open stitched end just enough to pull out knot; slip-stitch closed. Close other end of strip. Finished width is approximately ½″.

Zigzag stitch along both long sides of strip ⅛″ from edge. If fabric has stretched after turning, zigzag stitch down the middle of strip to adjust; to make narrower, hold fabric taut while feeding into machine; to widen, feed more rapidly.

Roll finished strip into an oval, pinning to maintain shape. Steam the roll of fabric on both sides. Remove pins; unroll. Strip is now ready to braid.

Planter No. 1

Left, page 40: (Size, approximately 5½″ deep, 8″ diameter.) From long burlap strip, cut five lengths, each 2 yards; cut one length, 7 yards (weaving strip). Fold each 2-yard strip in half crosswise; place over 7-yard weaving strip from right to left, starting 1 yard from right end of weaving strip and spacing strips so piece will measure about 5½″ wide. Hold in place with T-pins or staples (see Fig. 3).

With long end of weaving strip (left end), weave over, under, over, under, etc. each half of the 2-yard strips and right end of weaving strip. When you reach the other side, weave back in the opposite direction. Continue weaving back and forth until piece measures 27″ long. Pin end of weaving strip in place. Fit piece around pot and mark size. Trim ends if necessary. Overlap raw edge with finished edge and tack to secure.

Planter No. 2

Right, page 40: (Size, approximately 7½″ deep, 8″ diameter.) From long burlap strip, cut 30 lengths, each 16″ long. Cut one 26″ length for base; form into a ring; pin. Pin or staple five 16″ strips to outside of base side by side, working from left to right (see Fig. 4). Bend first strip in half; weave upper half under second, over third, under fourth, and over fifth strip. Pin end to inside of base, next to fifth

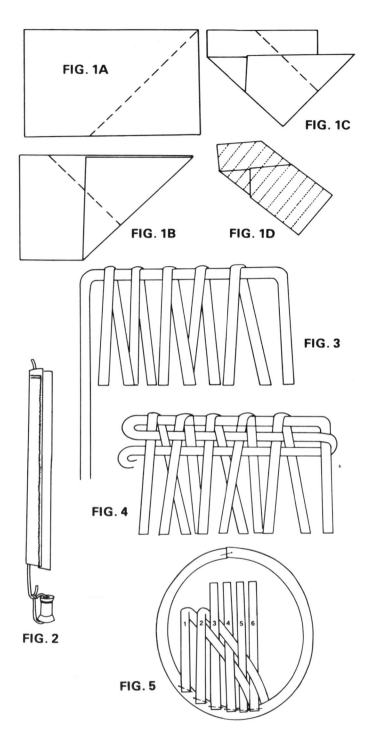

FIG. 1A

FIG. 1C

FIG. 1B

FIG. 1D

FIG. 3

FIG. 4

FIG. 2

FIG. 5

strip. Pin a sixth strip to outside of base, where woven first strip ends. Bending second strip in half, weave under third, over the fourth, under the fifth, and over the sixth strip. Pin end to base. Add a seventh strip where second strip ends. Continue to weave each strip in turn, pinning to base and adding an additional strip until all strips are used.

If base strip is too long, trim to fit. Tack ends of base strip together; tack raw edges of weaving strips to base on inside. Cut bias piece of burlap for binding, 27″ × 2½″. Pin one long raw edge of binding to raw edge of base strip on inside. Machine stitch ½″ from edge; fold over to outside; tack.

Cut three lengths of prepared strips for braiding, each about 1 yard long. Tack together at top; braid. Tack at bottom; cut off excess if necessary. Using twine, tack braid over binding on outside of planter. Turn raw edges under to make braid look continuous; tack.

From long burlap strip, cut a 28″ length. Pin to inside top of planter, about 1½″ from edge. Adjust weaving to shape and tack to strip. ◊

Songbird Set

Shown on page 53

SIZES: Needlebook, 4″ × 6¼″; pincushion, 3½″ × 4¼″.

EQUIPMENT: Tracing paper. Dressmaker's tracing (carbon) paper. Pencil. Ruler. Sewing and embroidery needles.

MATERIALS: White linen-like fabric, less than ¼ yard for both (two pieces 4½″ × 6¼″ for needlebook; two pieces 3¾″ × 4¾″ for pincushion). Crewel yarn (2-ply), one yard or less of the following: Dark blue (A); medium blue (B); pale blue (C); dark brown (D); russet (E); tan (F); green, red, white (G); black; on needlebook only, yellow. Bright blue cotton piping, 1 yard for both. Blue and white sewing thread. Stuffing for pincushion. Piece of pale blue felt 3½″ × 5½″ for needlebook.

Needlebook

Cut two pieces of fabric each 4½″ × 6¾″. Trace actual-size pattern; center design on right half of one piece of fabric and, using dressmaker's carbon, transfer to right side of fabric. Following letters for colors and referring to embroidery stitch details (see Contents), embroider design using single strand of yarn throughout. Fill blue areas in rows of outline stitch following contours of areas. Work upper part of breast in rows of chain stitch. Work lower chest in long and short stitch. Work all wing sections in satin stitch. Work legs and feet in outline stitch. Work beak in straight stitch. For eye, make French knot with back yarn. Using green, work leaves in satin stitch. Using red for petals and yellow for centers, work flowers in French knots. Using tan, work flower stems in outline stitch and lines under stems in straight stitch.

To assemble, place the two pieces of white fabric together with right sides facing; place piping between with raw edges out; baste. Stitch all around ¼″ from edge, rounding off corners; leave 2″ opening in center of one long side. Clip into curves at corners. Turn to right side. Turn edges of opening in ¼″ and slip-stitch closed. Center and pin piece of felt on side which is not embroidered. With white thread, stitch along crosswise center of felt and through all thicknesses of fabric. With scissors, round felt corners.

Pincushion

Cut two pieces of fabric each 4″ × 4¾″. Trace actual-size pattern and transfer to right side of one piece of fabric; embroider as for needlebook. Work branch in buttonhole stitch along one long side, then back again on opposite side (see Contents for stitch details).

Assemble with piping as for needlebook. Stuff fully before stitching closed. ◊

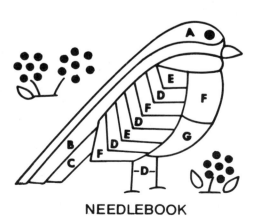

NEEDLEBOOK

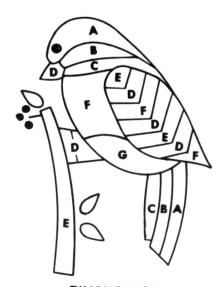

PINCUSHION

Geometric Pillows

Shown on page 54

EQUIPMENT: Pencil. Ruler. Thin, stiff cardboard. Scissors. Straight pins. Sewing needle.

MATERIALS: Closely woven cotton fabric with small print or stripe for part of design and pillow back: 36″ wide, ½ yd. for each. Small amounts of fabric for patch pieces (see photograph and individual directions). Matching sewing thread. Muslin, for inner pillow, 36″ wide, ½ yard for each. Polyester fiberfill for stuffing. Fine cording or string, about $\frac{1}{16}$″ thick, 1¼ yards for each.

GENERAL DIRECTIONS: Enlarge patterns for patch pieces by copying on paper ruled in 1″ squares; mark actual size of patterns on cardboard. Mark X on right side of each pattern. Cut each shape out with sharp scissors.

Press all fabric smooth. To determine straight of fabric, pull a thread. Arrows on patterns indicate straight of fabric. Place each pattern piece on wrong side of fabric, with X face down unless otherwise indicated, making sure each piece is placed in correct relationship to the straight of fabric. With pencil, trace around each pattern. When tracing a number of pieces on one fabric, leave enough space between patterns for seam allowances. Mark ¼″ seam allowance all around each piece. Cut out design pieces including border as indicated in individual directions and on diagrams. Patches may be stitched by machine or by hand. Pin patches together, right sides facing, following placement diagram. With sewing thread, carefully make tiny running stitches along marked outlines to join with ¼″ seams. Begin with a small knot; end with a few backstitches. To avoid

bunching of fabric, trim thickness of seams where a few points meet. When two bias edges come together, keep thread just taut enough to prevent seams from stretching. When piecing is completed, press all seams to one side.

Cut back the same size as finished front. To make narrow piping, cut bias strips $\frac{5}{8}$″ wide and long enough to fit around pillow front plus overlap (piece strips as needed to obtain required length). With wrong sides facing, fold strip in half lengthwise with cording between; stitch close to cord or string to complete piping. Baste piping on right side of front, around all sides, having raw edges flush, and joining piping ends in one corner. With right sides facing, sew front and back together making ¼″ seam; leave an opening in center of one side for turning and inserting inner pillow. Turn to right side. Push out corners.

To make inner pillow, cut two pieces of muslin, each ½″ larger all around than pillow cover. Sew the two pieces together making ¼″ seams; leave an opening in center of one side for turning. Turn to other side. Stuff pillow fully. Turn edges of opening in and slip-stitch closed. Insert muslin pillow in pillow cover. Turn edges of opening in and slip-stitch closed.

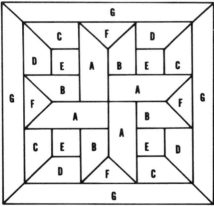

ENDLESS RIBBON

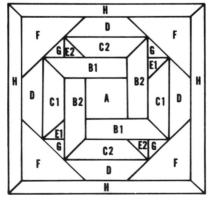

INTERLOCKING RECTANGLES

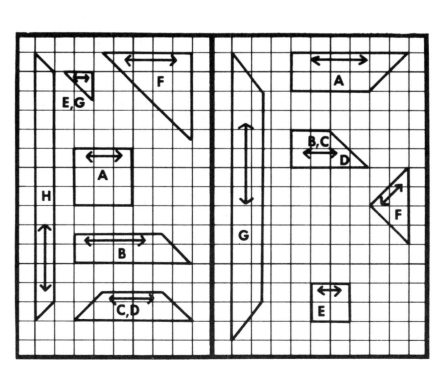

Endless Ribbon

(At left in illustration)

SIZE: 15″ square. All the design pieces (A, B, C, and D), and pillow back are cut out of red-and-white striped fabric. The stripes for all these pieces are to run horizontally to obtain a finished ribbon effect. The background pieces (E. F, and border G) are cut out of a small dark print. Cut four pieces A, four pieces B, and four pieces C: reverse pattern B with X face up and cut four pieces D. Cut four pieces E, four pieces F, and four pieces G.

Follow diagram and General Directions for piecing. Sew C to D, then sew to E; sew B to the C-D-E piece; sew on A. Repeat for the remaining three sets. Join all A's together and to edge of B's. Sew F in place at each side. Sew border strip G to each side, completing the front.

Interlocking Rectangles

(Right in illustration)

SIZE: 14 ″ square. The open rectangles are of two solid colors, 1 and 2 (pieces B, C, and E). The inner background is cut of polka dot fabric (pieces A, D, and G). The corners F and borders H, and pillow back are cut out of a small dark print. Cut one piece A, four pieces D, four pieces G. Cut two pieces C (using D pattern), two pieces E of one solid color. Repeat with other solid color for second rectangle. Cut four pieces F and four pieces H.

Follow diagram and General Directions for piecing. Sew D to C; sew E to G; sew E-G to D-C; sew on B. Repeat for remaining three sets. Join the four parts to A. Sew F to each corner. Sew border to each side, completing the front. ◊

Drunkard's Path Pillows

Shown on page 55

SIZE: 20″ square each.

MATERIALS: *For Each Pillow:* Closely woven fabric, 44″ wide: ¾ yard bold print and ¼ yard white. White cotton, 44″ wide, 1¼ yards (1¾ yards for two pillows), for lining and inner pillow. Polyester quilt batting and fiberfill. Matching sewing thread for patches and white silk buttonhole twist, one 10-yard spool, for quilting.

DIRECTIONS: *For Each Pillow:* Read General Directions for Quilting (see Contents). Before cutting patches from print fabric, cut one 20½″ square for

back and four strips 4″ × 20½″ for borders; these measurements include ¼″ seam allowance all around.

Trace actual-size square pattern, including curved bisecting line; glue tracing to cardboard and when dry, carefully cut out around square outline and then along curved inner line to make two patterns—A and B. Replace patterns as edges become worn. Following General Directions for cutting patches, cut eight of each shape from print fabric and eight from white fabric for blue pillow at left in photograph (piecing diagram 1) or red pillow (piecing dia-

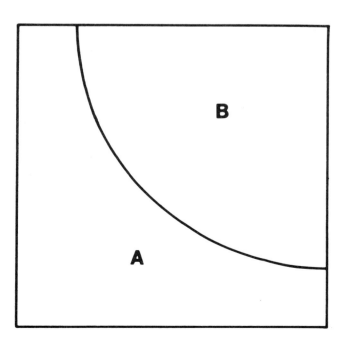

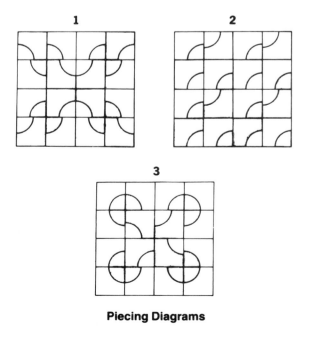

Piecing Diagrams

gram 2). For blue pillow at upper right in photo (piecing diagram 3), cut twelve of A, four of B from white fabric, and four of A, twelve of B from print fabric. In any case, you will have a total of 32 patches.

Note: Mark all patches on wrong side of fabric and add $\frac{1}{4}''$ seam allowance all around. To make $3\frac{3}{4}''$ squares, sew a print patch of one shape to a white patch of other shape along their curved edges; stitch along pencil lines, matching them carefully and easing the curves into one another. Clip into seam at curve; press seam under print fabric. Make 16 squares in this manner.

Following one of the piecing diagrams, stitch 16 squares together with right sides facing and making $\frac{1}{4}''$ seams to form a block. Block should measure $13\frac{1}{2}''$ square, including $\frac{1}{4}''$ seam allowance all around.

Pin a border strip to each side of pieced block, right sides facing and centering block so that equal lengths of border fabric extend at corners. Sew border strips to block, making $\frac{1}{4}''$ seams and leaving border ends free. To miter corners, place piece right side down on work surface, hold adjacent ends of border together with right sides facing. Keeping border flat, lift up excess and pin borders diagonally together from inner corner to outer corner; baste. Stitch on basting line. Cut off excess fabric to make $\frac{1}{2}''$ seam; press seams to one side.

Cut batting and white cotton piece for lining, both same size as pillow top. Place pillow top on lining with batting in between; baste through all thicknesses following General Directions. Using buttonhole twist and $\frac{1}{8}''$-long running stitches, quilt around outline of design created by print patches, stitching on white patches close to seamlines. Quilt around patchwork block, just inside border seamline.

Stitch pillow front to pillow back around three sides, right sides together and making $\frac{1}{4}''$ seams; turn to right side. Cut two $20\frac{1}{2}''$ squares from white cotton for inner pillow; stitch together, making $\frac{1}{4}''$ seams and leaving 6" opening in center of fourth side. Turn to right side and stuff with fiberfill; slip-stitch closed. Insert inner pillow into cover, slip-stitch closed. ◊

Scalloped Edging

Shown on page 56

SIZE: Edging, $1\frac{1}{4}''$ wide. Trimming, $2\frac{1}{2}''$ wide.

MATERIALS: J. & P. Coats Knit-Cro-Sheen: 2 balls (175 yds. each). Steel crochet hook size 7 (1.5 mm). Towel.

EDGING: Make a chain to measure 2" longer than width of towel, having 9 ch sts to 1".

Row 1: Hdc in 3rd ch from hook and in each ch across, having a number of sts divisible by 7 counting the ch-2 as one st. Cut off any remaining chain. Ch 1, turn.

Row 2: Sc in first 2 hdc, * ch 7, skip next 4 sts, sc in next 3 sts. Rep from * across, end last rep with sc in last st. Ch 4, turn.

Row 3: * Holding back on hook last lp of each dc, make 3 dc in next lp, thread over and draw through all lps on hook—cluster made; ch 3, in same lp make (cluster, ch 3) twice and cluster. Rep from * across, end with tr in last sc. Ch 1, turn.

Row 4 (right side): * Make 3 sc in next lp; in next lp make (sc, ch 3) 3 times and sc; 3 sc in next lp, sl st between next 2 clusters. Rep from * across, end with sl st in 4th ch of ch-4. Fasten off.

Trimming: Work as for Edging until Row 4 is complete. Fasten off. Now work along opposite side of starting chain as follows:

Row 1: With wrong side facing, join thread to first st, ch 2 hdc in each st across, having the same number of sts as on Row 1 of Edging. Ch 1, turn.

Rows 2-4: Rep Rows 2-4 of Edging. Fasten off. Sew strips in place as shown. ◊

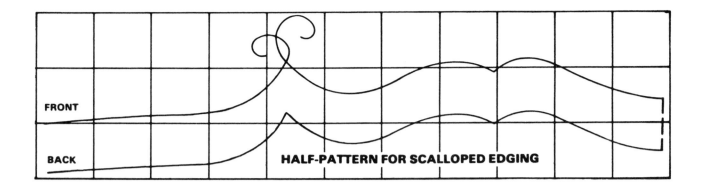

FRONT

BACK   **HALF-PATTERN FOR SCALLOPED EDGING**

Pillow Cases

Shown on page 57

EQUIPMENT: Zigzag sewing machine. Adjustable embroidery hoop, 8″ to 9″. Hard-lead pencil.

MATERIALS: Purchased pillow cases. Paper for patterns. Tracing paper. Dressmaker's tracing or carbon paper. Machine embroidery thread, #30 or #50, in colors desired.

DIRECTIONS: Read general directions for sewing machine embroidery on page 245. Enlarge patterns by copying on paper ruled in 1″ squares. Trace enlarged patterns; complete pattern for butterflies by reversing half-pattern along dash line indicating center of design. Trace actual-size pattern for cross-stitch design. Using carbon paper and hard-lead pencil, transfer traced designs to pillow cases. If using cross-stitch design, place the basic six-sided motif in the center, repeat three times on each side, and end with additional double-scroll motif and diamond shapes included in pattern.

Embroidery

Prepare machine for free-motion embroidery. Place top of pillow case in hoop, and work with length of case away from you.

To embroider the top design shown in photograph, begin with flower centers. Set zigzag dial at wide (4-5) when filling in solid areas such as flower centers and wider leaves. To outline flower petals, set zigzag dial at 3; satin stitch along line for each petal without rotating hoop, for thick-and-thin contouring. For accent lines within petals, set dial at 1. Outline and accent larger leaves in same manner. Work narrow solid leaves with satin stitch. Work tiny leaves with bar tacks. For stems, set stitch for wide and zigzag between and over marked lines.

Work remaining flower and butterfly designs in same manner, widening or narrowing the zigzag stitch as necessary. For pink dogwood design, fill in centers of flowers with wide stitch (4-5) in green, if using colors shown, then set zigzag dial at 2 and add yellow dots (hard to see in photograph, but clearly indicated on pattern). Fill in leaves, adding darker green center areas.

For bottom flower design shown in purple, embroider only dots in centers of flowers. If desired, inner areas of petals and leaves which are simply outlined in satin stitch can be cut away; use small scissors and cut close to stitching without clipping into stitches.

For cross-stitch design, set machine for narrow zigzag stitch and make lines of fine, even satin stitch; see general directions.

Finishing: When embroidery is complete, steam-press lightly on wrong side. To make scalloped edge shown in purple, complete half-pattern at bottom of opposite page and transfer to both open edges of pillow case. Satin stitch along marked lines and trim away excess fabric close to stitching.

For a crocheted edge, as shown with orange flower design at top of photograph, first cut edge of pillow case into shallow scallops. Then make a narrow hemstitched edge by machine and follow directions for crocheted edging below. You'll need one large ball of mercerized crochet cotton, size 30, in color desired (variegated thread was used for edging shown), and a steel crochet hook, No. 12.

Crocheted Edging

Rnd 1: Make lp on hook; sc in each hemstitched hole around edge, being sure not to pull in edge of pillowcase, sl st in first sc.

Rnd 2: Ch 1, * sc in each of 4 sc, 2 sc in next sc, repeat from * around. Sl st in first sc.

Rnd 3: Ch 3, dc in same sc with sl st, 2 dc in next sc, * ch 2, sk 2 sc, 2 dc in each of next 2 sc, repeat from * around, end ch 2, sl st in top of ch 3.

Rnd 4: Sl st in each dc to next ch-2 sp, ch 3, 3 dc in ch-2 sp; * ch 2, 4 dc in next ch-2 sp, repeat from * around, end ch 2, sl st in top of ch 3.

Rnd 5: * (Ch 2, sc in next dc) 3 times, 2 sc in ch-2 sp, sc in next dc, repeat from * around, end sl st in first ch. End off. ◇

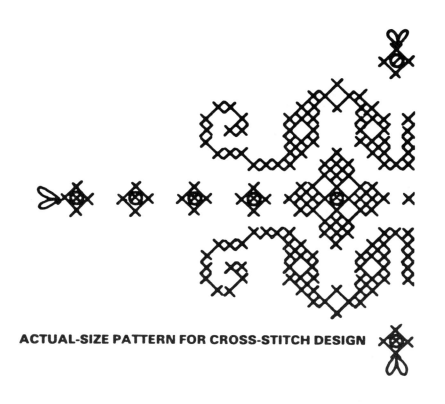

ACTUAL-SIZE PATTERN FOR CROSS-STITCH DESIGN

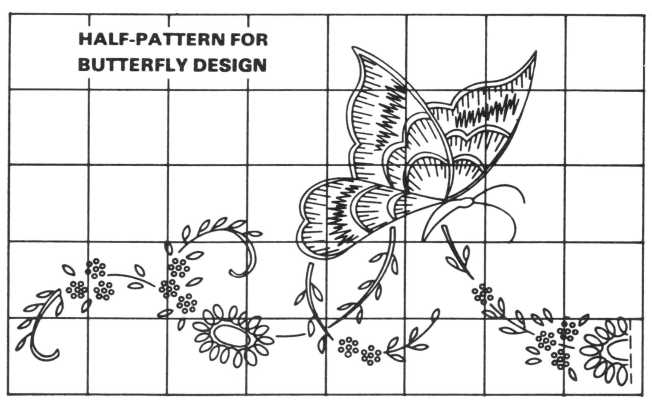

HALF-PATTERN FOR BUTTERFLY DESIGN

EMBROIDERY PATTERNS FOR PILLOW CASES

Covered Bottles

Shown on pages 58–59

EQUIPMENT: See General Directions for Macrame (refer to Contents).

MATERIALS: Bottles or jars in assorted sizes (see illustration for shapes and individual directions below for sizes). Medium-weight cotton cord in white or ecru (Mason cord or cable cord #18) about $\frac{1}{16}$" diameter (see individual directions for amounts). All-purpose glue. Felt for bottle bottom, optional.

GENERAL DIRECTIONS: Read General Directions for Macrame. Cut number and length of cords as indicated in individual directions. Use one cord as a mounting cord; pin to working surface. Fold the remaining cords in half and mount on cord (Fig. 1A). Place the mounting cord around the top of the neck of the bottle (fit it into the groove if there is one). Tie the ends of the mounting cord together tightly with a square knot (Fig. 2A-D). Use ends of mounting cord as working cords.

Continue, following individual directions. When you reach the bottom of the bottle, add a few more rows of knots, working tightly so macrame will turn under onto the base of the bottle.

To finish, cut cords close to the last row of knots. Coat the last row and cord ends with glue. When dry, apply a second coat of glue.

If desired, cut a circle of felt slightly smaller than the base of bottle and glue in place, to cover macrame ends.

Bottle #1

(Left, page 58): You will need a bottle 10" tall and 89 yds. of cord.

Cut 20 cords, each 90" long. Mount and tie around bottle neck, following General Directions above. Use the ends of the mounting cord as working cords, to get 40 in all.

Separate the cords into 10 groups of 4. With these groups, tie 9 rows of alternating square knots (Fig. 3A). Continuing to work with the last 4-cord grouping, tie flat sennits, 4 square knots in length.

As the circumference of bottle increases, you will need to add cords. Cut 20 cords, each 70" long; separate them into 10 groups of 2. Fold in half and pin the centers of each pair to a working surface. Tie a square knot with each pair of cords, using the 2 inner cords as filler cords around which the knot is tied. Place these separate square knots between last knots of sennits on the bottle, then mount by making an alternate row of square knots, * using 2 cords from added knot with 2 cords from adjacent square knots of sennit for each square knot. Continue by making 5 more rows of alternate square knots.* Using the last 4-cord grouping, make a flat square knot sennit 5 knots long. Work 11 rows of alternating square knots, keeping work tight and evenly spaced. Gradually increase the space between the knots if necessary to accommodate the circumference of bottle.

Tie flat sennits, 6 square knots long. Work rows of alternating square knots to bottom of bottle, then add several rows to turn under the bottom and finish, following General Directions above.

Bottle #2

(Right, page 58): You will need a bottle 11" tall and 95 yds. of cord.

Cut 20 cords, each 100" long. Mount and tie around bottle neck, following General Directions above. Use the ends of the mounting cord as working cords to get 40 in all.

Separate cords into 10 groups of 4. With these groups, tie 15 rows of alternating square knots (Fig. 3A). Separate the 4 cords as if to make another row of alternate square knots, but continue by making a sennit of Lark's Head knots, 8 knots long.

Cut 20 cords, each 70" long. Separate the cords into groups of 2. Pin to a working surface and tie square knots as for Bottle #1. Add one of these separate square knots between every 2 Lark's Head sennits on bottle; mount with a row of square knots, following directions for Bottle #1 from * to *.

To form the diamond pattern, divide the cords into 5 groups of 16 cords each (enough cords to make 4 square knots). Center these groups so that the apex of each diamond will be directly below one of the square knots added to the bottle. *Work 4 rows of alternating square knots with each group of 16 cords, decreasing the number of square knots in each row by one each time. Use all the cords for first row; for the second row, leave the outer 2 cords on each side of each group unknotted; for the third row, leave the outer 4 unknotted; for the fourth row, leave the outer 6 unknotted. To finish the diamond, work another 4 rows of alternating square knots, picking up cords on each side of the last knot as you work each row.* Repeat from * to * 4 times to complete 5 rows of diamonds.

Finish bottle by working rows of alternating square knots to the bottom of bottle, then add several rows to turn under. Finish, following General Directions above.

Bottle #3

(Left, page 59): You will need a bottle about $12\frac{1}{2}$" tall, 68 yds. of cord, and a crochet hook for popcorns.

Cut 22 cords, each 110". Mount and tie around bottle neck, following General Directions above. Use ends of the mounting cord as working cords to get 44.

Separate the cords into 11 groups of 4. With these groups, tie 10 rows of double alternating square knots (flat sennit, 2 square knots in length).

To make popcorn, separate the cords into groups of 4, taking 2 from every pair of adjacent knots. Tie a flat sennit, 4 square knots long. Using crochet hook, insert 2 center cords of group from front to back through work, directly above first knot of sennit. Pull cords through until the last knot of sennit touches the first knot of sennit and forms a ball. Separate the cords again into 2 pairs (2 cords each from adjacent knots) and work 2 rows of double alternating square knots; then make another sennit of popcorns as above. Work 2 rows of double alternating square knots.

Rather than add cords to accommodate the circumference of the bottle, at this point allow more space between each knot, keeping knots tight and evenly spaced. Proceed as follows: Tie a row of flat square knot sennits, 4 knots in length, then tie a row of double square knots, then repeat the square knot sennit, 4 knots in length. Continue with 6 rows of double alternating square knots. Then tie flat sennits of 6 square knots. Finish with 4 rows of double alternating square knots to the bottom of the bottle, then add several rows to turn under. Finish, follow General Directions above.

Bottle #4

(Right, page 59): You will need a rosé wine bottle 8″ tall, 71 yds. of cord, and a crochet hook to make popcorns.

Cut 20 cords, each 80″ long. Mount and tie around neck of bottle, following General Directions above. Use ends of mounting cord as working cords to get 40.

Separate the cords into 10 groups of 4 each. With these groups, tie 3 rows of alternating square knots. Continuing in alternating pattern, make 2 rows of popcorns as for Bottle #3, alternating with square knots. Make a single row of square knots all around, then 2 rows of popcorns alternating with square knots. Tie 9 rows of alternating square knots. Without alternating cords, make flat sennit of 2 square knots.

Cut 20 additional cords, each 50″ long. Separate the cords into groups of 2. Pin to a working surface and tie square knots as for Bottle #1. Add one of these separate square knots between every 2 sennits on the bottle by continuing with 3 rows of alternating square knots. Work a row of popcorns alternating with square knots.

Divide the cords into 2 groups of 40 each to cover each flat side of the bottle. At each side seam of bottle, tie one square knot with 4 cords at end. Group 2 cords from one side with 2 cords from the other and tie a flat sennit, 2 square knots long.

With the 16 cords at the center of one flat side, tie a row of 4 square knots with 2 knots on each side of the center. Make a row of popcorns alternating with square knots. Make another row of 4 square knots. Put these center cords aside for the time being.

Pick up 8 cords at each side of the 16 cords just set aside. Tie 3 rows of alternating square knots with each set of 8 cords. Drop 2 cords of each set closest to the center of the flat side and pick up 2 cords close to each side seam, keeping 8 cords in each group. Tie one row of square knots. Drop 2 more

cords closest to the center of the bottle and pick up 2 more cords close to the seam (these are the cords remaining from the square knot sennit previously made along the bottle seam). With these 8 cords, tie 2 rows of alternating square knots. Repeat to make each side identical.

At each side seam of the bottle, tie a flat sennit, 2 square knots long, using 2 cords from each side of bottle. Pick up 4 more cords (2 from each flat side group) and tie a row of square knots, then by another flat sennit, 2 square knots long.

At the center of each flat side, divide the 36 out of the 40 cords into 2 equal groups. Separate each group of 18 into 4 groups of 4, plus 2 cords at each side (you still have 4 cords at each side seam: 2 from the front groups and 2 from the back). With each group of 4, tie 7 rows of square knots on a diagonal by dropping 2 cords closest to the center of the flat side and picking up 2 cords closest to the seam side, so that you are not working with 4 groups of 16 cords. With these groups, tie 3 diagonal bars as close to the square-knot rows as possible.

With the center 4 cords on each flat side, work a twisted sennit, 21 half knots long. Set these aside for now. Skip the next 2 cords on each side of the center. Pick up the next 4 cords on each side of the 8 center cords and tie a twisted sennit, 14 half knots long. Skip the next 2 cords to each side of the center 16 cords. Pick up the next 4 cords on each side of the 20 center cords and tie a twisted sennit 5 half knots long. Work 3 diagonal bars of double half hitches with the center 32 cords to complete the center diamond motif.

With the 4 cords at each side beyond the diamond, tie a single square knot even with the center of the diamond. Separate these cords, so that 2 go to the side and 2 to the center. With these 36 cords tie 8 rows of alternating square knots on a diagonal by dropping 2 outer cords and picking up 2 inner cords with each row.

Tie 5 rows of alternating square knots with center 20 cords on each flat side.

With the 4 cords at each side seam, work a sennit, 2 square knots long. Adding 4 cords to each row, tie 4 rows of alternating square knots (you should now have 20 cords included in the pattern at the side seams). Reverse the pattern by decreasing the number of working cords of each row by 4 and work 4 rows of alternating square knots to create a diamond pattern at each seam.

To finish bottle, use all 80 cords on the bottom to work 5 rows of alternating square knots. This will stretch the macrame over the bottle and hold it in place. Cut and glue cords, following General Directions above.

Bottle # 5

(Center, page 58): You will need a French mustard jar about 5″ tall and about 50 yds. of cord.

Cut 28 cords, each 70″ long. Mount and tie around neck of bottle, following General Directions above.

Continued on page 81

To make edge-trimming points, you simply fold fabric squares into triangles. Then dress up a garment bag, brighten a baby bib, or trim a toy turtle. Or, embroider your gingham for a "Home Sweet Home" sampler.

Dress up your home in cheery gingham. Great in gingham are a kitchen apron, carry-all bag and cross-stitch sampler.

Brighten a table with prairie-point place mats, tea cozy, and basket liner. Gingham bird holds a small plant. Directions for all begin on page 83.

It doesn't take much to spruce up your kitchen shelves: fabric liners are bordered in red zigzag stitching and finished with embroidered flowers. For fun, add fabric covers to jars. Directions for Shelf Decor begin on page 89.

Grandma and her cuddly cat will sit pretty in your kitchen, but they're also terrific toys for kids. Easy to sew in two browns with embroidery. Directions for Grandma Doll and Cuddly Cat begin on page 87.

Pretty pot holders to crochet —square is double-thick with ripple band; round is felt-backed with flower motif. Orange, apple and pear are really balls of string covered with felt. Small opening on bottom lets you use without

tangles. Mother Hen and her family of pot holders guard eggs in the basket of woven calico, $8\frac{1}{2}'' \times 5''$. Directions for Crocheted Pot Holders, page 90; String Holders, page 90; Hen and Family Pot Holders; page 91.

Use up leftover yarn from canvas projects to make a hot mat, then back it with felt. White flowers bloom

on a field of brown gingham, making every meal a picnic. Tablecloth, place mat and napkins are bordered in white and finished with floss. Directions for Brown Gingham Set, page 103; Crocheted Mats begin on page 101.

Green and white crochet cottons stripe an interesting mat worked in a four-row double crochet pattern. Stripy Duo place mat and coaster are crocheted in an easy stitch with leftover crochet cottons. So colorful under clear glass!

Sunny sets to
sew: bright
fruits and
fruit slices
are giant pockets
on cotton cobbler-type aprons, as well as perky motifs for matching
pot holders. Designs are machine-appliqued; machine-stitching creates
some details: green rind on the watermelon, markings on the pineapple,
and core of the apple. Other details on all are hand embroidered.
Ties from bib slip through plastic curtain rings at sides, making the
apron adjustable—you may wear it as high or as low as you need!
Designed by Wendy Mills. Directions for
Kitchen Ensembles begin on page 105.

White stars emblazon a tricolor apron and hot mitt.
Stars and stripes are machine-appliqued. Mitt is
quilted. Denim ''chain'' trims front of a second apron.
''Ball'' is a quilted pot holder! Apron has modified
neck strap to follow chain motif. Directions for
Apron Sets begin on page 106.

Sponge off spills on our
rubberized kitchen aprons.
Mom's little helper wears
a multi-pocketed apron.
Stenciled pockets are
catch-alls for goodies. The

makings of a great salad
are appliqued to form a
pocket on Mom's apron.
Directions for Pocket and
Salad Bowl Aprons
on page 108.

Bake a box to hold a gift of goodies from your kitchen! Basic shapes are easy to find around the house—just use simple boxes of any size or even a gelatin mold. Baker's clay recipe and directions for Baked Boxes are on page 121.

Continued from page 72

Use the ends of the mounting cord as working cords to get 56 in all.

Separate the cords into 14 groups of 4 each. Tie one row of square knots. Alternating cords, tie a flat sennit of 1½ square knots. Alternating cords, tie a flat sennit of 2 square knots.

Redivide the cords into groups of 4, using 2 cords from each pair of neighboring sennits. Following Details A-C, make a Josephine knot with each group of 4. Make another row of Josephine knots below first row, leaving about ½″ of space between rows. Using 2 cords from each Josephine knot, regroup

Josephine Knot

Detail A   **Detail B**   **Detail C**

into 4 cords. Make a flat sennit, 2 square knots long. Alternate cords and make a flat sennit, 1½ square knots long. Alternate cords and make another flat sennit 3 square knots long. Cut cords and glue. Finish, following General Directions. ◊

Shell Mirror

Shown on page 60

SIZE: 8″ square.

EQUIPMENT: Pencil. Ruler. Saw. Small paintbrush. Sandpaper. Hammer. Miter box and back saw.

MATERIALS: Plywood ½″ thick, 7½″ square. Pine or hardwood strips as follows: ¼″ thick, 1¾″ × 34″; ⅛″ thick, ⅜″ × 26″; ¼″ thick, ½″ × 14″; ⅛″ thick, 3/16″ × 12″. Paint: small amounts of gray, cream, and white. Assorted seashells. Mirror, 2½″ square. Cardboard backing, 8″ square. Wire brads, ½″ long. All-purpose glue. Clear acrylic spray. Fixture for hanging.

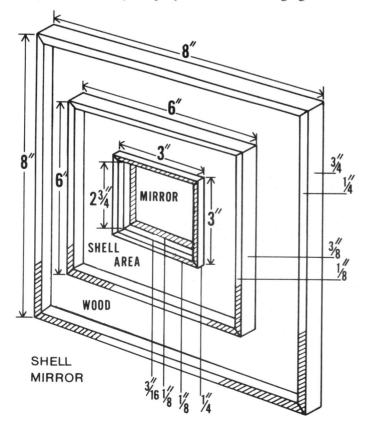

GENERAL DIRECTIONS: Following the Shell Mirror diagram, cut wood strips according to the marked measurements, being sure to miter all corners. Sand strips lightly. Cut out a 3″ square from the center of the plywood to accommodate framing strips and mirror.

Paint plywood and strips on all surfaces gray except the 3/16″ × ⅛″ innermost strip. Paint the plywood in the border area cream, and paint the shell area white. Paint the innermost strip cream. Apply as many coats as necessary, letting each dry between applications. Using brads and glue, assemble frame as diagrammed; glue and nail inner framing strips around mirror opening. Cover back of frame with cardboard backing piece; glue and nail in place. Touch up brads with matching paint. Set in mirror; glue inner holding strips or quarter round molding to frame over mirror.

Decorate shell areas as desired. Lay out design in area first; when arrangement is satisfactory, remove each piece, apply glue, and affix in place. When design area is completely dry, cover mirror with piece of heavy paper, then spray frame with clear acrylic. Apply two or three coats, letting each coat dry between sprayings. Attach hanging fixture. ◊

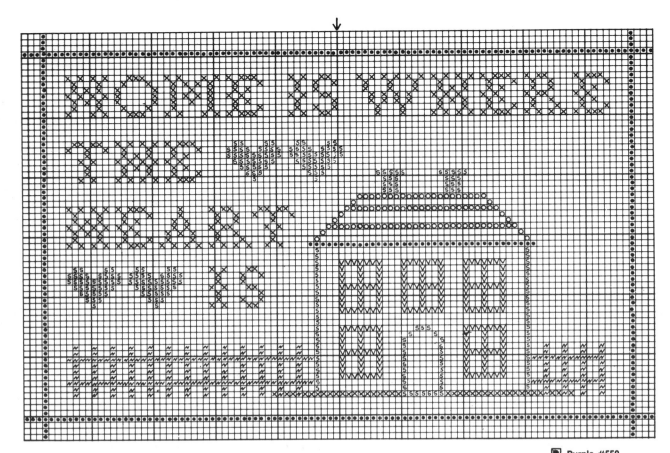

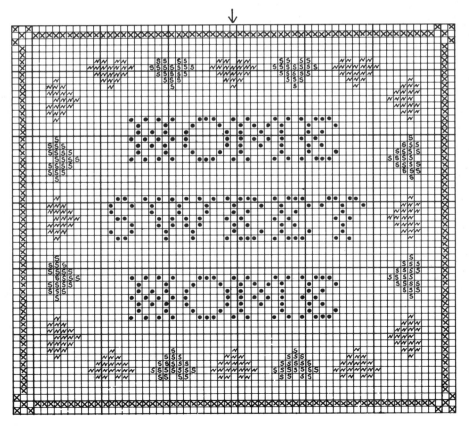

Purple #550
Bright Green #702
Hot Pink # 603
White
Ice Blue #747
Deep Blue # 517

Deep Blue #517
Hot Pink #603
Yellow Orange #971
Blue Green #943

Gingham Samplers

Shown on page 73

FINISHED SIZES: "House," 12″ × 16″; "Home Sweet Home", 10″ square.

EQUIPMENT: Ruler. Pencil. Scissors. Embroidery hoop and needle. Straight pins. Steam iron. Sewing machine (optional).

MATERIALS: Gingham fabric with $\frac{1}{8}$″ checks, orange and yellow, $\frac{1}{2}$ yard each. *Note:* In some gingham fabrics, the checks are not perfectly square; cut gingham and work samplers so that the greater number of checks per inch run horizontally. Cut orange 21½″ × 17⅞″ (21½″ is horizontal measurement) for "House." Cut yellow 16⅛″ square for "Home Sweet Home." Six-strand embroidery floss, one skein of each color in color key. Artist's stretcher strips 12″ × 16″ for "House" and 10″ square for "Home Sweet Home." White cotton duck fabric 45″ wide, $\frac{1}{2}$ yard (for both). Deep color grosgrain ribbon $\frac{3}{4}$″ wide, 2 yards for "House"; 1½ yards for "Home Sweet Home." Staple gun and staples. All-purpose glue.

GENERAL DIRECTIONS: To prevent fabric from raveling, whipstitch edges by hand, or machine-stitch $\frac{1}{8}$″ in from all edges. Cut floss or yarn into 18″ strands. To begin a strand, leave an end on back and work over it to secure; to end, run needle under four or five stitches on back. Do not use knots. When working cross-stitches, keep all crosses in the same direction; work underneath stitches in one direction and top stitches in the opposite direction, making sure that strands lie smooth and flat. Make all crosses touch by inserting needle in same hole used for adjacent stitch (see Contents for stitch details).

Each symbol on chart represents one stitch on fabric. Work stitches over checks, so that one complete cross-stitch covers one check.

Place fabric in hoop, making sure horizontal and vertical threads are straight and even; move hoop as needed. Work design, following individual directions, chart and color key. Place finished embroidery, face down, on padded surface and steam-press lightly from center outward. Finish, following individual directions.

Samplers

Read General Directions; stitch fabric edges. Each square on chart represents one check on gingham. Each symbol represents one cross-stitch. Place orange gingham with short edges at sides. Fold each piece in half to find vertical center; mark at top edge with pin. Measure down 3½″ to correspond with arrow on chart.

To Stitch "House," count four checks down from arrow to begin purple border; complete, following chart and color key.

To Stitch "Home Sweet Home," count two checks down from arrow to begin blue border; complete, following chart and color key. Press embroideries, following General Directions.

To Finish: Assemble frame, following manufacturer's directions. Cut duck fabric 2½″ larger all around than outside frame dimensions. Center frame on duck; stretch fabric around frame edges, folding excess to back. Making neat mitered corners, staple fabric edges to frame back. Repeat with embroidered gingham, centering design carefully; pin excess gingham to duck at frame edge before stapling, and check that stitched borders are parallel to frame edges; adjust if necessary. Staple as for duck. Glue ribbon, cut to fit, around frame edges; overlap ends at bottom corner. ◊

Prairie Point

Shown on page 73

EQUIPMENT: Colored pencil. Pencil. Ruler. T- or carpenter's square. Paper and thin, stiff cardboard for patterns. Scissors. Seam ripper. Tape measure. Compass. Straight pins. Dressmaker's tracing (carbon) paper. Dry ball-point pen. Pinking shears. Zigzag sewing machine. Sewing and embroidery needles. Embroidery hoop. Iron.

MATERIALS: Gingham fabric 45″ wide (with $\frac{1}{4}$″ checks unless otherwise indicated): yellow with $\frac{1}{8}$″ checks (A); orange with $\frac{1}{8}$″ checks (B); orange (C); pink (D); lavender (E); blue (F); navy (G). Solid-color cotton or cotton-blend fabric 45″ wide: bright yellow (H); orange (J); kelly green (K). Batting and fiberfill. Thread to match fabrics. See individual directions for fabric yardage and additional materials.

GENERAL DIRECTIONS: Using sharp colored pencil, draw lines across patterns, connecting grid lines. Enlarge patterns by copying on paper ruled in 1″ squares; complete half-patterns, indicated by long dash lines. Mark outline of pattern on wrong side of designated fabric, leaving at least $\frac{1}{2}$″ between pieces; cut out $\frac{1}{4}$″ beyond marked outline (seamline) for seam allowance. Cut additional pieces from fabrics as directed; measurements include seam allowance. Stitch pieces together with right sides facing and raw edges even, making $\frac{1}{4}$″ seams. Press seam allowances to one side unless otherwise directed.

To make a "prairie point," cut 3″ square from fabric; fold square in half diagonally, right side out, forming a triangle. Fold triangle in half, bringing raw edges together; baste across raw edges; press. To form edging, stitch each prairie point to right side of fabric with raw edges even, so points are facing toward center of piece; overlap raw edges 1½″ (half way).

Clothes Bag

(About 19″ × 40″). Fabric: E, ⅝ yard; ⅜ yard each C, D, F; ⅛ yard each A, B, H. White cotton or cottonblend lining fabric 45″ wide, 1 yard. Yellow novelty wide-toothed zipper, 22″ long. Plastic hanger.

Enlarge pattern for top section of clothes bag, following General Directions; use pattern to cut two pieces from C, adding ½″ seam allowance to center edge and ¼″ to all other edges. Cut two 9″ × 12¾″ pieces from D; cut two 9″ × 17″ pieces from F. Cut one 18″ × 39″ backing piece from E; set aside. Following General Directions, make 100 prairie points,

using all fabrics; with raw edges even, overlap and baste five points to one 9″ (top) edge of each D and F piece, centering points between sides. With raw edges even and points in between, stitch top of each D piece to bottom edge of each top section. Stitch top edge of each F piece to bottom edge of each D piece in same manner. Press points toward bottom. Pin strips together along center edges, matching seams; machine-baste ½″ from edges. Press seam open. Position pieced front, wrong side up, on work surface. Place zipper over basted seam 6″ down from top; mark fabric at top and bottom of zipper. Stitch seam above and below marked positions, then stitch zipper to basted seam, following manufacturer's directions; open up basted area over zipper, using scissors or seam ripper.

Use pieced front as a pattern to cut backing to fit from reserved E piece; also cut two matching lining

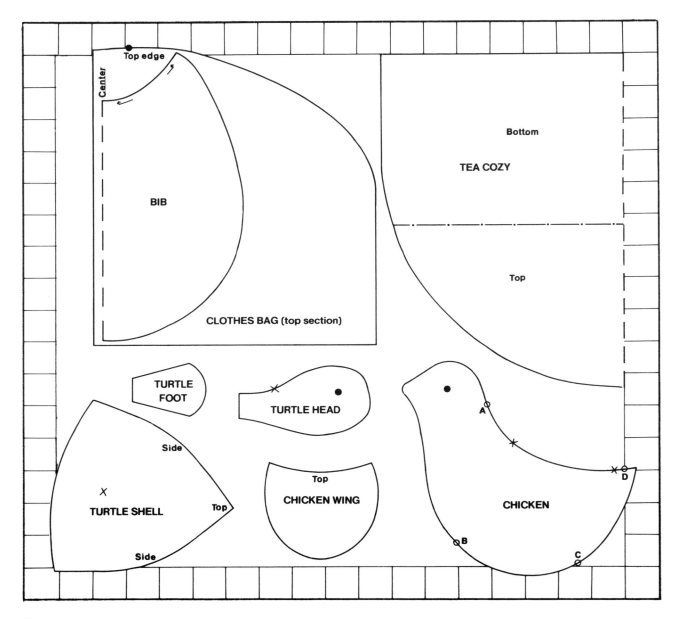

pieces from white fabric. Stitch points all around pieced front. With right sides facing and points between, stitch front to backing, leaving open between large dots at top.

Cut one lining piece in half lengthwise; place each half over pieced front and mark top and bottom of zipper along center edges of lining pieces. Stitch lining pieces together above and below marked positions, making $\frac{1}{4}''$ seam; press raw edges of open section $\frac{1}{4}''$ to wrong side. Stitch outer edges of lining pieces together, leaving opening between large dots at top; turn lining to right side.

With wrong sides facing, insert outer section, with zipper open, into lining; pin and slip-stitch together along sides of zipper and at large dots at top, turning raw edges to inside. Turn clothes bag to right side; insert hanger through top hole.

Bib

Fabric: $\frac{1}{4}$ yard each D, F; scraps A, B, E. Rickrack $\frac{1}{2}''$ wide, $\frac{3}{4}$ yard desired color. Double-fold bias seam tape, $1\frac{1}{8}$ yards desired color.

Enlarge bib pattern, following General Directions; complete half-pattern. Use pattern to cut two bib pieces, one each from F and D. On right side of one piece, center rickrack over seamline around edge (omitting neck); baste in place. Cut one piece of batting $\frac{1}{4}''$ smaller than piece all around; center and baste on wrong side of one bib piece. Stitch bib pieces together with right sides facing and rickrack in between, leaving neck edge open. Turn to right side, enclosing batting; remove basting. Make four prairie points from scraps, following General Directions. Pin and baste to neck edge of desired side of bib with raw edges even, overlapping points to fit. Center bias seam tape at neck edge of bib and sandwich top raw edges of bib between folded edges of tape, leaving excess tape free for ties. Topstitch edges of tape together, making ties and finishing top edge of bib; zigzag raw ends.

Turtle Toy

Fabric: $\frac{1}{4}$ yard each D, G, H, J; $\frac{1}{8}$ yard K; scraps of all colors. Two black $\frac{1}{2}''$ shank-type buttons.

Enlarge patterns for turtle head, foot and shell, following General Directions. Use patterns to cut two heads and eight feet from J, and two shell pieces each from D and G. Using compass, mark 8''-diameter circle on H; cut out along marked line.

Alternating colors, stitch shell pieces together along side edges. Make 18 prairie points, using all fabrics and following General Directions. With right sides facing and raw edges even, overlap and stitch prairie points all around bottom of pieced shell. Stitch four pairs of feet together, leaving straight edge open. Turn to right side; stuff lightly with fiberfill. With raw edges even, center one foot over each seam of shell; stitch in place over prairie points. Make head same as for feet, stuffing firmly; flatten straight edge, centering and matching seams. Choose the outside center of one shell piece for head placement. Using

seam ripper, open seam where prairie point is stitched to shell edge to fit straight edge of "neck." Insert head between shell and point with X on head facing shell; stitch head and point in place. Pin circle to bottom of body with right sides facing, and with prairie points, head and feet in between; stitch, leaving opening for turning. Turn to right side; stuff firmly with fiberfill. Fold raw edges at opening to inside; slip-stitch closed. Sew button eyes to each side of head at large dots. To hold head up, tack to shell at X.

Napkins

(14'' square): Fabric (for 4 napkins): D, $\frac{7}{8}$ yard; scraps A, C, E, F.

Cut four 15'' squares from D. Turn raw edges under $\frac{1}{4}''$ twice; press; stitch in place, mitering corners. Make four prairie points from scraps, following General Directions. Pin a point in one corner of the right side of each napkin, with outer edges even and raw edges facing center of napkin. Zigzag-stitch in place along raw edge.

Placemats

(About $18\frac{1}{2}''$ diameter): Fabric (for 4 placemats): $\frac{1}{2}$ yard each A, B, D, F; 1 yard desired color for lining; scraps of all colors.

Using compass, draw $17\frac{1}{2}''$-diameter circle on paper for pattern. Use pattern to cut one circle each from A, B, D, F, and four circles from lining fabric. Following General Directions, make 140 prairie points. With raw edges even, overlap and stitch 35 points around each gingham (top) circle.

Use pattern to cut four pieces of batting; trim batting $\frac{1}{4}''$ smaller than circles all around. Baste batting to wrong side of each lining piece. With right sides facing and points in between, stitch linings to tops, leaving opening for turning. Turn to right side; sew opening closed; remove basting. Topstitch $\frac{1}{4}''$ away from edge of circle all around.

Tea Cozy

(About 16'' × 10''): Fabric: $\frac{1}{2}$ yard each G, J; scraps of all colors.

Enlarge pattern for tea cozy, following General Directions; complete half-pattern. Use outline of full pattern to cut two lining pieces from J. Cut pattern into two pieces on dot-dash line for top and bottom; cut two tops and two bottoms from G. Following General Directions, make 41 prairie points. With raw edges even, overlap and stitch 10 points to upper edge of each bottom piece, $\frac{1}{4}''$ in from each side edge. Stitch each top to bottom with points in between; press points toward bottom. Stitch 21 prairie points all around curved edge of one G piece, beginning and ending $\frac{1}{4}''$ above straight bottom edge. Stitch each G piece to a lining piece along straight bottom edges, for two oval pieces. Cut two pieces of batting $\frac{1}{4}''$ smaller than each oval piece all around. Baste batting to wrong side of each piece. With right sides facing and points in between; stitch pieces together around all edges, matching fabrics and seams and leaving opening for turning. Turn to right side; sew opening closed. Push lining up into G front and back.

Basket Liner

Fabric: Approximately $\frac{1}{2}$ yard desired color for a small basket (adjust yardage for different size baskets); scraps of all colors.

Make pattern for base of basket by placing paper inside basket and cutting to fit. Remove paper; fold into quarters and adjust lines. Cut two bases from fabric, adding $\frac{1}{4}$" seam allowance. Measure for side panel as follows: Place tape measure inside top edge of basket and measure perimeter; add 1" to measurement. Measure height; add $\frac{1}{2}$". Cut two side panels from fabric, using these measurements. Stitch short edges of each together, making two tubes.

Following General Directions, make enough prairie points to cover one edge of one side panel; overlap and stitch points to fabric with raw edges even. On opposite edge, machine-baste $\frac{1}{8}$" in from edge; machine-baste one edge of other side panel. Pull basting, gathering panels to fit around bases; stitch each side panel to a base, adjusting gathers. With right sides facing and points in between, pin and stitch panels together at raw edges, leaving opening for turning. Turn to right side; sew opening closed. Push one piece into the other and tack at bottom seam; insert liner into basket.

Apron

Fabric: 2 yards desired color; scraps of all colors.

Cut the following: two $8\frac{1}{2}$" $\times$ 8" bibs; four $2\frac{1}{2}$" $\times$ 35" straps; two 21" $\times$ $2\frac{1}{2}$" waistbands; two 34" $\times$ 5" ties; one 61" $\times$ 26" skirt; one 61" $\times$ 2" facing for skirt hem. Stitch pieces together as directed below with right sides facing, making $\frac{1}{2}$" seams.

Make 96 prairie points, following General Directions. For straps, overlap and stitch 24 prairie points to one long edge of two straps. With raw edges even and prairie points in between, stitch same long edge to a plain strap. Press opposite long edge $\frac{1}{2}$" to wrong side on each strap piece.

Stitch six prairie points across one 8" edge (top) of one bib; stitch bib pieces together along top edge with raw edges even and points in between. Turn to right side and press; baste other three edges together. Sandwich $8\frac{1}{2}$" edges of bib between pressed edges of straps, with bottom edges flush. Topstitch straps to bib, starting at bottom and continuing to ends of straps.

To make ties, fold long edges of each piece $\frac{1}{4}$" to wrong side twice; press and topstitch in place. For pointed ends, fold down one corner of each tie, matching end to side with wrong side out, to form a diagonal; stitch in place along side; turn to right side. Machine-baste raw short edge of each tie; pull stitches to gather to $1\frac{1}{2}$" width. With raw edges even,

stitch gathered ties to center of each end of one waistband piece, leaving $\frac{1}{2}$" on either side of tie. Press raw edges toward waistband. With right sides facing, center and pin bottom edge of bib/strap section to one long edge of waistband with ties. To make facing for waistband, press one long edge and both short edges of remaining waistband piece $\frac{1}{2}$" to wrong side. With raw edges even, pin waistband pieces together with bib/strap section in between. Stitch $\frac{1}{2}$" from raw edges through all layers; turn waistband to right side, exposing bib.

Stitch remaining prairie points to one long (bottom) edge of skirt. Press one long raw edge of skirt facing $\frac{1}{2}$" to wrong side; stitch. With right sides together and raw edges even, stitch facing to bottom of skirt with prairie points between. Turn to right side; press. Slipstitch top of facing to skirt. Turn side edges of skirt $\frac{1}{4}$" to wrong side twice; topstitch in place. Machine-baste $\frac{1}{2}$" and again $\frac{1}{4}$" from remaining raw edge. Pull bobbin threads to gather fabric to fit waistband. With right sides facing and raw edges even, pin gathered edge of skirt to bottom edge of waistband, keeping waistband facing free; adjust gathers and stitch $\frac{1}{2}$" from raw edges. Press raw edges toward center of waistband. Pin pressed edge of waistband facing over gathered edge of skirt and ties; slip-stitch in place; press.

Try on apron to adjust straps; slip-stitch ends of straps to back of band.

Drawstring Bag

(About 15" high): Fabric: D, $\frac{1}{4}$ yard; G, $\frac{1}{3}$ yard; H, $\frac{1}{2}$ yard; scraps in all colors. White fabric-covered cord, 2 yards.

For bag, cut one $24\frac{1}{2}$" $\times$ 6" lower section and one $7\frac{1}{2}$"-diameter circle from D. Cut one $24\frac{1}{2}$" $\times$ $11\frac{1}{2}$" upper section from G. For lining, cut one 15" $\times$ $24\frac{1}{2}$" piece and one $7\frac{1}{2}$"-diam. circle from H.

Following General Directions, make 15 prairie points from scraps; overlap and stitch prairie points to one long edge of lower section; stitch lower and upper sections together at long edges, with prairie points in between. Stitch side edges together, matching seam, to make a tube. Pin bottom of lower section to circle D, easing fabric; stitch. Press top raw edge of bag $\frac{1}{4}$" to wrong side, then $1\frac{3}{4}$" again for facing. Turn bag to right side, and unfold facing. Stitch 15" edges of lining together, making a tube; stitch circle H to lining as for bag.

Insert lining into bag with wrong sides facing; pin top edges together so raw edge of lining is flush with pressed crease of facing. Make 1"-long vertical buttonholes $\frac{1}{2}$" below facing crease on opposite sides of bag, keeping facing free. Fold facing over to lining side; stitch facing to fabric above and below buttonholes to make casing. Cut cord into two one-yard lengths; insert each through buttonholes, drawing ends out on opposite sides. Knot ends to secure. ◊

Grandma Doll and Cuddly Cat

Shown on page 74

SIZES: Grandma: About 12½" tall. Cuddly Cat: About 10" tall.

EQUIPMENT: Paper for patterns. Pencil. Colored pencil. Ruler. Scissors. Embroidery needles. Large-eyed needle. Compass. Sewing machine with zigzag attachment. Iron.

MATERIALS: *For Grandma:* Brown calico 45" wide, ¼ yard. Brown polka-dot fabric 45" wide, ½ yard. Pinky-beige cotton knit, 7" square. Scrap ⅜"-wide lace or tatted edging. Three ¼"-diameter pearl buttons. Small amount of gray yarn for hair. *For Cuddly Cat:* Brown polka-dot fabric 45" wide, ½ yard.

Scrap brown calico. Scrap beige felt or chamois. *For Both:* Matching sewing thread. Scrap six-strand embroidery floss in bright blue, black and rose. Stuffing.

Grandma

Using colored pencil, draw lines across patterns, connecting grid lines. Complete half-patterns indicated by dash lines and enlarge patterns for body, face, bonnet back and front, arm and hand by copying on paper ruled in 1" squares. Cut pieces as follows, adding ½" seam allowance all around unless

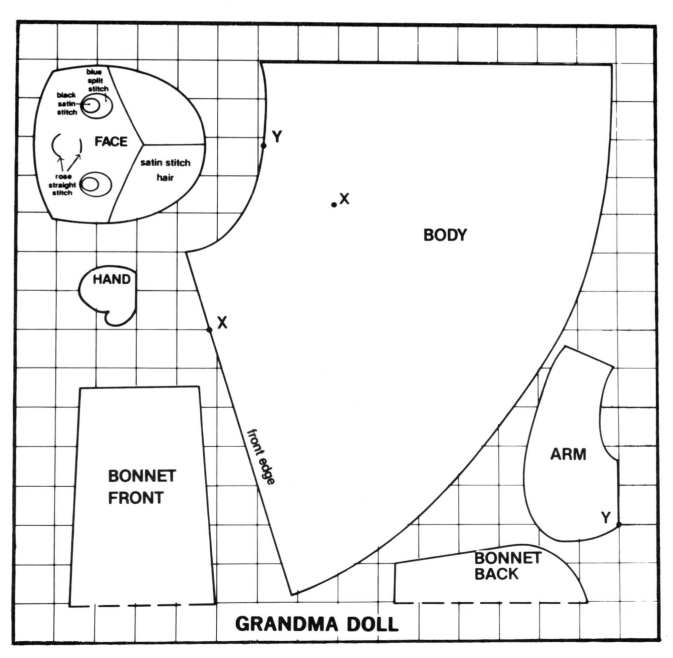

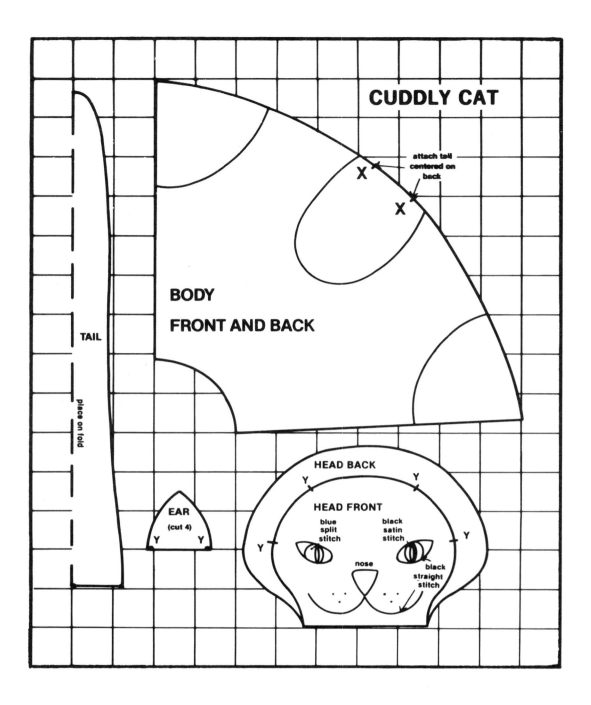

otherwise indicated: From brown polka-dot fabric, cut two bodies and two arms, using patterns (reverse arm pattern for right and left side and add seam allowance to straight edges only); also cut 9″-diameter circle. From brown calico, cut one bonnet back and one bonnet front, using patterns; also cut 7″ × 18″ piece for apron, two 2″ × 9″ strips for apron ties, and one 2½″ × 18″ strip for bonnet ruffle. From pinky-beige cotton knit, use pattern to cut face and single hand, adding seam allowance to wrist of hand only.

Make ¼″ hems along 7″ side edges of apron. Along one 18″ edge, machine-stitch two rows of long basting stitches. For apron ties, fold each 2″ × 9″ strip in half lengthwise, wrong side inward and with raw edges tucked in; topstitch along open long edge. Tuck in raw edges at one end on each tie; topstitch. With right sides facing, pin bonnet back to bonnet front, easing at top as necessary; stitch. For bonnet ruffle, fold 2½″ × 18″ strip in half lengthwise, wrong side inward; stitch along 18″ edge. Turn in raw edges at each end; topstitch. Pleat ruffle strip to measure about 11″; press and stitch to hold pleats along raw edge. Pin ruffle to right side of front edge of bonnet; stitch. Trim bonnet along ruffle with lace edging as in color illustration; slip-stitch in place. Pin right side of face to wrong side of bonnet front edge; stitch. Referring to pattern, mark placement and embroider facial features and hair (see Contents for Stitch Details). Work eyes in six strands of blue and black floss as indicated. Work mouth and nose in two strands of rose floss as indicated. Satin-stitch yarn hair from center part to outer edges of face as in illustration. Seam body pieces together, right sides facing. Machine-stitch two rows of long basting stitches along bottom edge of body (skirt). Gather skirt edge to fit circle. With right sides facing, pin and stitch circle to body; turn.

To assemble Grandma, gather long edge of calico apron to fit between dots marked X on body; baste in place. Pin arms in place, lining up dots on arm and neck edge of body marked Y and overlapping left arm, wrist edge on top of right arm. Make certain lower edge of arms overlaps apron top edge. Tuck in raw end of apron tie at lower back edge of arm. Appliqué arms to body, using white thread and close zigzag stitch. Do not stitch overlapped wrist edges. With right sides facing, pin hand to left wrist; stitch. Add lace edging and slip-stitch in place. Attach open edges of hand to right arm, using buttonhole stitch and matching sewing thread (see Contents for Stitch Details). Lightly pad arms. With right sides facing, pin head to neck edge; stitch, leaving opening to stuff. Stuff fully; tuck in raw edges at opening; slip-stitch closed. Pin and hem lower edge of apron. Add three small buttons down back seam of body, beginning at neck edge. Tie apron ties in bow.

Cuddly Cat

Enlarge patterns for cat as described for Grandma doll. Adding $\frac{1}{2}''$ seam allowance all around, unless otherwise indicated, use patterns to cut two body pieces, one tail, two ears and back and front head pieces from brown polka-dot fabric. Also cut an 8''-diameter circle from polka-dot fabric. Referring to pattern, mark placement for leg details on body front along lower edge. Use close zigzag stitch to embroider details in brown thread. With right sides facing, stitch body pieces together at side seams. Machine-stitch two rows of long basting stitches along bottom edge of body. Fold tail in half lengthwise, right side inward; stitch and turn tail. Also make basting stitches around head back piece. Use patterns to cut two beige felt or chamois ears and one nose. Fold and press raw side edges of polka-dot ears to wrong side. With wrong sides facing, use buttonhole stitch and matching thread to join beige ear to polka-dot ear. Use buttonhole stitch to attach nose to head front piece. Referring to pattern, mark placement for eyes and mouth on front. Work eyes in six strands of blue and black floss as indicated. Work mouth in two strands of rose as indicated. For whiskers, use doubled strands of black floss, and thread needle so that doubled ends go through needle eye. Following dots around mouth, insert needle; remove needle and thread loose ends of floss through loop at opposite end; pull up and knot. Trim to $2\frac{1}{2}''$.

To assemble cat, pull up basting stitches at lower edge of body to fit circle. With right sides facing, pin circle to body, adding tail at dots marked X, center back; stitch. Turn. Pull up basting stitches around back of head and with right sides facing, pin back to front. Add ears at dots marked Y. Stitch, leaving neck edge open. With right sides facing, pin head to body; stitch, leaving opening. Turn; stuff cat; turn in raw edges and slip-stitch opening closed. Make collar from scrap calico. Cut collar strip to 2'' × 7''. Fold and press long edges to center on wrong side, then fold strip in half again lengthwise. Fit collar around neck; sew in place. ◊

Shelf Decor

Shown on page 74

EQUIPMENT: Pencil. Ruler. Scissors. Scalloping shears. Tracing paper. Dressmaker's tracing (carbon) paper. Dry ball-point pen. Sewing machine with zigzag attachment. Iron.

MATERIALS: *For Scalloped Shelving:* White cotton fabric (see below for amount). Sewing thread for edging and floral motif in desired colors. White thumbtacks. *For Jar Covers:* Cotton print fabric (see below for amount). Thread. Rubber bands.

DIRECTIONS: *For Scalloped Shelving:* Measure length of shelf, then measure width plus desired overhang. Cut fabric to these measurements, adding $\frac{1}{2}''$ to one long edge and to each short end. With a ruler and pencil, lightly mark off evenly spaced areas for motifs. With scalloping shears, cut along entire length on one side, indenting as shown.

On tracing paper, plan a simple stylized flower (see illustration) to fit in each scalloped area. Transfer design to right side of fabric with dressmaker's carbon and dry ball-point pen. Remove tracing and carbon.

With machine set for very close zigzag stitch, satin-stitch flower petals, center, stem, leaves, and edging. Press extra fabric to wrong side; tack to shelf.

For Jar Covers: Cut fabric circle 2'' larger than jar lid. Fold under $\frac{1}{4}''$ all around circle; clip curves and press. Turn folded edge under $\frac{1}{4}''$; hem.

Secure cover to lid with rubber band. ◊

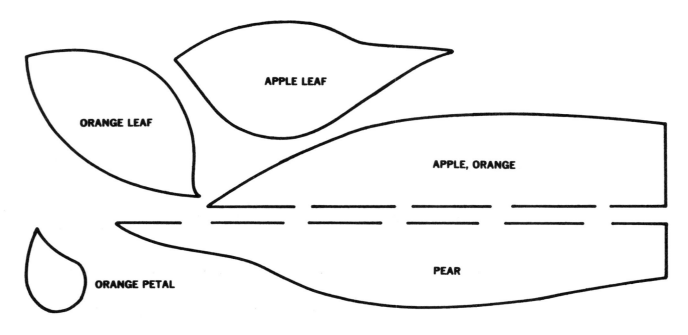

APPLE LEAF

ORANGE LEAF

APPLE, ORANGE

ORANGE PETAL

PEAR

String Holders

Shown on page 74

EQUIPMENT: Paper for patterns. Pencil. Ruler. Scissors. Sewing and embroidery needles. Safety pin.

MATERIALS: Felt: 9″ × 12″ each of red, orange, light olive green; scraps of white, brown, and bright green. Matching sewing thread. Orange, green, and red yarn. Light orange embroidery floss.

DIRECTIONS: *Note:* Each fruit is a holder for a 160-yard ball of parcel-post twine.

Trace actual-size patterns for fruit and leaves above; complete half-patterns indicated by dash lines. For each fruit, cut six of each main shape from appropriate color felt, adding ⅛″ to curved edges and ¼″ to straight bottom edge. Sew pieces together side by side with ⅛″ seam, leaving bottom open. Fold bottom edge under ½″, then sew ¼″ from fold to make casing. Cut small slit in the casing. With safety pin, insert matching-color yarn into slit, around through casing, and out through slit. Turn to right side.

For apple, cut two leaves of bright green felt; sew to top. For orange, cut two leaves of green felt (one bright green, one light olive) and five petals of white felt. Sew leaves to top. Sew the petals together at center with French knots, using light orange floss (see Contents for Stitch Detail); sew to leaves. For pear stem, cut ¾″ × 1¼″ piece of brown felt. Fold in thirds lengthwise and whip long edge together; sew one end to top. ◇

Ripple Band Pot Holder

Shown on page 74

SIZE: 6½″ square.
MATERIALS: Coats & Clark's Speed-Cro-Sheen, 1 100-yard ball each of White (W), Yellow (Y) and Tango (T). Steel crochet hook size 0.
GAUGE: 5 sts = 1″; 6 rows = 1″.

Pot Holder

Front: With W, ch 33.

Row 1 (right side): Sc in 2nd ch from hook and in each ch across—32 sc. Ch 1, turn each row.

Rows 2-4: Sc in each sc across.

Row 5: Working 1 st in each sc across, work (2 sc, 1 hdc, 2 dc, 2 tr, 2 dc, 1 hdc) 3 times, sc in each of last 2 sts. Change to T in last sc by pulling T through last 2 lps on hook. Cut W. With T, ch 1, turn.

Row 6: Sc in each st across. Change to Y. Cut T. With Y, ch 1, turn.

Rows 7-11: Sc in each sc across. Change to T at end of row 11. Cut Y. With T, ch 1, turn.

Row 12: Sc in each st across. Change to W. Cut T. With W, ch 4, turn.

Row 13: Sk first sc, tr in next sc, (dc in each of next 2 sc, hdc in next sc, sc in each of 2 sc, hdc in next sc, dc in each of next 2 sc, tr in each of next 2 sc) 3 times. Ch 1, turn.

Rows 14-38: Sc in each st across. Ch 1, turn each row. End off.

Back: With Y, ch 34. *Row 1:* Dc in 4th ch from hook (counts as 2 dc), dc in each remaining ch—32 dc. Ch 3, turn.

Rows 2-17: Sk first dc, dc in each dc across, dc in top of ch 3. Ch 3, turn. When back is same length as front, end off.

Finishing: Place front, right side up, over back. With T, beg at upper right corner, sc front and back tog, working 3 sc in each of first 3 corners. At last corner, sc in corner st, ch 24 for hanger, 2 sc in same st. End off. ◇

Hens and Basket

Shown on page 74

SIZES: Basket, 5″ × 8½″ × 3½″ deep. Hens, 8″, 7″ and 6″ across.

EQUIPMENT: Paper for patterns. Pencil. Ruler. Scissors. Straight pins. Sewing and embroidery needles. Sewing machine with zipper foot attachment. Pinking shears.

MATERIALS: *For Hens:* Three different cotton calico prints in red, green, and blue: 11″ × 17″ for large hen and two basket bows; 7½″ × 15″ for medium hen, 7″ × 13″ for small hen. Polyester fiberfill batting. Rickrack in colors to contrast with fabrics, 24″, 20″, and 17″ lengths. Six-strand embroidery floss to match rickrack. Sewing thread to match fabrics. *For Basket:* Yellow calico cotton, 36″ wide, ¾ yard. Four-ply soft cable cord, size 250, 7 yards. Yellow sewing thread. All-purpose glue.

DIRECTIONS: Enlarge patterns on next page by copying on paper ruled in 1″ squares. Dot-dash lines indicate a second pattern piece (for underbodies). Short dash lines indicate topstitching. When sewing pieces together, make ¼″ seams (patterns include seam allowance).

To Make Each Hen: Fold fabric in half crosswise, right side out. From double fabric, cut two complete body pieces and two underbody pieces.

Sew rickrack to each complete body piece, on right side of fabric, ¼″ in from lower edges, between X's. Sew a piece of rickrack to one body piece at head, on right side of fabric and ¼″ in from raw edge, between X's. Embroider eye on each body piece with satin stitch (see Contents for stitch details); use three strands of floss in needle, matching color to rickrack. With right sides facing, pin body pieces together; sew seam from dot-dash line at throat around head and back to dot-dash line under tail.

With right sides facing, pin underbody pieces together; sew seam from outer ends of straight edge to crosslines, leaving middle of seam open.

With right sides facing, pin underbody to body. Sew one side at a time, making seam ¼″ in from raw edges and sewing over rickrack stitches. Turn hen to right side.

Stuff head and tail with polyester batting. Using underbody pattern, cut two pieces from batting; trim each ¼″ all around and slip one into each hen side. Slip-stitch underbody seam closed. Topstitch lower edge of each hen side where indicated by short dash lines, sewing through all thicknesses. Tack both sides of hen together at lower neck and under tail.

To Make Basket: Basket is woven of fourteen 1″-wide padded strands. Padded strands are made from fabric-covered cord.

From yellow calico, cut the following 3″-wide strips: seven, 11″ long; four, 14½″ long; four, 26″ long (reserve one 26″ strip for rim). Cut lengths again from four-ply cable cord, cutting only three 26″ lengths.

Following Diagram 1, make padded strands as follows: Unwind a length of cord and separate the four plies. Place the four plies lengthwise and close

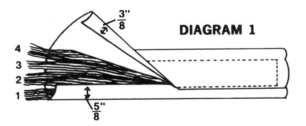

together on wrong side of fabric strip. Fold bottom long edge of fabric up ⅝″ over cord; turn top long edge of fabric under ⅜″ and fold over cord overlapping bottom edge of fabric; pin. Topstitch with zipper foot through all thicknesses ¼″ in from both long edges, stitching between cord plies 1 and 2, and 3 and 4, and across both ends; trim excess cord. Make 14 padded strands in this manner.

For Basket Bottom: Following Diagram 2, weave

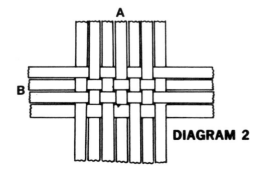

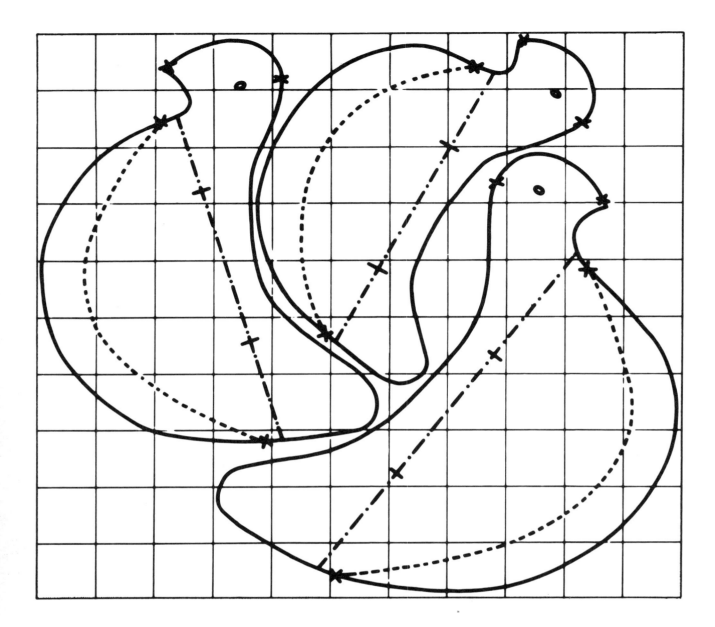

14½" strands (sides B) through 11" strands (sides A), seam sides up. Unwoven ends should measure 3½" each; they will become the 22 stakes for the basket sides.

For Basket Sides: Starting between the stakes at one side B, weave 26" strands through stakes, turning the stakes up as you weave around the basket. Weave strands so that all seams face inside. Overlap ends of each strand on inside of basket; turn under raw edge and slip-stitch closed. When weaving last strand, put a dab of glue between strands and stakes where they overlap. Trim all stakes ¼" below edge of top strand at the stitching line.

For Basket Rim: Fold both long edges of remaining 26" strip under ⅜"; topstitch ¼" in from both edges. Drape strip right side up evenly over top edge of basket; slip-stitch strip edges to both inside and outside of basket. To give rim a padded look, tack all around to outside of basket at topstitching line.

From fabric for large hen, cut two 1" strips, 17" long, with pinking shears. Pass each through weaving at upper end of basket rim and tie into bow (see color illustration). ◇

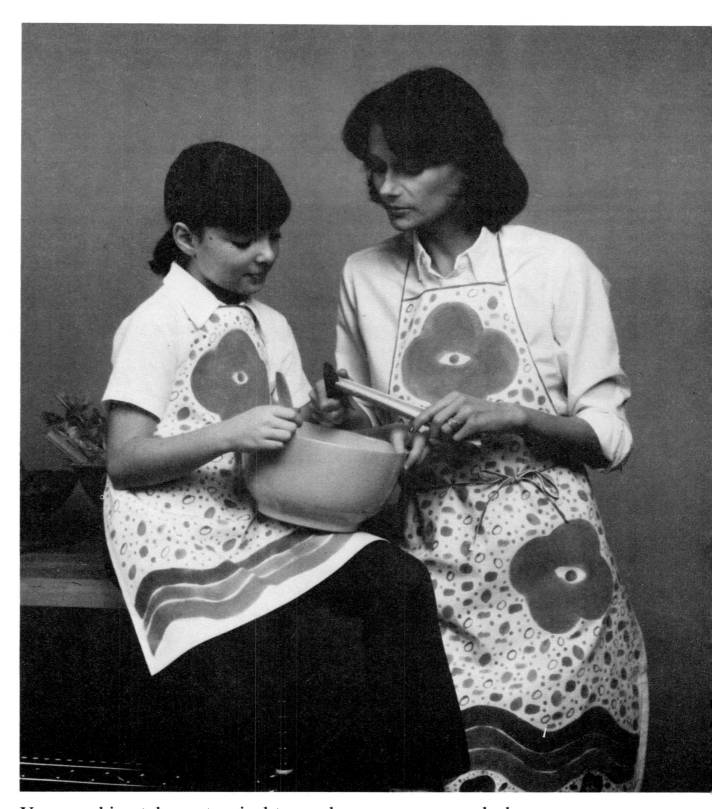

Your cooking takes a tropical turn when you wear a splashy cotton duck apron. We have apron patterns sized for a child and an adult. Use our luscious shades—sapphire blue, seafoam green and tangerine—or choose your own favorites. Directions are included with Fabric Painting instructions, beginning on page 41.

Beehive cozy holds tea hot in the pot. Felt hive is
machine quilted, joined with buttonhole stitching.
Calico lines the cozy, and covers napkin rings.
Bees buzz all around! Directions for
Beehive Cozy and Napkin Rings, page 111.

Make a recipe notebook from a loose-leaf binder covered with fabric. Cutouts are appliqued with machine stitching; cover slips off for washing. Recipe Notebook directions begin on page 122.

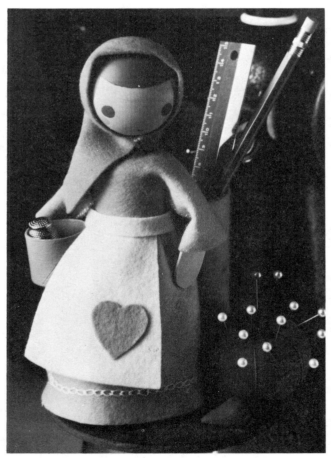

Felt items are great for bazaar gifts. Country lass keeps your sewing notions close at hand. She's made with a dowel and finial and outfitted in felt. Directions, page 111.

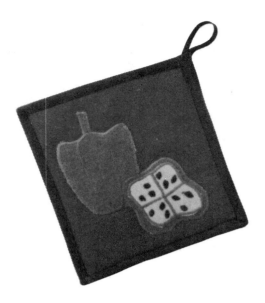

Garden pot holders: fruit and vegetable motifs
are appliqued to heavy cotton pot holders with
iron-on bonding net; all the edges of the appliques
are done in zigzag stitch on a sewing machine.
Details on the designs are embroidered by hand.
Bias tape forms hanging loop. Directions for
Garden Pot Holders begin on page 122.

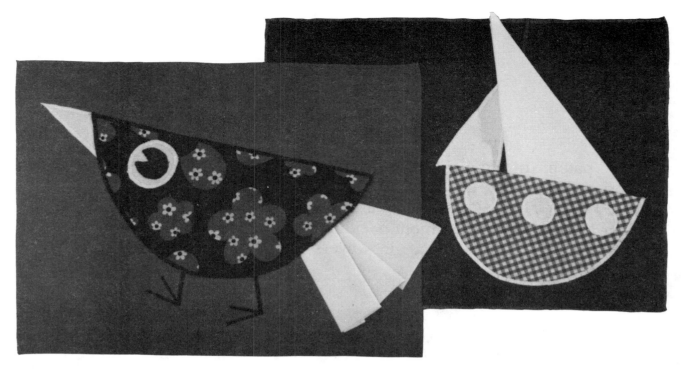

Color every meal happy with these machine-appliqued
place mats. A layer of fusible web makes the mats
more durable, and an innovative placement of napkins
makes each design really unique. See if you can
find them! One is the bird's tail; another, the
boat's mainsail; and third, the clown's tie.
Directions for Cheerful Place Mats, page 125.

It's a "patch" of bunnies! If you're hunting for fresh ideas
in spring decorating, try our adorable Easter Egg Hunt appliques!
White bunnies hop about, hiding a basketful of fabric-scrap
Easter eggs. You can see them peeking from behind bright
yellow-colored eggs decorated in flowers, polka dots, and swirls.

Even the cheeriest kitchen seems brighter with Bunny Pot Holders; make a whole hutch of them in no time! Decorate in simple applique, then bind fabric and batting with yellow bias tape. Bias tape loops make them easy to hang.

Three-sided tea cozy is machine-quilted, appliqued and stitched with bias tape binding. It's so simple, you'll have it done almost before the tea has brewed! Pillow for living room or bedroom completes the great Easter egg hunt. To sew Bunny Patch Pot Holders, Pillow and Tea Cozy, see page 128.

Place mats that look good enough to eat can be embroidered on a
sewing machine, shading delectable-looking fruit by changing thread
colors as you stitch. Shaded grapes center the tray-shaped mat,
easily trimmed to its curvaceous shape after embroidery is completed.
Strawberries-in-a-basket make an ingenious motif for a place mat,
with each matching napkin trimmed with a single ripe berry.
Directions for Tray-Shaped Mat, page 126; Strawberry Mat, page 129.

Flower Pot Holder

Shown on page 74

SIZE: 7¼" diameter.

MATERIALS: Coats & Clark's Speed-Cro-Sheen, 1 100-yard ball each of white, main color (MC) and green, contrasting color (CC). Crochet hook size E. White felt circle, 7⅛" diameter. Matching sewing thread.

GAUGE: 5 sts = 1"; 2 dc rnds = 1".

Pot Holder

Front: Beg at center with MC, ch 6. Join with sl st in first ch to form ring.

Rnd 1: Ch 1, 16 sc in ring. Sl st in first sc.

Rnd 2: Ch 3, dc in next sc, * ch 5, dc in each of next 2 sc, repeat from * around, end ch 5, sl st in top of ch 3—8 lps.

Rnd 3: Sl st in next dc, ch 1, * 9 sc in next lp, repeat from * around, sl st in first sc. End off.

Rnd 4: Join CC in same sc with sl st, sc in st, * ch 5, sk 2 sc, sc in next sc, repeat from * around, end ch 5, sl st in first sc—24 lps.

Rnd 5: Sl st in first lp, ch 1, sc, hdc and dc in same lp, * yo hook, insert hook in next lp and draw up a lp to measure ½", complete a dc—long dc made; 1 more long dc in same lp, yo hook twice, draw up a lp in same lp to measure ½", complete a tr—long tr made; in same lp make 7 more long tr and 2 long dc; in next lp, make dc, hdc and sc; in next lp make sc, hdc and dc, repeat from * around, end dc, hdc and sc in last lp. Sl st in first sc—8 scallops. End. Stretch out scallops.

Back: Beg at center with MC, ch 5. Sl st in first ch to form ring. *Rnd 1:* Ch 1, 8 sc in ring.

Rnd 2: Ch 1, 2 sc in same sc as sl st, 2 sc in each sc around. Sl st in first sc—16 sc.

Rnd 3: Ch 3, dc in same sc as sl st, 2 dc in each sc around. Sl st in top of ch 3—32 dc.

Rnds 4 and 5: Ch 3, dc in same st as sl st, * dc in next dc, 2 dc in next dc, repeat from * around, end dc in last dc. Sl st in top of ch 3—72 dc.

Rnd 6: Ch 3, dc in same st as sl st, * dc in each of next 8 dc, 2 dc in next dc, repeat from * around, end dc in last 8 dc. Sl st in top of ch 3—80 dc.

Rnd 7: Ch 3, dc in same st as sl st, * dc in each of next 9 dc, 2 dc in next dc, repeat from * around, end dc in last 9 dc. Sl st in top of ch 3—88 dc.

Rnd 8: Ch 1, 2 sc in same st as sl st, * sc in each of next 10 dc, 2 sc in next dc, repeat from * around, end sc in each of last 10 dc. Sl st in first sc—96 sc.

Rnd 9: Ch 1, sc in same st as sl st, sc in each of next 10 sc; pick up front section and hold in front of work, right side up; insert hook in sp between center 2 tr of any scallop and through next sc on back, work 1 sc, work another sc in same sp and st, * sc in each of next 11 sc, make 2 joining sc through next scallop and sc, repeat from * around. Sl st in first sc.

Rnd 10: Ch 1, 2 sc in same st as sl st, * sc in next 12 sc, 2 sc in next sc, repeat from * around, end sc in last 12 sc. Sl st in first sc—112 sc. End off.

Edging: Join CC in same sc as sl st. Ch 1, sc in same sc, sc in each sc around. Sl st in first sc. Ch 14 for hanger, sl st in same st as sl st; turn, sl st in each of 14 ch. End off.

Pin felt circle to wrong side just inside top of edging sts. With matching sewing thread, sew lining in place. ◇

Green and White Mat

Shown on page 75

SIZE: 12" × 18".

MATERIALS: Southmaid Crochet Cotton, 2 550-yd balls each of white (W) and green (G), enough for 2 mats. Steel crochet hook No. 1.

GAUGE: 6 dc = 1"; 3 rows = 1" (double strand).

Notes: Use cotton double throughout. When changing colors, work last dc of color until there are 2 lps on hook, finish dc with new color. Work over unused color to hide it in work.

Mat

Beg at one end, with G, ch 66.

Row 1 (right side): Dc in 4th ch from hook (counts as 2 dc), changing to W (see Notes); * with W, dc in each of next 2 ch, change to G; with G, dc in each of next 2 ch, change to W; repeat from * across, end 2 W dc—64 dc. Do not change to G. With W, ch 3, turn.

Row 2: Sk first dc (ch 3 counts as first dc), dc in next dc, change to G; * with G, dc in each of next 2 dc, change to W; with W, dc in each of next 2 dc, change to G; repeat from * across, working last G dc in top of ch 3. Ch 3, turn.

Rows 3 and 4: Work 2 more rows of G dc in G dc, W dc in W dc. At end of row 4, change to W in last dc. With W, ch 3, turn.

Row 5: Work W dc in G dc, G dc in W dc across.

Rows 6-8: Work G dc in G dc, W dc in W dc. At end of row 8, change to G. Continue in this manner, working 4 rows of G on G and W on W, then reverse colors for next 4 rows until there are 48 rows.

Edging: Rnd 1: From right side, with G, work around 4 sides of mat in sc, working 2 sc in side of each dc row, sc in each st on ends of mat and 3 sc in each corner st. Sl st in first sc.

Rnd 2: Ch 1, sc in each sc around, working 3 sc in each corner sc. Cut G; with W, sl st in first sc.

Rnds 3 and 4: With W, work sc in each sc, 3 sc in each corner sc. Join each rnd.

Rnd 5: Working from left to right, sc in each sc around. Join; end off. ◊

Cross-Stitch Hot Mat
Shown on page 75

SIZE: Approximately 7″ square.

EQUIPMENT: Pencil. Ruler. Large-eyed needle. Scissors. Sewing machine.

MATERIALS: Counted thread cloth for 6 stitches per inch, 9″ square. Medium-weight yarn in colors and amounts indicated in color key. Red felt for backing, 8″ square. Sewing thread, dark blue and red.

DIRECTIONS: With pencil, mark 6″ square in center of cloth, for charted design area.

Work design in cross-stitch; see Contents for stitch details. To make cross-stitches, begin by leaving an end of yarn on back and working over it to secure; run end of strand in on back of work to finish off. Do not make knots. Work all underneath threads in one direction and all the top threads in the opposite direction. Keep the stitches as even as possible. Make all crosses touch by putting your needle in same hole used for adjacent stitch. Keep yarn smooth and flat.

Follow chart to work one half of design. For second half, repeat first half in reverse, omitting center row. Then work a border of long-legged cross-stitch all around design, using medium blue yarn. Work a second border row around first, using dark blue.

When all cross-stitching has been worked, turn excess cloth to back; trim corners. Center piece, right side up, on red felt. Machine-stitch close to outer edge of cross-stitch, using blue thread in needle and red thread in bobbin. Trim felt so that it extends $\frac{1}{4}$″ beyond edge of cross-stitch. Round off corners. ◊

LONG-LEGGED CROSS-STITCH

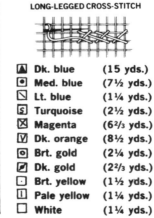

▲	Dk. blue	(15 yds.)
⊙	Med. blue	(7½ yds.)
◥	Lt. blue	(1¼ yds.)
S	Turquoise	(2½ yds.)
✕	Magenta	(6⅔ yds.)
V	Dk. orange	(8½ yds.)
◉	Brt. gold	(2¼ yds.)
◪	Dk. gold	(2⅔ yds.)
⬚	Brt. yellow	(1½ yds.)
⊔	Pale yellow	(1¼ yds.)
☐	White	(1¼ yds.)

Stripy Duo
Shown on page 75

SIZE: Mat, 11½″ × 17″; coaster, 4½″ square.

MATERIALS: Coats & Clark's Speed-Cro-Sheen, 1 100-yd. ball each of 5 colors: Red (R), gold (G), blue (B), orange (O) and green (GR). Steel crochet hook No. 0.

GAUGE: 5 sts = 1″; 6 rows = 1″.

Mat

With R, ch 145. *Row 1:* Hdc in 2nd ch from hook and in each of next 52 ch, yo hook, pull up a lp in each of next 3 ch, yo and through all 5 lps on hook (mark this st for corner), hdc in each remaining ch. Ch 1, turn.

Row 2: Hdc in each hdc to 1 st before marked st, yo hook, pull up a lp in each of next 3 sts, yo and through all lps on hook (mark for corner), hdc in each remaining hdc to last hdc, yo hook, pull up a lp in last hdc, cut R, finish st with G. With G, ch 1, turn.

Row 3: Working over ends to hide them, hdc in each hdc to 1 st before marked st, dec as before, hdc in each remaining hdc. Ch 1, turn.

Row 4: Hdc in each hdc to 1 st before marked st, dec as before, hdc in each hdc to last hdc, complete last hdc with B. Cut G. With B, ch 1, turn.

Continue in this manner, working 2 rows of a color and decreasing 2 sts at corner every row. Work striped pat of R, G, B, O and GR or any desired colors. When all sts have been worked off on short end of mat, end off. With any desired color, work 2 rnds of sc around mat, working 3 sc in each corner each rnd.

Coaster

With R, ch 46. *Row 1:* Hdc in 2nd ch from hook and in each of next 20 ch, yo hook, pull up a lp in each of next 3 ch, yo and through all 5 lps on hook (mark this st for corner), hdc in each remaining ch. Ch 1, turn. Work as for mat until all sts have been worked off. Work edging as for mat. ◊

Brown Gingham Set
Shown on page 75

SIZES: Bridge Cloth, about 44″ square. Napkins, 13″ square. Place Mats, 11½″ × 17½″.

EQUIPMENT: Paper for pattern. Ruler. Dressmaker's tracing (carbon) paper. Dry ball-point pen. Tracing paper. Colored pencil. Scissors. Straight pins. Embroidery needles. Embroidery hoop. Sewing machine. Padded ironing board. Steam iron.

MATERIALS: Brown-and-white checked gingham (¼″ squares) 44″-45″ wide: 1¼ yards for cloth; 1 yard for four napkins; 1⅓ yards for four place mats. White bias tape, 1″ wide: five yards for cloth, seven yards for napkins, seven yards for place mats. Six-strand embroidery floss: For cloth: seven skeins white, three skeins of dark green, and one skein each dark brown and yellow; for napkins: one skein each white, dark green, dark brown, and yellow. For place mats: Same amounts and colors as cloth. Muslin, 36″ wide, ¾ yard for place mats.

GENERAL DIRECTIONS: Trace complete motif on next page for cloth and place mats; trace the single motif indicated for napkins. Using dressmaker's carbon and dry ball-point pen, transfer motif to right side of fabric as indicated in individual directions. Remove tracing and go over any design lines to clarify if necessary.

To Embroider: Refer to Contents for stitch details. Place fabric in hoop, making sure fabric is taut and not distorted. Cut floss into 18″ lengths. Use three of the six strands in needle for daisy unless otherwise indicated. Use two strands for border. Do not make knots. To start, leave 1″ end of floss on underside of cloth and work over it to secure. Begin and end successive strands by running ends under stitches on back of work.

Embroider daisy petals in satin stitch with white. Complete petal by working outline stitch at center. Work leaves as for petals with dark green. Outline stems in chain stitch with dark green, then fill center of each in rows of outline stitch. Work each daisy center in French knots, using six strands of yellow. Press each motif on wrong side.

To Finish: Cut lengths of white bias tape as indicated in individual directions. Miter corner and assemble as follows: Open up tape at one end. Place two strips together, one on top of the other, right lines facing. Fold end up so that end is flush with top edge (see Figs. 1 and 2). Unfold and stitch along crease ¼″ in from each edge (between the folds). Open out strips (see Fig. 3). Trim seam; press open

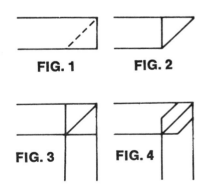

FIG. 1   **FIG. 2**

FIG. 3   **FIG. 4**

(see Fig. 4). Repeat with two remaining strips. Then miter the corners of each pair of strips together to form a border of tape. Pin border around outside edge on wrong side of fabric. Machine-stitch along outer tape fold. Turn tape to right side, pushing out corners. Slip-stitch inner edge in place.

With dark brown floss, make outline stitch at inner edge of white binding. Then, using seam allowance of binding as a guide, work another row of outline stitch about ¼″ away all around. With dark

green floss, work all around. With dark green floss, work feather-stitch between the two rows of outline stitches.

Bridge Cloth

Working on one corner at a time, transfer daisy motif 3″ in from edge and 4″ in from point of cloth.

For border, cut four strips of white tape 44″-45″ long.

Napkins

(Make 4): For each napkin, mark and cut a $13\frac{1}{2}$″ gingham square. Trace, transfer, and embroider single daisy about $2\frac{1}{4}$″ in from lower right corner.

For border, cut four $13\frac{1}{2}$″-long strips of white tape.

Place Mat

(Make 4): For each place mat, mark and cut two gingham pieces 12″ × 18″; mark and cut one muslin piece the same size. Trace, transfer, and embroider complete daisy motif about 4″ in from top left corner of one gingham piece.

With wrong sides of gingham facing, place the muslin piece between the gingham pieces. Pin and baste all around.

For border, cut four strips of white tape, two 12″ long and two 18″ long. Place longer strips on top and bottom, shorter strips at sides. ◇

Kitchen Ensembles

Shown on pages 76–77

EQUIPMENT: Pencil. Ruler. Scissors. Paper for patterns. Embroidery needle. Sewing machine with zigzag attachment.

MATERIALS: Heavy cotton fabric, 45″ wide, 1 yd. main color for each; small pieces of other colors shown for fruit appliqués. Sewing thread to match fabrics. Six-strand embroidery floss: blue, yellow, and orange. Fusible web for appliqués. Plastic curtain rings, 1″ diameter, four for each apron. Thin cotton lining fabric for pockets, about 12″ square for each. For Pot Holders: bias binding tape to match background fabric; cotton batting 7″ square for each.

Apron

Enlarge apron pattern and pocket fruit patterns on paper ruled in 2″ squares; complete half-patterns indicated by long dash lines. Enlarge fruit patterns for pot holders on 1″ squares. Cut apron from main color fabric. For binding, cut 1½″-wide strips of main color across fabric; join strips to make lengths required. Fold strips in half lengthwise and turn in long edges and ends ¼″; press. Machine-stitch bindings in place as follows: Bind bottom curved edge

of apron skirt from middle of each side (side curtain rings), down around bottom. Bind top straight edge. Leaving a 1″ tab of binding strip extending at each end, bind curved sides of apron bib from top corner down to middle (the tabs are for attaching rings). For ties, cut two strips 2″ wide, each 44″ long. Fold each in half lengthwise, turn in long edges and ends ¼″; stitch open edges together. Insert one end of ties through curtain rings; fold over 1″ and sew to secure ring. Fold 1″ of tab at top of apron through tie rings and sew to back, thus attaching a tie at each side of top. In the same manner, sew a ring to each tab at middle of sides of the apron.

For pocket appliqués, cut complete fruit shape of lining fabric. Cut each part of fruit design from fusible web and heavy cotton in colors shown. Place fruit pieces over lining piece with fusible web in between; press with iron to bond appliqués to lining for added stiffness.

Use matching sewing thread in machine; zigzag-stitch appliqué pieces to fruit shape with narrow satin stitch; satin-stitch across top edge between crosslines on pattern; do not stitch leaves or stems

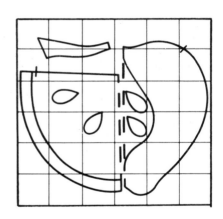

APRON AND POCKET FRUIT PATTERNS

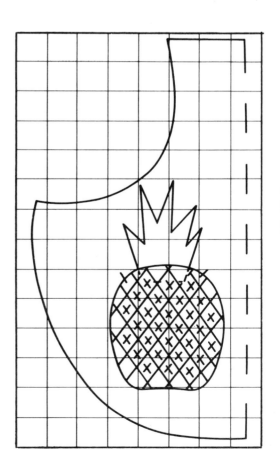

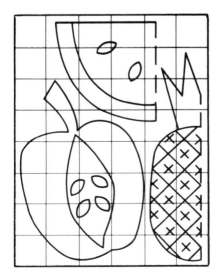

POT HOLDER FRUIT PATTERNS

yet. Satin-stitch fruit seeds in place. On pineapple, satin-stitch the diagonal lines with orange thread. Hand embroider the crosses using full six strands of yellow floss in sewing needle. On apple, zigzag-stitch yellow line down center.

Place pocket on apron as shown, with stem and pineapple leaves under top of pocket; baste. With matching thread, satin-stitch stem and pineapple leaves to apron. Satin-stitch pocket to apron around sides and bottom of pocket; leave top between crosslines open.

Pot Holder

For each, cut two pieces of main color fabric 6¾" square. Cut appliqué pieces of fabric and fusible web. Place appliqués on one piece of main color fabric for front with fusible web between. Following directions on package, bond appliqués to fabric. With matching thread and zigzag attachment, satin-stitch appliqué pieces to fabric all around edges of each piece. On pineapple, satin-stitch diagonal lines with orange thread; hand embroider crosses with six strands of yellow floss. Hand embroider seeds in apple and watermelon with satin stitch, using six strands of blue floss for watermelon, six strands of orange for apple.

Place the two fabric pot holder pieces together with cotton batting between; baste. Machine-stitch around each fruit shape with thread to match background, straight-stitching through all thicknesses.

With tape to match main color, bind edges of pot holder, starting at top corner; leave a 3½" end of tape at top corner. Stitch open edges of tape end together; fold in half to form a loop and stitch to back. ◇

Kitchen Stars

Shown on page 78

EQUIPMENT: Paper for patterns. Tracing paper. Pencil. Ruler. Scissors. Straight pins. Sewing machine with zigzag attachment.
MATERIALS: Purchased pattern for man's apron. Fabric: red denim, 44" wide, ⅞ yard; blue and white denim 44" wide, ⅜ yard each; small amount of thin cotton for hot mitt lining. Sewing thread to match. Batting for hot mitt.
APRON: Using purchased pattern, cut apron of red denim and neck strap of blue. Enlarge pattern by copying on paper ruled in 1" squares; complete half-pattern crosswise. Then continue pattern lengthwise to make about 30" long, repeating stars the same distance apart and making top end of pattern straight. Trace pattern. Cut blue and white denim 12" × 30". Pin white on blue. Pin tracing on white fabric, with bottom edge of curve flush with bottom edge of fabric. On machine, satin stitch around each star. Then pin fabric, centered, to apron front, with top edges flush. On machine, satin stitch along both border lines through all thicknesses. Tear away tracing paper. Being careful not to cut through blue fabric, cut away white fabric in center area around stars and inner edge of border, close to stitching. Cut away blue and white fabric around outside of border close to stitching. Trim arm area of design border to ½", following contour of apron. Cut away red fabric on wrong side within center panel area; do not discard; use for hot mitt. Complete apron following purchased pattern instructions.

Hot Mitt

Enlarge pattern on this page, on paper ruled in 1" squares. Using pattern, cut two complete mitts of lining fabric, and one of red denim (back) adding ¼"

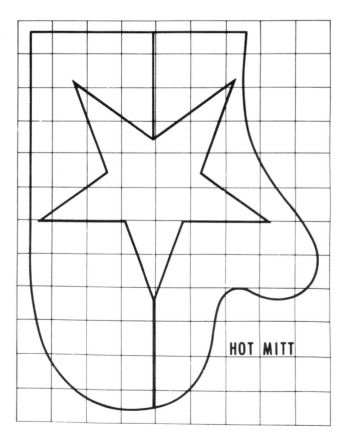

all around for seam allowances. Cut two of batting (slightly smaller than pattern). Cut front of mitt from blue and red denim (see illustration), adding ¼" all around for seam allowances. Cut star of white. With right sides facing, sew center seam of blue and red front pieces. Lay front piece out flat and referring

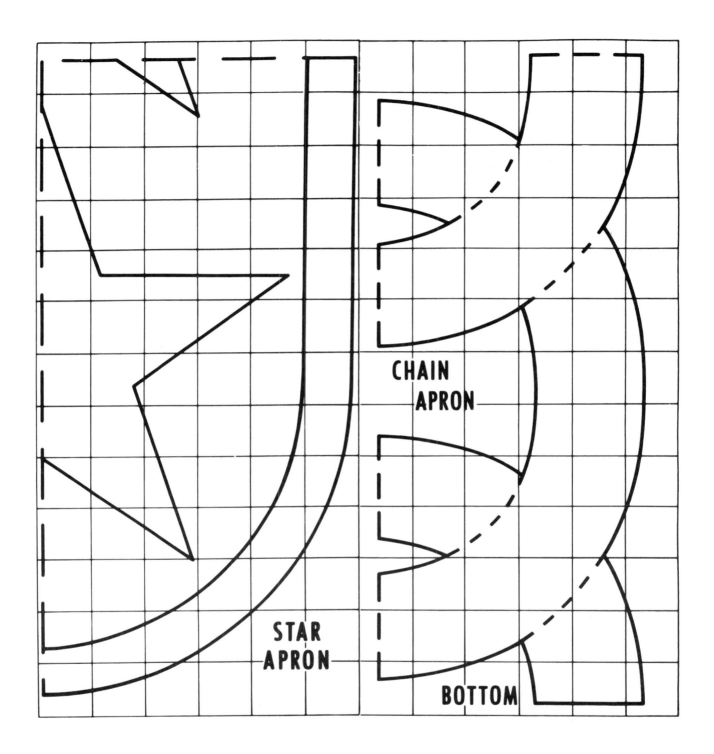

STAR
APRON

CHAIN
APRON

BOTTOM

to pattern, pin star in place. Machine-stitch star to front with satin stitch along edges. With wrong sides facing, place front and lining together and a layer of batting between; baste together. Do the same with back piece. Cut a mitt shape of tracing paper. On this, mark lines diagonally about 1″ apart in one direction and then in opposite direction. Pin tracing on front piece. Baste along diagonal lines through all thicknesses; do not baste over star. On machine, stitch over basted lines, through all thicknesses. Quilt the back in same manner. Tear away tracing paper.

Place front and back together, right sides facing, and sew all around, making $\frac{1}{4}$″ seams. Zigzag-stitch over raw edges of seam. Turn to right side. To bind open edge, cut bias strip of red denim $1\frac{1}{2}$″ × 14″. Fold in half lengthwise, then fold long edges to center; insert raw edges of mitt into fold. Stitch binding to mitt, close to edges. For hanging loop, cut strip of red denim $1\frac{1}{2}$″ × $5\frac{1}{2}$″. Fold in half lengthwise; turn raw edges in and sew edges together. Fold in half crosswise to form loop; sew ends together and to inside top of mitt. ◇

Ball and Chain Set

Shown on page 78

EQUIPMENT: Paper for patterns. Tracing paper. Pencil. Ruler. Compass. Scissors. Straight pins. Sewing machine with zigzag attachment.

MATERIALS: Purchased pattern for man's apron. Fabric: black sailcloth, 45" wide, ⅞ yard. Tan cotton denim, 44" wide, ¾ yard. Sewing thread to match fabric. Flannelette for pot holder, 8" square.

DIRECTIONS: Using purchased pattern, make complete apron, without neck strap, of black fabric; leave bottom edge unhemmed. Enlarge pattern, page 107, copying on paper ruled in 1" squares; complete half-pattern crosswise and repeat pattern lengthwise for 2½ more rings. Trace complete pattern and pin tracing to tan fabric, having fabric extend 12" beyond top of pattern. Continue marking chain strip at each side, to top of 12" extension for neck strap; allow ¼" at edges of neck strap for seams. Cut design out of tan fabric. Pin chain design down center of apron with bottom edges flush. On sewing machine with zigzag attachment, satin stitch along all edges of tan fabric and along short dash lines (see pattern); stitch only up to top edge of apron. To form strap, bring ends of strips together with right sides facing and sew across with ¼" seam. Cut a strip of tan fabric 3" × 22½": zigzag stitch across ends to keep them from raveling. With right sides facing, pin this strip to neck strap with about 1" of strip extending below top edge of apron. Sew inner edges together, making ½" seam. Turn right side out. Turn outer edges to inside ½" and topstitch along edge ⅛" in from edges. Tack ends to apron on wrong side. Make ½" hem at bottom edge of apron.

Ball Pot Holder

With compass, mark two 8"-diameter circles on tan fabric and one on flannelette; cut out. Pin tan pieces together with flannelette between. To quilt on machine, make line of topstitching horizontally and vertically across center, then make two additional lines of stitching 1¼" apart on each side of and parallel to each of the center lines. For binding, cut bias strip of tan fabric 1½" × 26". Fold in half lengthwise, then fold sides in to center. Insert raw edges of circles into fold. Zigzag stitch over edges of binding through all thicknesses.

For hanging loop, cut bias strip of tan fabric 1½" × 6". Fold in half lengthwise; fold each long edge to center. Zigzag stitch along edges and ends. Fold strip in half crosswise to form loop and stitch ½" from ends to edge of pot holder. ◇

Pocket Apron

Shown on page 79

MATERIALS: Purchased apron pattern, Child's 2-6X. Rubber-and-cotton backed fabric for apron (see pattern for amount); additional small pieces of apron fabric in colors desired for the four pockets. Stencil with ¾" letters. Pinking shears. Black permanent marker.

DIRECTIONS: Following pattern directions, make apron; do not cut pocket, if included in pattern.

To Make Pockets: Use various colors of rubberized fabric for the pockets. With pinking shears, cut center bottom pocket included with the apron pattern along stitching line (or use our pattern, adding 1½" all around for seam allowance). For top pocket and two side pockets, trace full-size pattern, at right; dash line indicates half-pattern. Cut out pockets with pinking shears.

Stencil label across pockets with permanent marker; space letters evenly across pockets measuring 2" up from bottom on center bottom pocket and 2¾" up from bottom on the other three pockets. Fold pocket hemline under. Place pockets on apron as shown in color illustration. Center side pockets across side seams of apron. Stitch pockets to apron. ◇

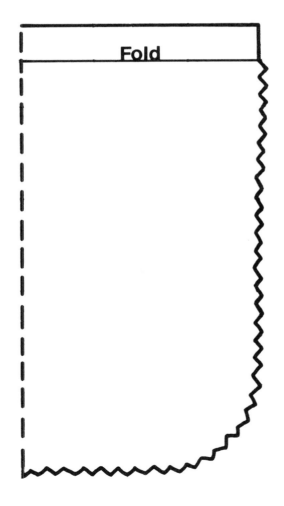

Fold

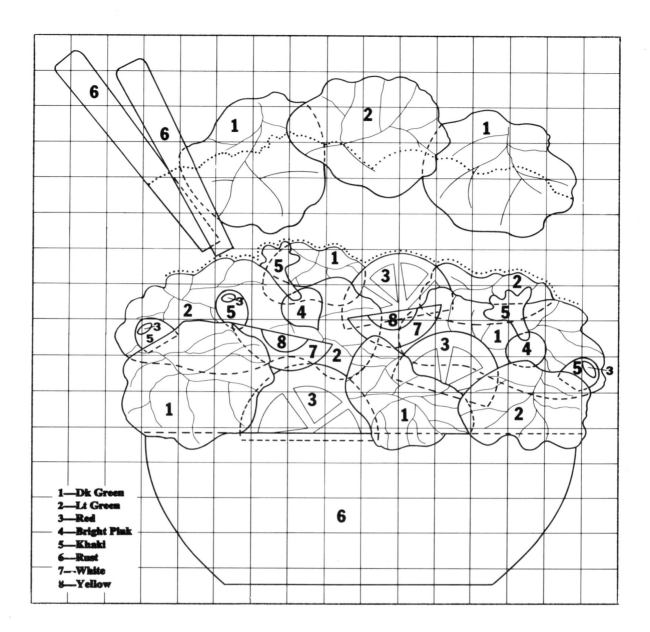

1—Dk Green
2—Lt Green
3—Red
4—Bright Pink
5—Khaki
6—Rust
7—White
8—Yellow

Salad Bowl Apron

Shown on page 79

MATERIALS: Purchased apron pattern Misses' Small-Large. Rubber-and-cotton backed fabric for apron (see pattern for amount); additional fabric scraps for appliqué. Thread to match all colors. Dressmaker's carbon. Tracing wheel.

DIRECTIONS: Following pattern directions, make apron.

To Appliqué Pocket: Enlarge salad bowl design by copying on paper ruled in 1″ squares. Dash lines indicate overlapping pieces; heavy lines indicate cutting lines, thin lines indicate machine embroidery. Salad bowl design is given in two pieces: bowl and part of salad form pocket; upper portion of salad and utensil handles are appliquéd onto apron underneath. Following pattern and color key, trace each part of design onto wrong side of scraps of rubberized fabric with dressmakers' carbon and a tracing wheel. Cut out each piece of fabric. With matching thread, stitch interior lines of salad with tiny zigzag satin stitches, following pattern.

Note: Light and dark lettuce leaves are stitched internally with medium green thread. Following pattern, stitch appliqué pieces together, using matching thread and zigzag medium satin stitch. Attach utensils and upper lettuce leaves to apron with zigzag satin stitch; attach bowl and salad to apron, matching dotted lines. Stitch around sides and bottom only, being sure not to attach top of salad since it forms a pocket. ◇

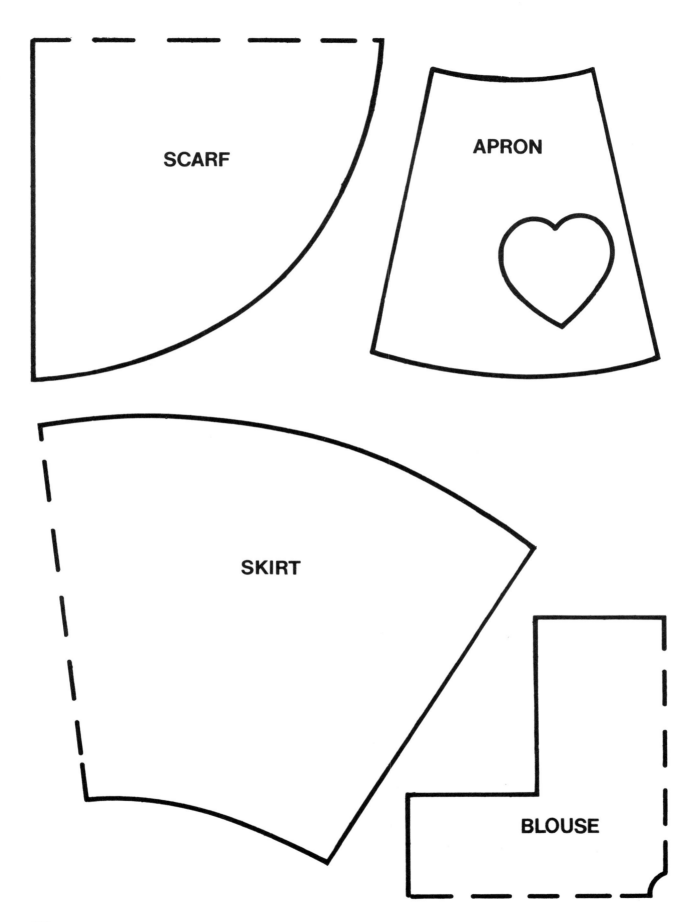

SCARF

APRON

SKIRT

BLOUSE

Sewing Maid

Shown on page 94

EQUIPMENT: Paper for patterns. Pencil. Ruler. Scissors. Single-edged razor blade. Sewing needle. Small paintbrush. Compass. Drill with ⅜″ bit. Hammer.

MATERIALS: Large scraps of felt: pink, yellow, light and dark orange, white and bright green (or desired colors). White heavy duty thread or buttonhole twist. Wooden dowels: one piece 5¼″ long, 1¼″ diameter; one piece 1″ long, ⅜″ diameter. Wooden ball finial 1⅝″ diameter. Piece of heavy cardboard 5″ × 10″. Two cardboard tubes: one 1¾″ diameter, one 1¼″ diameter. Wooden ice cream spoon. Brown, green and pink acrylic paints. All-purpose glue. Ready-made pincushion (ours is tomato design).

DIRECTIONS: For base, cut two circles of cardboard each 5″ diameter. Cut and glue a 5″-diameter circle of green felt on one cardboard circle. Drill hole ¼″ deep in one end of larger dowel and in ball finial (if it does not already come with hole). Glue undrilled end of larger dowel on felt-covered circle to one side of center; hammer nail through bottom of circle into dowel to secure. Glue second cardboard circle to bottom of base. Glue small dowel into top of large dowel; glue on finial. Referring to illustration, paint features on finial: make hair and eyes brown, mouth and cheeks pink. Paint edges of base brown.

Trace full size patterns; complete half- and quarter-patterns indicated by dash lines. Cut blouse of light orange felt; fold in half along shoulder line; slash from neck to bottom on center of one side for back. Whip underarm seams together. Place on dowel with opening in back; whip back edges together. For hands, cut wooden ice cream spoon in half; glue one cut end inside end of each blouse sleeve. Cut skirt of yellow felt; make line of chain stitch (see Contents for stitch details) near wider (bottom) edge. Place around dowel, overlapping bottom of blouse; whip back edges together; gather skirt at waist to fit and tack skirt to blouse. Cut apron of white felt; cut heart of light orange felt; glue heart in place. For apron tie and waistband, cut strip of white felt ⅜″ wide, 8″ long. Place apron on front of skirt and glue waistband around top edge and around girl's waist; overlap and glue ends in back. Cut headscarf of pink felt. Wrap around head; sew ends together and glue in place under "chin" and at center back.

With razor blade, cut wider tube down to 4″ long; glue piece of cardboard over one end to cover. Cover entire tube except open end with dark orange felt; glue. Glue this tube to base at side back of girl. Glue pin-cushion to base just in front of this tube. Cut smaller tube down to 1″ long. Glue piece of cardboard to one end to cover. Paint this tube green. When dry, glue to one hand and to body side as shown in illustration. ◇

Beehive Cozy Set

Shown on page 94

EQUIPMENT: Ruler. Pencil. Paper for pattern. Tissue paper. Straight pins. Scissors. Sewing needle. Paring knife. Sewing machine.

MATERIALS: Felt 36″ wide, ½ yd. gold; scraps of brown and white. Dark print gingham 36″ wide, ½ yd. Cotton batting. Bumblebees, available in florist, millinery, or party supply stores. Gold sewing thread. Thin, stiff cardboard for napkin rings. All-purpose glue.

Beehive

Cut two pieces of gold felt, two of gingham fabric, and two of batting, each measuring 11″ × 13″. On a flat surface place a piece of gingham fabric right side down, a layer of batting, and a piece of felt. Baste the three pieces together for front of hive.

Enlarge pattern for beehive (on page 112) by copying on paper ruled in 1″ squares. Cut out pattern. Pin pattern on top of layered pieces. With pencil mark around beehive design; cut away excess material. Remove pattern and trace on tissue paper.

Place tissue paper pattern on beehive. Baste across with long stitches through dash lines of pattern. Tear away paper pattern. Machine-stitch across hive following basting stitches.

From calico cut larger hive opening, adding ¼″ seam allowance all around. Turning in edges ¼″, slip-stitch calico in place. From brown felt cut smaller hive opening; glue in place.

Make back of hive with remaining pieces in same manner, omitting opening. Using gold thread, work small, close buttonhole-stitching through the three thicknesses across bottom edges of front and back pieces (see Contents for stitch details). Pin front and back together, calico sides facing, and buttonhole-stitch around sides and top of hive to join. Sew bees on front and back of hive as desired.

Napkin Ring

From cardboard cut strip 1½″ × 6¼″. With knife score across strip at 1″ intervals along the length of the cardboard. Bend on scored lines to form ring.

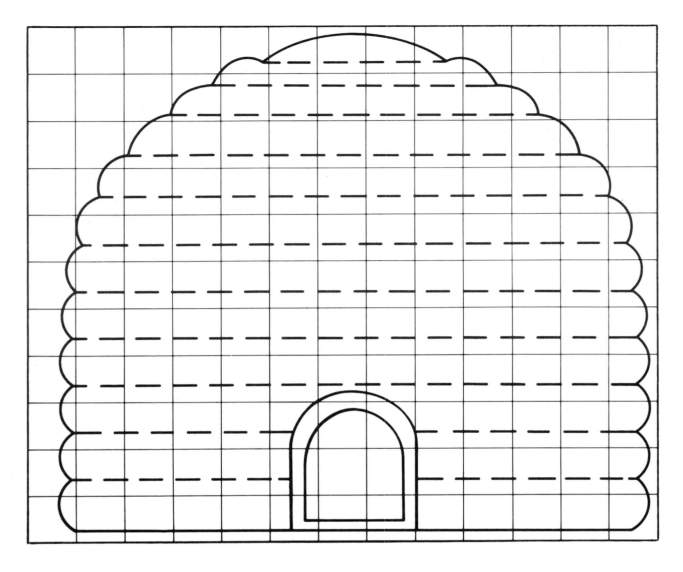

From calico cut strip 2″ × 6¾″. Place calico right side down on flat surface. Apply glue to outside of cardboard strip; center on calico and press flat. Fold ¼″ edges of fabric over cardboard; glue in place.

Cut strip of gold felt 1½″ × 6⅝″. Apply glue to other side of cardboard and press felt in place, overlapping ends ¼″ to form napkin ring; glue ends. Trace actual-size flower pattern; cut outer piece of white felt and center of gold felt. Slip-stitch yellow center onto white, stuffing with a little batting as you go. Sew bumblebee to center. Glue flower onto ring. ◇

Fluffy, snow-white poodle is crocheted, but sports a "fleecy" coat. Orlon yarn, looped on the body, is cut, then brushed with steel bristles for the fuzzy effect. Features on the 12″ high poodle are embroidered, pink leash is slip-stitch crochet.

Sleepy-eyed pup is sure to be perky when loved by an adoring youngster. Long, floppy ears and body are made from soft, furlike fabric; the snout is appliqued, and friendly features and paw pads are of felt. It's 14″ of cozy fun. Directions for Fluffy Poodle, page 132; Cuddly Pup, page 147.

Flip-Over Doll is really two dolls in one! With her gingham skirt down, she's a wide-eyed brunette. Flip the skirt over, and a sleepy-eyed blonde in a flannel nightie appears. She's 11½″ tall and fun to make. Directions for Flip-Over Doll are on page 144.

Sweet little Sleepy Sock Doll has a papier-mâché face formed over a jar lid, with a tiny bead for a nose. Head and features then come alive with enamel paint. Soft sock body is stuffed with batting and stitched. Don't forget the soft flannel sleeper and, of course, a cuddly blanket. Directions for Sleepy Sock Doll are on page 148.

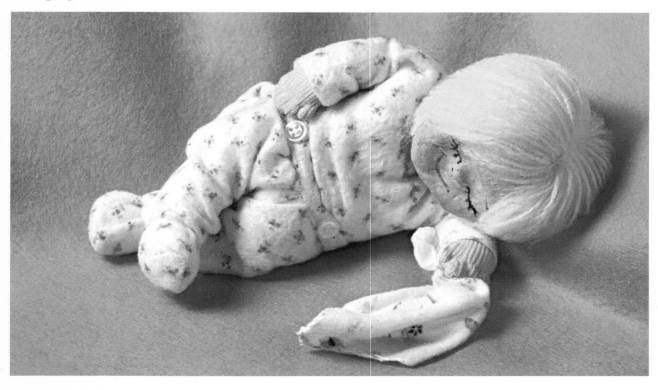

Baby-in-a-Bootie is a huggable sleeptime pal. Of pink fabric and only 7½″ long, she will sleep sweetly in her felt bootie "crib" or in a baby's loving arms. Directions begin on page 141.

Soft Terry Babies are lovable dolls. Their bodies are cut from a foam rubber chair pad (one pad makes two), covered with terry cloth, then embroidered and dressed. So easy to make and completely washable. Directions begin on page 146.

Rainbow rickrack flashes across rich black felt for an easy-to-make trio. Pieces are lined; round-the-neck bagette has braid trim and a long strap, closes with a snap. Soft sculpture sedan and propeller plane (with an 18"-wing span) make up our own fly and drive plan, right for both girls and boys. They're sewn in sturdy fabrics, then firmly stuffed. Designed by Jane Slovachek. Directions for Felt Set, page 152; Fabric Transports, page 150.

Wiggly snake and lanky pals are fun to make with rickrack. And a simple gathering stitch is all you have to do! Rickrack hair is stitched to the pals' stocking heads; finish snake with bright scraps of felt. Best of all, they are just the right size for little hands, and they love to travel in pockets. Each doll is 7" long. For Rainbow Toys, see page 162.

Three little friends from covered wagon days will settle right into your heart! Princess Lost Feather wears beaded mocs; Patience and Prudence wear lace. Little Miss Dolls designed by Nora Dilks, page 163. Giant car (23″ long) makes a perfect seat for TV watching! Directions for Giant Car, page 171.

117

Strawberry:
Embroidered lines,
glue-on face.

Orange:
Leaf, eyes, mouth
and chin are
glued in place.

Lime:
Applique eyes,
mouth and leaf to body.

Green Pepper
Eyes, mouth
and cheeks
are glued on.

Apple:
Face consists of
eyes, smiling mouth,
cheeks, leaf
and stem.

Pear:
Glue on eyes
mouth, cheek
and top leaf.

AND VEGETABLES

Carrot:
Yarn beard is stitched in place. Eyes and mouth are appliqued to the body.

Lemon:
Bright and sunny felt shapes accent mouth, eyes and leaf.

Peas in a Pod:
Glue stem, eyes, mouth and five peas to pod body.

Radish:
Make beard of yarn pieces, stitch in place under chin.

Banana:
Tall and lean with contrasting spots; eyes and mouth.

Tomato:
Ripe and plump with eyes, mouth, cheeks and leaf.

Directions for all begin on page 167.

Play-pillow toys in bright colors and
varied fabrics form the gayest zoo.
Fabric and 1″ foam rubber padding for owl,
chick, mouse, and rabbit are cut from
the same basic pattern. You can ad-lib
your own pet animals with details
of felt, buttons, pompons.
Directions for all begin on page 171.

Baked Boxes

Shown on page 80

EQUIPMENT: Measuring cup. Large mixing bowl. Plastic bags. Rolling pin. Wax paper. Sharp knife. Scissors. Flat cookie sheets. Toothpick. Tile or other flat, oven-tempered object for weight (optional). Aluminum foil. Tape measure. Paintbrush. *For Charlotte Russe Box:* Two oven-tempered plates and one fancy metal gelatin mold.

For Brownie Box: Small cardboard jewelry box about $2'' \times 3'' \times \frac{3}{4}''$ for mold.

MATERIALS: *Basic Clay Recipe:* 2 cups flour, 1 cup salt, 1 cup water, 1 ounce liquid glycerine (optional). Large cotton fabric scraps for lining. Small can of high-gloss polyurethane. All-purpose glue. *For Cookie Jar Box:* Cardboard powdered chocolate-drink container with metal ends. *For Dumpling Dish:* Cardboard salt container.

GENERAL DIRECTIONS: In mixing bowl, mix flour and salt together. Add water, a little at a time, until dough forms a crumbly but not sticky ball (dough will change after kneading). Use more or less water depending upon the humidity. Knead for 10 minutes until texture is smooth. If desired, divide dough into portions and knead one at a time. Keep unused portions of dough in an airtight plastic bag to keep it moist. Leftover dough will keep refrigerated for a week in this way.

When working on very large projects, add up to 1 ounce of glycerine, if desired, to make dough more pliable. Dough with glycerine will require longer baking time.

All projects require one batch of dough, with the exception of Charlotte Russe Box, which requires two.

Some molds are part of the finished container. Those that are to be removed must be covered with aluminum foil first.

Roll kneaded dough onto wax paper to desired thickness. Walls must be at least $\frac{1}{4}''$ thick to stand. Keep turning dough over as you roll to make sure both sides are smooth. Smooth surface cracks by rubbing water into dough with fingers. Shape all containers, following individual directions. To bond two pieces together, apply water to both surfaces and press together; smooth with fingers.

Bake all items on flat baking sheet until dough is thoroughly dry. Baking times vary with each item, because of thickness and size. They can be baked at 150°F overnight or at 350°F for 1-5 hours. We suggest you bake at the lower temperature overnight, because chances of the dough puffing up are reduced. If dough does puff up while baking, prick it with toothpick and press air out. If it continues to puff up, weight it down.

Bake items and molds and do not remove mold until dough is cool. If the mold does not come away easily, the dough has not baked long enough.

To Line Containers: Cut cotton fabric the same shape as container area plus 1″ all around. Fold raw edges under 1″ and glue lining in place.

After containers are lined, apply several coats of polyurethane to entire container, drying completely between each coat. Coat bottom last to prevent sticking.

Cookie Jar Box

With knife, remove metal top of chocolate drink container. For bottom of cookie jar, press bottom of container down on rolled dough firmly enough to make an outline. With knife, cut away dough beyond outline. For sides of cookie jar, cut rectangle from rolled dough 1½″ longer than height of container and slightly longer than its perimeter. Starting at one corner, wrap slab of dough around container. Using water, press seam together, then bond bottom to sides. Fold excess dough over top edge of container (container is a permanent part of Cookie Jar Box). If necessary, reinforce side seam with small strip of dough over joint.

For lid, turn Cookie Jar Box upside down on rolled dough. With knife, cut around box shape and remove excess. For knob, loosely crumple a piece of aluminum foil into a ball. Roll out circle of dough and wrap it around ball to cover. Using water, bond knob to center top of lid.

After baking, line inside of box (excluding inner rim) and lid as directed above.

Charlotte Russe Box

For top of box, cover mold with aluminum foil. Roll out circle of dough large enough to cover entire outside of mold. Press dough firmly and smoothly down over mold; cut off excess dough around edges. Trim surface with coils and circles of dough; press on and bond with water. Make small knob in same manner as for Cookie Jar Box.

For bottom, lay rolled dough between two oven-tempered plates (size should be right for molded top). Trim excess dough.

Bake with mold and plates in place. Line center bottom of plate.

Dumpling Dish

Cut salt container to height of 2½″; discard upper portion. Wrap outside of lower half with aluminum foil. Place piece, bottom side up, on baking sheet. Cut 9″-diameter circle of rolled dough. Drape over container, letting edges of circle flare out onto baking sheet. Bake with dough draped over container. After dough begins to harden, turn piece over and continue to bake right side up. Line inside bottom only.

Brownie Box

For box, wrap outside of bottom half of cardboard jewelry box with aluminum foil. Cut a rectangle from rolled dough the size of box bottom plus the sides. From each corner of dough, cut away a square the depth of box side. Center jewelry box on dough and bring sides of dough up and together at corners; using water, pinch and smooth dough until seams are invisible.

For lid, cut two rectangles from rolled dough, one the size and shape of box and the other $\frac{3}{8}''$ smaller all around. With water, bond smaller rectangle to center of larger one.

After baking, line inside of box as directed above, leaving lid unlined. ◊

Recipe Notebook
Shown on page 95

EQUIPMENT: Paper for patterns. Pencil. Ruler. Scissors. Straight pins. Sewing machine with zigzag attachment.

MATERIALS: Heavy cotton fabric 36″ wide, $\frac{1}{3}$ yard blue; large and small pieces of orange, yellow, and orange-yellow stripe. Yellow baby rickrack $\frac{3}{4}''$ yard. Sewing thread: blue, yellow and orange. Rigid loose-leaf notebook 10″ × 11″ × 2″ thick.

DIRECTIONS: Enlarge patterns by copying on paper ruled in 1″ squares. Solid lines are cutting lines; dotted lines are embroidery. Cut letters, pepper mill, salt shaker of orange fabric. Cut whisk handle, spoon, bowl top of yellow fabric. Cut bowl sides of striped fabric.

Cut blue fabric 12″ × 30″. Turn in $\frac{1}{4}''$ across each end and stitch across each. Turn in $\frac{3}{8}''$ on each long edge and $3\frac{1}{2}''$ on each end; press. Unfold, then fold in half crosswise, right side out. Pin cut pieces in place on half of blue fabric for front, within area of folds with about $\frac{1}{2}''$ margin (from folds) at top and bottom. Start letter ''R'' $1\frac{1}{2}''$ in from center fold and arrange other pieces in relation to this. Stitch all pieces in place around edges with satin stitch and matching thread on sewing machine. Dotted lines on pattern indicate additional narrow machine satin stitching. Cut three pieces of rickrack: $10\frac{1}{2}''$, $9\frac{1}{4}''$, and $6\frac{1}{4}''$. Pin and sew longest piece under letters, next one down center (under letter ''C''), and shortest under the striped bowl as shown in photograph.

Fold $3\frac{1}{2}''$ ends over in opposite direction of original

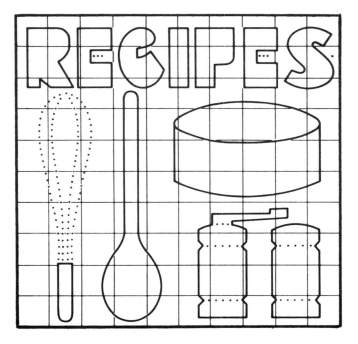

fold (right sides facing). Stitch doubled edges together at top and bottom of each end with $\frac{3}{8}''$ seams. Turn right side out. Refold $\frac{3}{8}''$ along top and bottom long edges, stitch across each $\frac{1}{8}''$ from fold.

Insert edges of notebook front and back into ''pockets'' of fabric cover. ◊

Garden Pot Holders
Shown on page 96

EQUIPMENT: Paper for patterns. Pencil. Ruler. Scissors. Sewing machine with zigzag attachment. Iron. Large-eyed needle.

MATERIALS: Cotton fabric 8″ × 16″ main color for each; small pieces of various colors for appliqués. Thread to match fabrics. Fusible bonding web, $1\frac{1}{2}''$ or 5″ wide. Wide bias binding tape to match appliqué colors. Cotton batting $6\frac{1}{2}''$ square for each.

DIRECTIONS: For each, cut two pieces of main color fabric 7″ square. Trace full size patterns, pages 123 and 124; dash lines show overlapping pieces, dotted lines are stitching lines. Cut appliqué pieces of fabric in colors desired. For front, place appliqués on one piece of main color fabric, with bonding web between. Press with iron to bond appliqués to fabric. With matching thread and zigzag attachment, satin-stitch appliqués to fabric all around edges of each piece; satin stitch along all dotted lines. With needle and six strands of appropriate color floss, embroider seeds (shaded areas), making tomato seeds in French knots, pepper, orange, and apple seeds in satin stitch (see Contents for stitch details).

Place the two fabric pot holder pieces together, right side out, with cotton batting between and baste together. Machine stitch around outside of appli-

quéd shape with thread to match background, straight stitching through all thicknesses.

With bias tape to match appliqué, bind edges of pot holder, starting at top corner; leave a 3½″ end of tape at top. Stitch open edges of tape end together; fold in half to form loop, stitch to back. ◊

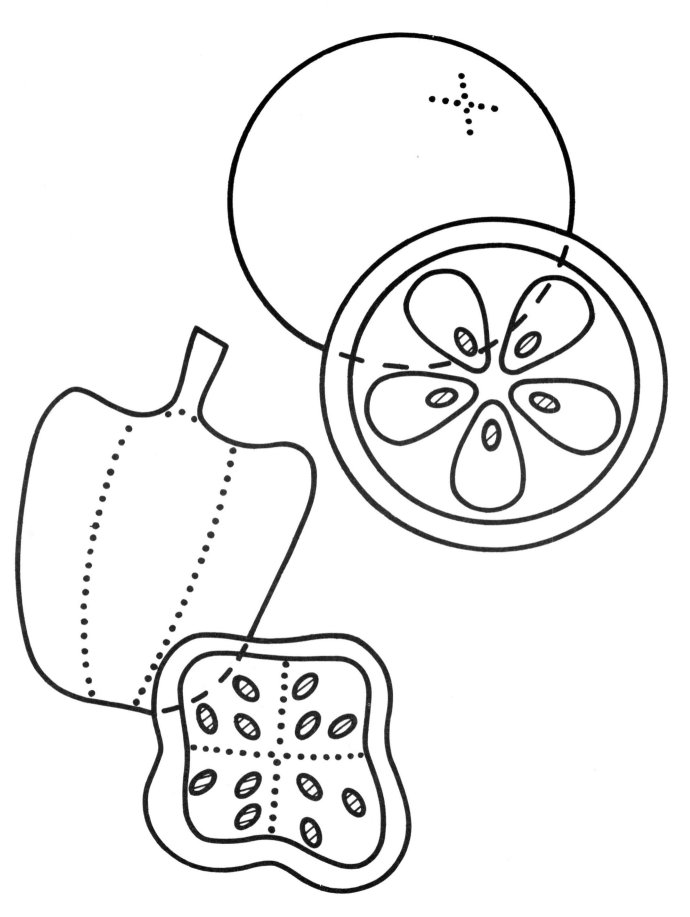

Cheerful Place Mats

Shown on page 97

EQUIPMENT: Pencil. Ruler. Scissors. Paper for patterns. Straight pins. Zigzag sewing machine.

MATERIALS: Medium-weight cotton fabric, 36″ wide, $\frac{1}{3}$ yd. for each place mat in colors desired; $12\frac{1}{2}$″ square for each napkin (in matching or contrasting color); large and small pieces for designs. Fusible web for bonding, 11″ × 15″ for each. Sewing thread to match or contrast with fabric.

DIRECTIONS: Enlarge patterns by copying on paper ruled in 1″ squares; complete half-patterns indicated by long dash lines. Short dash lines indicate where pieces overlap. Solid lines on pattern indicate cutting outlines. Dotted lines indicate lines, in addition to outlines, which are to be satin stitched.

For each place mat, cut two pieces of fabric and one of fusible web, each 11″ × 15″. Place the fabric together with wrong sides facing and with fusible web between. Following directions that come with fusible web, bond the two pieces of fabric together. Zigzag-stitch edges of place mat. To make stitching easier and edges neater, stitch around the edge twice with stitching spaced a little instead of close stitching once. For napkin, make $\frac{1}{2}$″ hem all around $12\frac{1}{2}$″ square; straight-stitch.

Cut two of each design piece of fabric and one of fusible web; bond together as for place mat. Pin design pieces on place mats and napkin; using closely worked zigzag stitch, satin-stitch around edges and along dotted lines (see individual directions) to secure to place mat or napkin.

Sailboat

Instead of cutting two boat bottoms, fold fabric for boat in half and place top edge of boat pattern along fold. Keeping fabric folded, bond the two halves together. Do not stitch along fold; leave unstitched when stitching to place mat. For mast, stitch line of satin-stitch directly on place mat. For mainsail, fold napkin and insert in opening of boat.

Bird

Before stitching bird on place mat, stitch edge between X's; leave this area unstitched when stitching onto place mat. Fold napkin and insert into opening on the bird as shown. Stitch bird legs directly on place mat.

Clown

Satin-stitch mouth directly on place mat after stitching on pieces. For bow tie loop, cut piece of fabric 2″ × 3″ to match napkin fabric; turn edges and ends under $\frac{1}{4}$″; straight-stitch. Satin-stitch ends to place mat under clown head (see illustration), so that center extends out from place mat to form a half loop. Insert napkin through loop.

Flowers

Before stitching on top flower petal pieces, stitch around edges of each, then pin center in place on each of these pieces and secure to bottom petal pieces on place mat by stitching only around centers, leaving petal edges unstitched. For butterfly on napkin, stitch the antennae directly on napkin. ◇

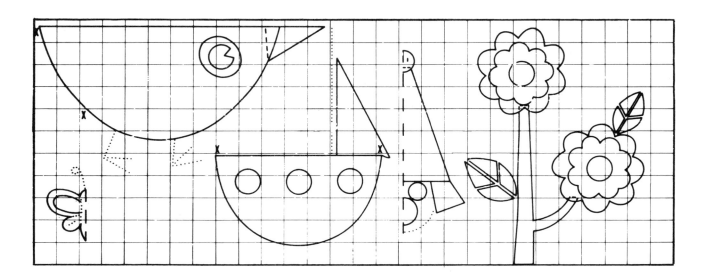

Tray-Shaped Placemat

Shown on Page 100

SIZE: $15\frac{1}{2}'' \times 12\frac{3}{4}''$.

EQUIPMENT: Zigzag sewing machine. Embroidery hoop, preferably plastic, 8″ to 9″. Ruler. Blue pencil. Scissors.

MATERIALS: White organdy, 36″ wide, 1 yard for four place mats. Machine embroidery thread #50: dark purple, medium purple, fuchsia, peach, lavender, dark olive green, bright green, yellow-green, dark brown, medium brown, tan, royal blue, cornflower blue, medium grey-blue. Paper for pattern. Tracing paper.

DIRECTIONS: Enlarge tray pattern by copying on paper ruled in 1″ squares. Full-size pattern is supplied for grape motif, page 127. For each mat, cut a piece of organdy 14″ × 17″. Center organdy right side up over pattern and lightly trace all outlines with blue pencil, omitting the fine interior lines that indicate darkest shadings of color. Do not cut tray shape out. Read general directions for machine embroidery (see Contents). Prepare machine for free-motion embroidery.

Grapes: Set stitch-width dial at 4-5. Place center of fabric in hoop. Shading is done by changing thread color as you work, stitching partially over the previous color. Start each grape in center, using peach thread. Change to fuchsia and stitch partially over and around peach area. Using medium purple, stitch partially over fuchsia and slightly over peach in spots. Using dark purple, work partially over medium purple and out to edge of grape, stitching in direction indicated by fine lines. Change to a narrow stitch and outline each grape with a line of lavender stitching. Work leaves in same manner, starting with dark olive green along fine lines that indicate veins, changing to yellow-green, then working bright green lightly over yellow-green. Refer to color photograph as you work. Fill in most of stem with tan thread, shading with medium brown and then dark brown where indicated by fine lines on pattern. Work bright green lightly over tan thread in spots, continuing into bright green tendril.

Shaded Areas of Tray: Set stitch at 0. Using grey-blue thread, work inner and outer shaded areas indicated by solid black on pattern. Graduate direction of stitches as you go around tray, so stitches radiate from center of mat.

Latticed Areas: Stitch a bright green flower in each diamond-shaped space by moving hoop to form four small loops, beginning and ending each loop at the same point in center of diamond. Using cornflower blue, stitch along each line of lattice three times.

Defining Lines: Remove fabric from hoop, replace presser foot, and work remainder of embroidery in a close zigzag stitch, with tracing paper under organdy for firmness. Using cornflower blue with stitch set at $\frac{1}{16}''$ wide, stitch along outer edge of inner shaded area. Change stitch width to $\frac{1}{8}''$; stitch along lower and right edges of tray and along broken lines. Change thread to royal blue and stitch around latticed areas; stitch around outline of place mat at left and top, continuing onto inner edge of outer shading at right and bottom of tray.

Carefully trim away organdy around tray shape close to stitching; steam-press on wrong side on a padded surface. ◊

Kitchen Bunnies

Shown on pages 98-99

SIZES: Pot Holder, 7″ square; Pillow, 13″ square; Tea Cozy, 9″ × 11″.

EQUIPMENT: Colored pencil. Pencil. Paper for patterns. Ruler. Scissors. Straight pins. Sewing needle. Zigzag sewing machine.

MATERIALS: *Pot Holder, Pillow, Tea Cozy:* Green heavy cotton fabric 45″ wide, $\frac{3}{4}$ yard for all three, or see individual directions. Scraps of heavy cotton fabric in plain white and both plain and printed gold, for appliqués. Gold sewing thread. *Pot Holder, Tea Cozy:* Batting. Gold doublefold bias tape $\frac{1}{4}''$ wide, 1 package. *Tea Cozy:* Soft fabric for lining 36″ wide, $\frac{1}{3}$ yard. Gold 1″-wide bias tape 28″. *Pillow:* Fiberfill.

GENERAL DIRECTIONS: Using sharp colored pencil, draw lines across patterns, connecting grid lines. Enlarge patterns needed by copying on paper ruled in 1″ squares; complete half-patterns indicated by dash lines. Cut out patterns.

To cut appliqués, place bunny pattern on right side of white fabric and bushes (or "eggs") on various gold fabrics, as directed; mark around. (For bushes, vary size and shape of our patterns as desired; see color illustration.) Cut out appliqués $\frac{1}{4}''$ beyond marked lines.

Cut background piece from green fabric as directed. Following photograph for placement, pin bunny and bushes on background piece, overlapping as shown; do not turn under excess fabric. If bushes overlapped by bunny are too visible under the white fabric, mark bunny outline on bushes while pieces are still pinned in place; unpin and trim bushes to $\frac{1}{4}''$ outside new lines; repin pieces to background. Using gold thread, straight-stitch around appliqués on marked lines. Trim away excess fabric to $\frac{1}{8}''$ from straight stitching. Set sewing machine for close zigzag (satin) stitch and stitch around appliqués, cov-

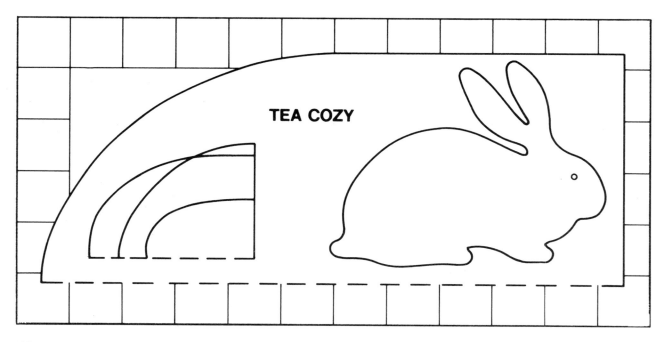

ering straight stitching and excess fabric. For bunny eye, zigzag-stitch or hand embroider a tight circle. Finish as directed below.

Pot Holder

Read General Directions. Make patterns for bunny and bushes. From green fabric, cut two pieces 7″ square. Cut and appliqué one white bunny and four gold bushes to one green square, as directed. Cut two 7″ squares of batting. With right sides facing out, pin and baste green squares together with batting between. Cut one yard of gold $\frac{1}{4}$″ double-fold bias tape. Place pot holder with bunny in horizontal position. Starting 1″ to right of top corner, pin bias tape all around pot holder, enclosing edges in fold and with wider half of tape on bottom; do not cut off excess tape. Topstitch tape in place, close to inner edge; continue stitching at end to overlap beginning slightly. To make hanging loop, stitch edges of excess tape together. Fold end under and stitch to pot holder, at left of top corner.

Pillow

Read General Directions. Make patterns for bunny and bushes. From green fabric, cut two pieces 14″ square. Cut and appliqué two white bunnies (reversing pattern for second bunny) and about 20 gold bushes to one green square, as directed; do not place any appliqués closer than $\frac{3}{4}$″ from edges of piece. Place the two green pieces together, right sides facing; stitch around with $\frac{1}{2}$″ seams, leaving 6″ opening in one side; trim corners. Turn piece to right side, stuff fully, turn in edges of opening $\frac{1}{2}$″ and slip-stitch closed.

Tea Cozy

Read General Directions. Make patterns for tea cozy, bunny, and bushes; make bunny pattern flat across bottom, drawing straight line from front paws to tail. Using pattern, mark three tea cozies on green fabric; cut out on marked lines. Cut three linings and six layers of batting same size. Cut and pin one bunny and about 10 bushes to each green piece; place bottom edge of appliqués $\frac{1}{4}$″ from bottom edge of green piece. Straight-stitch and trim appliqués as directed. For each side of tea cozy, place lining, wrong side up, on flat surface; place two layers of batting on top; place a green piece, right side up, on batting. Pin and baste layers together. Finish by zigzag-stitching around appliqués as directed, thus quilting piece. Using wide zigzag stitch, sew all around edges of each side piece.

Cut 28″ length of gold $\frac{1}{4}$″ double-fold bias tape. Mark center top of each side piece. Place two pieces together, wrong sides facing. Starting at bottom left, pin bias tape around pieces to center top, enclosing both edges in fold and with wider half of tape underneath; leave excess tape free at top. Topstitch tape in place, close to inner edge. Fold underneath side piece in half, with free half against attached half; pin to hold. Place third side piece underneath assembled piece, wrong sides facing. At center top, slit underneath half of tape widthwise, then enclose both edges of side pieces in tape from center top to bottom right; pin and stitch as before; cut off excess tape at end. Cut 18″ length of $\frac{1}{4}$″ tape. Unpin folded side and join free edges of underneath pieces from bottom to center top; enclose edges in tape and stitch as before, leaving excess tape free at top. To make loop, stitch edges of excess tape together; fold end under and stitch to front side of first tape. Cut 28″ length of wide gold bias tape. Fold almost in half lengthwise (making a double-fold tape) and press. Enclose bottom edge of tea cozy in fold of tape, widest half inside, and topstitch in place; at end, cut off excess beyond $\frac{1}{2}$″; turn end under $\frac{1}{4}$″, and stitch over beginning. ◇

Strawberry Place Mat

Shown on page 100

SIZE: Approximately $11\frac{1}{2}$″ × $17\frac{1}{2}$″.
EQUIPMENT: Hard-lead pencil. Ruler. Straight pins. Scissors. Zigzag sewing machine. Adjustable embroidery hoop, 8″ to 9″. Steam iron. Two terrycloth towels for pressing.
MATERIALS: White fabric, 45″ wide, 1 yard for two sets of place mat and napkin, or $\frac{1}{2}$ yard for two place mats. Lightweight Pellon, 36″ wide, $\frac{1}{2}$ yard for two place mats. Paper for pattern. Tracing paper. Dressmaker's tracing or carbon paper. White sewing thread. Machine embroidery thread #50 in following colors (amounts vary, but a set can be done with less than one spool each): bright red, dark red, black, white, bright yellow, light green, medium green, beige, medium brown.

DIRECTIONS: Read general directions for machine embroidery (see Contents). Trace actual-size half-pattern on pages 130–131 for mat by copying on paper ruled in 1″ squares; trace and complete pattern by reversing strawberry-and-flower design along dash line, but continue basket weave border design in same direction all around mat. Enlarge and trace corner strawberry design (page 132) if making matching napkins. You need not trace seed marks on strawberries nor the fine lines which indicate shading.

Cut $22\frac{1}{2}$″ × $16\frac{1}{2}$″ piece of fabric for each place mat. Using dressmakers' carbon paper and hard-lead pencil, transfer design onto right side of fabric, leaving $2\frac{1}{2}$″ margin all around. Do not cut out. Cut piece

A

B

A

B

of Pellon the same size as fabric and pin to wrong side; machine-stitch together ½″ beyond outline of place mat.

For each napkin, cut a piece of fabric 19″ × 20½″. On tracing paper, mark a 14″ square. Matching heavy, straight lines of pattern with lower right corner of ruled square, trace the single strawberry and three leaves onto the tracing paper. Using dressmaker's carbon paper and hard-lead pencil, transfer the complete napkin design to fabric, placing it so 2½″ of fabric extends beyond any marking.

Embroidery: Prepare sewing machine for free-motion embroidery. Set zigzag stitch dial to wide (4-5) unless otherwise instructed. Place fabric in hoop. To shade embroidery, change thread color and zigzag over the edge of previously embroidered area.

Fine lines on pattern indicate approximate placement of shaded areas and need not be followed precisely.

Begin embroidery by filling in the strawberries, using bright red thread for outer areas and shading inner areas with dark red. Using black thread, make small bar tacks for seeds. Fill in petals of flowers with white, then the centers with bright yellow. Change stitch dial to fine or 0 and stitch around petals with bright yellow. Fill in strawberry caps with medium green and stems with light green. Fill in leaves with light green, then use medium green for shading around outer edges. Satin stitch over the edges of leaves which extend beyond outline of place mat or napkin.

For basketwork border on place mat, work fill-in embroidery with beige thread, turning hoop so stitches follow basket outline. Work the fine lines indicating shading in brown, with the stitch dial set at fine or 0. Embroider the crisscrossing outlines that make the border look like basketwork in brown also, in a narrow satin stitch.

Finishing: To finish edge of mat, raise feed dogs, replace presser foot, set zigzag dial for medium width and slowly stitch around mat while moving fabric to follow outline. Finish edges of napkin with matching satin stitch worked over ruled outline. When all embroidery is complete, trim excess fabric away close to outer stitching. Turn mat to wrong side and carefully trim away excess Pellon from center of mat, close to inner stitching. Place embroidery face down between two terry towels and steam-press on wrong side. ◇

Fluffy Poodle

Shown on page 113

SIZE: 12″ high.

MATERIALS: Orlon 4-ply yarn of knitting worsted weight, 1 4-oz. skein white, small amount of black and pink. Crochet hook size G. Tapestry needle. Stuffing.

GAUGE: 4 sc = 1″.

Poodle

Body: Beg at neck, ch 8, sl st in first ch to form ring.

Rnd 1: Ch 1, 16 sc in ring. Do not join rnds; mark end of rnds (center back).

Rnds 2 and 3: Sc in each sc around.

Rnds 4 and 5: Inc 4 sc evenly spaced around—24 sc.

Rnd 6: Work even.

Rnd 7: Repeat rnd 4—28 sc.

Rnd 8: Sc in 3 sc, 2 sc in next sc, sc in each sc to last 4 sc, 2 sc in next sc, sc in last 3 sc—30 sc.

Rnd 9: (Sc in next sc, 2 sc in next sc) 3 times, sc in each sc to last 6 sc, (2 sc in next sc, sc in next sc) 3 times—36 sc.

Rnd 10: (Sc in next 2 sc, 2 sc in next sc) twice, sc in each sc to last 6 sc, (2 sc in next sc, sc in next 2 sc) twice—40 sc.

Rnd 11: Work even.

Rnds 12-14: Repeat rnds 10, 11 and 10—48 sc. Work even for 5 rnds.

First Hind Leg: Rnd 1: Sc in next 11 sc, ch 13, sl st in first sc of rnd to form circle.

Rnd 2: Sc in 11 sc, sc in each of 13 ch—24 sc.

Rnd 3: Work even.

Rnd 4: Dec 2 sc evenly spaced—22 sc.

Rnd 5: Work even.

Rnds 6-8: Repeat rnds 4, 5, and 4.

Rnds 9-13: Work even on 18 sc.

Rnds 14 and 15: Dec 3 sc evenly spaced each rnd—12 sc.

Continued on page 141

Vegetables from a jolly giant's garden
make charming toss-about pillows.
Summer squash, cucumber, carrot,
eggplant, and lima bean pod are
cut from polished cottons or wool,
boldly embroidered with tapestry yarn
in simple stitches. Carrot has a
shaggy topknot of green wool yarn.
Pillows range from 16″ to 24″ in size.
Directions for Vegetable Pillows
begin on page 173.

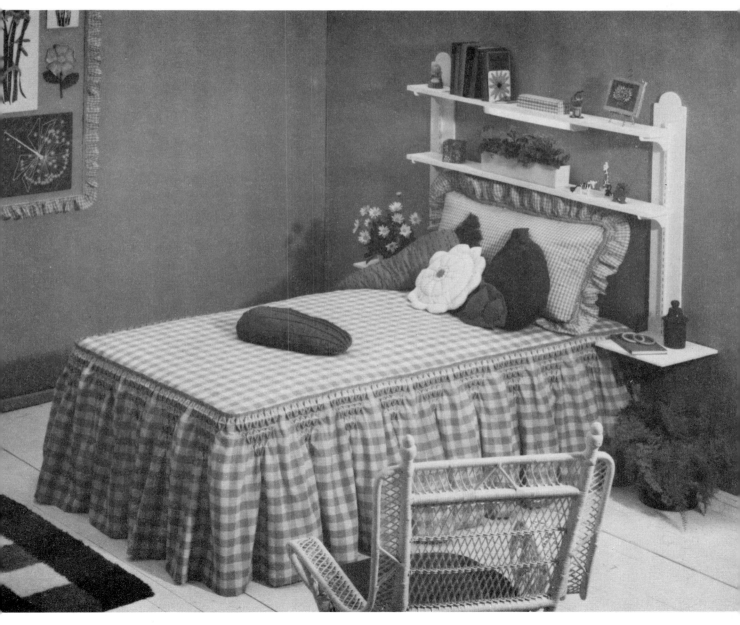

Switch plate dress-ups add an amusing splash of color and make a merry decor for a playroom, bedroom or nursery.
Directions are on page 174.

This fanciful elephant is a fairy-tale figure
come to life in lavish embroidery worked/
on a background of rich orange fabric.
The 16″-long toy is a gift that will be
treasured for years to come. Directions
for Fantasy Elephant are on page 192.

Stand-up pets are fun to make
with cotton fabric scraps.
Stuff with foam to make them
completely washable—perfect
for tots. Giraffe, 10½″ tall.
From Jane Slovachek.
Directions for Fabric Pets
begin on page 177.

Gingham girl and cowboy pal are going
square dancing tonight. Cuddly dolls make
a happy armful for little girls and boys.
The stuffed bodies are costumed in
character, from yarn hair to felt shoes
—with pretty panties and petticoats for our
Gingham girl. Simple embroidery defines
their faces. Designed by Marion Gloeggler.
For directions, see page 193.

138

Five wooden blocks will make learning a game! Put blocks together
to make one of two clocks—then teach a tot to tell time. Or, use sides
of blocks to build an alphabet or the numbers from 1 to 24! Design is
from Tomas Junta. Each of the blocks is painted on front and back,
numbers and letters on the sides. Arrange blocks to form a pretty
little cuckoo clock, or turn them over for bright green-faced
clock (opposite). Movable hands spin on a wooden peg which fits in the
center block. Corner blocks, $3\frac{1}{2}''$ square; long center block is $3\frac{1}{2}'' \times 7''$.
Directions for Block Clock are on page 198.

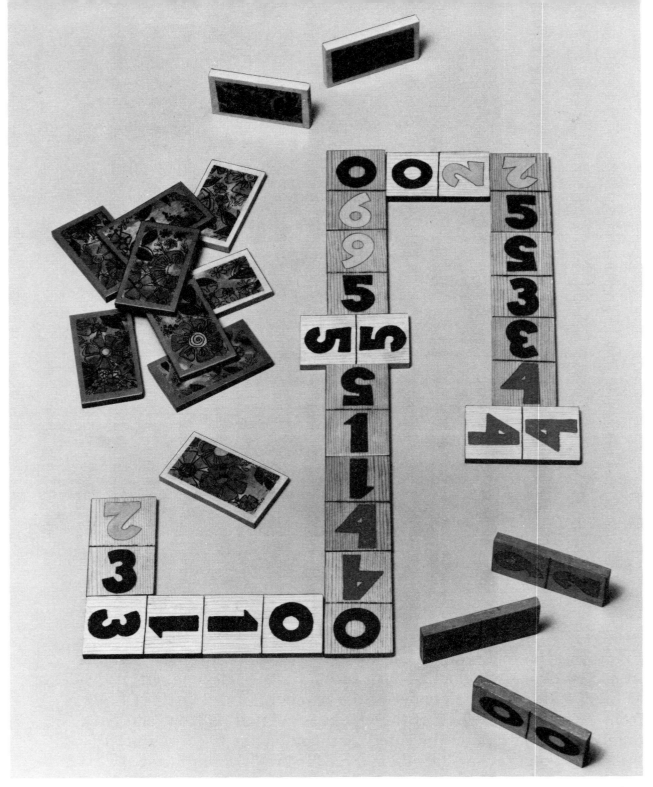

Big, bright dominoes are fun to play with, easy to make. Giant dominoes
are created from flat wooden molding. The number combinations are
painted on one side of each tile; plain sides of tiles are decorated
with a patch of gift-wrap paper in a bright print. Directions
include actual-size patterns for numbers.
Directions for Super Dominoes are on page 200.

Continued from page 132

Rnd 16: Dec 6 sc. End off; close up leg with yarn end.

First Front Leg: Rnd 1: Sk next 4 sc on last rnd of body following hind leg, sc in next 9 sc, ch 11, sl st in first sc of this rnd.

Rnd 2: Sc in each sc and ch—20 sc.

Rnd 3: Work even.

Rnd 4: Dec 2 sc evenly spaced.

Rnds 5 and 6: Repeat rnds 3 and 4.

Rnds 7-11: Work even on 16 sc.

Rnds 12-14. Dec 4 sc evenly spaced each rnd. End; close up leg with yarn end.

2nd Front Leg: Sc in next free st on last rnd of body and in next 8 sc, work as for first front leg.

2nd Hind Leg: Sk next 4 sc on last rnd of body, sc in next 11 sc, ch 13, work as for first hind leg. Sew first 8 free sc of both hind legs tog; sew first 7 free sc of front legs tog.

Underbody: Beg at front, ch 10. Work even on 9 sc for 5 rows. Ch 1, turn each row. End off. Stuff body and legs; sew underbody in place.

Head: Beg at nose, ch 2. *Rnd 1:* 6 sc in 2nd ch from hook. Do not join rnds; mark ends of rnds.

Rnd 2: 2 sc in each sc around.

Rnds 3-6: Work even on 12 sc.

Rnd 7: (Sc in next sc, 2 sc in next sc) 6 times—18 sc.

Rnd 8: (Sc in next 2 sc, 2 sc in nex sc) 6 times—24 sc.

Rnd 9: Inc 6 sc evenly spaced around.

Rnd 10: Work even—30 sc.

Rnds 11-14: Repeat rnds 9 and 10 twice—42 sc.

Rnd 15: Inc 3 sc evenly spaced around.

Rnd 16: Work even—45 sc.

Rnd 17: Dec 3 sc in rnd—42 sc.

Rnds 18-23: Dec 6 sc each rnd, stuffing head at same time. Close up head with yarn end.

Ears (make 2): Ch 10.

Row 1: Sl st in 2nd ch from hook, sc in each ch to last ch, 3 sc in last ch; working on opposite side of ch, sc in each ch to end, sl st in last ch. Ch 1, turn each row.

Row 2: Sl st in sl st, sc in each sc to rounded end, inc 2 sc around end, sc in each sc, sl st in sl st.

Rows 3 and 4: Work as for row 2, inc 4 sc around rounded end. End off.

Tail: Beg at tip, ch 2. *Rnd 1:* 4 sc in 2nd ch from hook.

Rnd 2: 2 sc in each sc. Work even on 8 sc until there are 12 rnds. End off. Stuff.

Collar

With pink, ch 24. Dc in 4th ch from hook and in each ch. End off.

Leash

With pink, ch 40; sl st in 8th ch from hook and in each ch. End off.

Finishing: Thread tapestry needle with double strand of yarn. Make loops about 1½" to 1¾" long on legs, starting about 1" up from bottom and making loops about ½" apart; catch each lp with a short back st to keep from pulling out. Cover legs, then body, sewing tail on in upright position after first row of loops on body. Cover snout and top of head with 2" loops. Sew loops on ears. Sew on ears. Cut loops, comb and brush with steel brush. With black, embroider satin st nose; embroider inverted T under nose for mouth; embroider 4 little loops for each eye. Sew ends of collar tog around neck; attach leash. ◇

Baby-in-a-Bootie

Shown on page 114

EQUIPMENT: Tracing paper. Ruler. Pencil. Dressmaker's tracing (carbon) paper. Scissors. Straight pins. Embroidery and sewing needles. Leather punch.

MATERIALS: *For Doll:* Pink cotton fabric, at least 9" × 12". Small print flannel for gown, 8" × 17". White flannel for diaper, 8" × 9". Sewing thread to match. Small amounts of six-strand embroidery floss in light brown, dark brown, and pink. Small amount of yellow knitting worsted for hair. Pink satin ribbon, ¼" wide, 15". Rouge. Stuffing. *For Bootie:* White felt, 10" × 12". Pink satin ribbon, ¼" wide, 24". Small amount of pink knitting worsted.

DIRECTIONS: Trace patterns on pages 142–143; complete half-patterns indicated by long dash lines. For doll, fold pink fabric in half; cut out body pattern and two arms through double thickness, adding ¼"

seam allowances on all edges. Using dressmaker's carbon, trace features on right side of one body pattern. Thread embroidery needle with two strands of floss and embroider face in outline stitch (see Contents for stitch details) as follows: eyelashes and eyebrows, dark brown; nose, light brown; mouth, pink. Rouge cheeks slightly.

With right sides facing, sew body pieces together, making ¼" seams and leaving one side open between the top and the leg and neck. Clip into seam allowance at outer ankle bend, inner knee bend, crotch, hip, and neck. Turn right side out; stuff legs to hipline, then stitch across dotted line on pattern. Stuff doll fully; slip-stitch closed.

With right sides facing, seam two arm pieces together, leaving straight end open; repeat for other

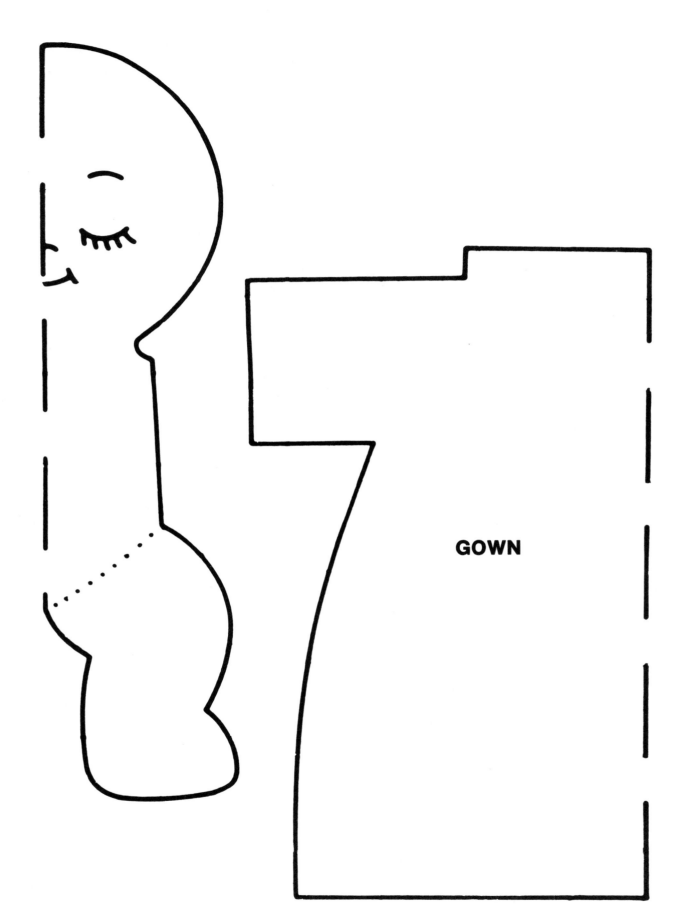

GOWN

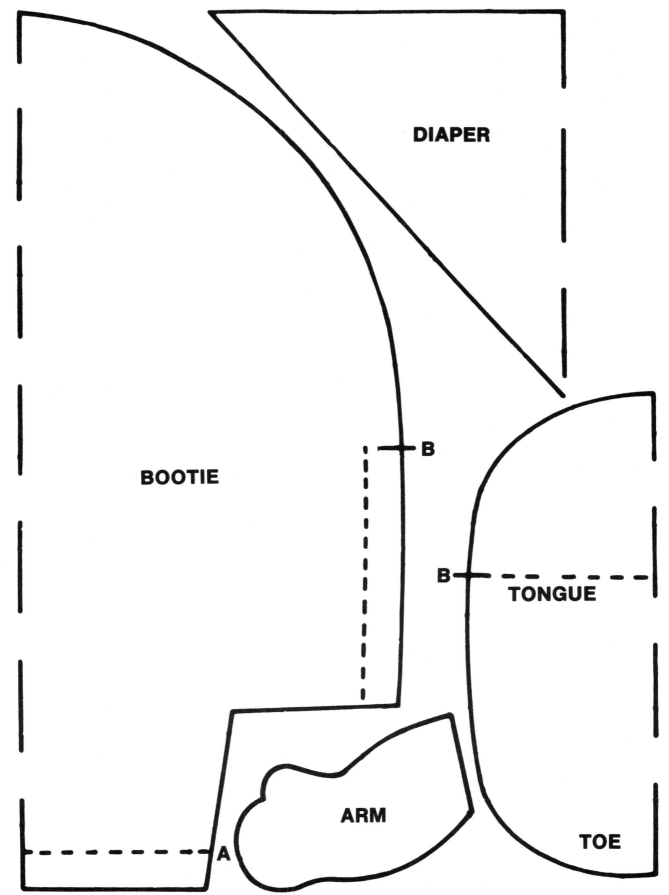

DIAPER

BOOTIE

B

B TONGUE

A

ARM

TOE

143

arm. Clip into seam allowances between thumb and fingers. Turn right side out; stuff fully. Turn open edges in; slip-stitch closed. With thumbs up, stitch arms to each side of body just below neckline.

For hair, thread embroidery needle with convenient length of yellow yarn. Beginning along seamline of head, catch yarn in doll's head. Using whip-stitch motion, draw yarn through fabric along seamline, leaving loops of yarn about 1" long; make loops down sides to about eye level. Make about three rows, each ¼" from the last at both front and back of first row. Clip some loops and trim as desired. From 7" length of satin ribbon, make bow; tack in hair.

Diaper: Fold white flannel in half crosswise, then lengthwise. Place pattern with right angle lying on folded corner; cut flannel along diagonal line adding ¼" for seam allowance. Unfold flannel lengthwise; refold crosswise with right sides together. Leaving ¼" seam allowance, stitch around two open sides leaving a 2" opening to turn. Turn right side out; slip-stitch closed. Fit on doll; stitch in place.

Nightgown: Fold print flannel in half. Using complete pattern, cut two gown pieces, adding ¼" seam allowance. With right sides facing, stitch ¼" seams across sleeve tops, under sleeves, and down sides. Make narrow hems in ends of sleeves and bottom edge of gown. Slit flannel about 1" down center line of back. Hem neck edges ⅛". Using two strands of pink floss, make running stitch around the neck ⅜" from top edge, leaving long ends of floss. Put gown on doll; slip-stitch slit closed. Pull floss ends to gather neckline; knot; trim ends. Make bow from 7" length of ribbon; tack at front neck of gown.

Bootie: Cut one each of bootie and tongue pieces. Bring points A of bootie together with right sides facing out. Thread needle with pink worsted. Using running stitch, stitch bootie together between letters A ⅛" in from edges. With right sides facing out, place tongue on shoe, matching letters B at sides. Using pink worsted, seam edges together around toe line between points B; gather sides of shoe to fit tongue. Using pink worsted, embroider curved edge of tongue with blanket stitch (see Contents for stitch details). Whip floss through running stitches on top of bootie. With punch, make small holes every ⅜" around side and back edges of shoe and across tongue at dash line on pattern. Thread with pin ribbon and tie bow.

Fit doll into shoe, stuffing at toe. ◇

Flip-Over Doll

Shown on page 115

EQUIPMENT: Tracing paper. Ruler. Pencil. Dressmaker's tracing (carbon) paper. Scissors. Pins. Sewing and embroidery needles.

MATERIALS: Fabric, 36" wide: Pink cotton, ¼ yd. for two-headed body; flannel print, ¼ yd.; checked gingham, ¼ yd. Narrow white satin ribbon, 1¼ yds. Narrow white lace trim, 2 yds. Knitting worsted: Approximately ½ oz. each of dark brown and gold for hair. Six-strand embroidery floss for features: pink, blue, light brown, dark brown. Sewing thread to match all fabrics. Polyester or cotton fiberfill for stuffing. Two pink pompons from ball fringe. Rouge.

DIRECTIONS: The doll is made with one head at each end of a torso, each having a pair of arms, but no legs. A completely different doll appears when the skirt of one is pulled over the head of the other.

Enlarge patterns onto grid with 1" squares; complete half and quarter-patterns indicated by long dash lines. Add ¼" seam and hem allowances to all pieces, unless otherwise indicated.

Body: From pink cotton, cut two head-torso pieces and eight arms, reversing pattern for four. Using carbon, transfer features to each head on one head-torso piece: put awake face on one and asleep face on the other. Using two strands of floss in needle and following stitch details (see Contents), embroider features as follows: Using dark brown floss on awake face, work eyebrows, eye outline, and eyelashes in outline stitch. Using blue, outline eyes in outline stitch, then fill in eyes with satin stitch. Using light brown, embroider nose and dimple in outline stitch; using pink, embroider mouth in outline stitch. Using dark brown floss on asleep face, embroider eyebrows, eye outline, and eyelashes in outline stitch; using light brown, work nose in outline stitch; using pink, embroider mouth in straight stitch and satin stitch.

Place two head-torso pieces together with right sides facing; sew together, leaving side open between two slash marks, as indicated on pattern. Clip into seam allowance at curves. Turn to right side. Stuff fully; slip-stitch closed.

For each arm, place two pieces together; with right sides facing, stitch each pair together, leaving straight ends open. Clip into seam allowance at curves. Turn to right side. Stuff fully; turn in fabric end and stitch closed. Slip-stitch arms, with thumbs pointing up, to each side of both ends of torso, as indicated by X's.

Brown Hair: Wind knitting worsted around one finger four times to make one ringlet loop; cut yarn. Stitch individual ringlets to head with matching wool, using continuous strand for stitching on ringlets. Repeat until top, sides, back of head are covered (as

144

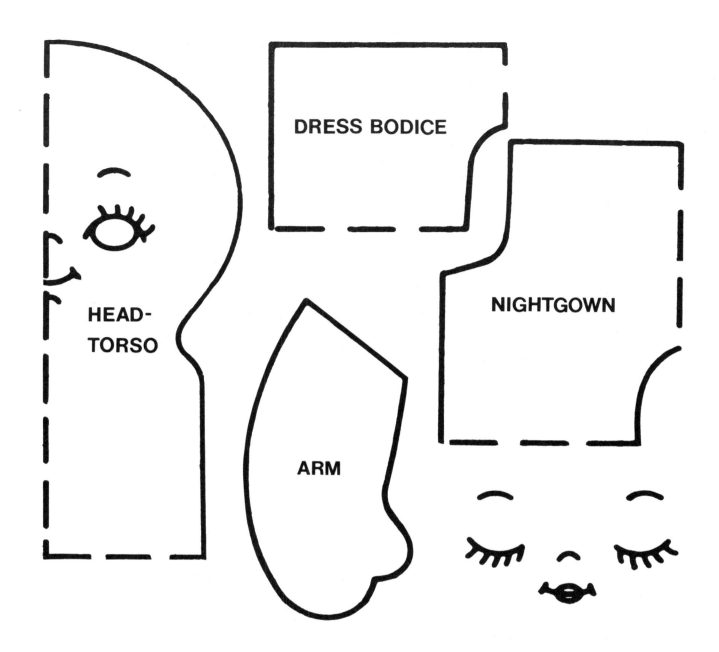

pictured). **Blond Hair:** Wind knitting worsted around two fingers four times to make larger ringlet loop; stitch.

Gingham Dress: Cut bodice in one piece. Slit center back from neck to bottom. Press hem allowance of sleeve and neck edge to wrong side; sew hems. Trim sleeve edges with single strip of lace. Trim neckline with two pieces of gathered lace for double ruffle. With right sides facing, fold bodice in half at shoulder line; sew side and underarm seams. Clip into seam allowance at curve. Turn to right side.

For skirt, cut a piece of gingham 24″ × 7½″. Sew a strip of lace trim lengthwise across skirt, 2¾″ from one edge (this will be top). Press bottom skirt hem allowance to wrong side. Fold skirt in half crosswise with right sides facing; sew ends together 4½″ up from bottom, leaving remainder of seam open. Gather top edge of skirt to fit bodice. With right sides facing,

sew bodice to skirt, along seamline. Put dress on doll. Fold seam allowance to wrong side, along one edge of bodice back; lap folded edge over raw edge; slip-stitch. Fold seam allowance to wrong side along both edges of skirt opening at back.

Flannel Nightgown: From flannel, cut bodice; cut skirt 24″ × 7½″. Follow same directions as for dress, omitting lace trim. Sew two pompons down center front. When garments are on each side of doll, top-stitch both skirt bottoms together, close to hem folds. Sew lace trim around bottom edge of gingham side. Match folded edges of back skirt opening, with wrong sides facing; slip-stitch folded edges together.

From satin ribbon, cut a piece 20″ long; tie around waist of gingham dress. Make three small bows with remaining ribbon. Stitch one bow to each side of brown head; stitch one bow to one side of blond head. ◇

Terry Babies

Shown on page 114

EQUIPMENT: Scissors. Needle. Paper for patterns. Tracing paper. Pencil. Ruler. Straight pins. Ball-point pen. Lightweight cardboard.

MATERIALS: Terrycloth toweling 36″ wide, ½ yard for each; matching sewing thread. Foam rubber cushion pad 16″ square, 1″ thick (makes two). Large scraps of cotton fabric in a variety of colors and prints; bias tape to match or blend with fabrics; matching sewing thread. Ribbon. Embroidery floss. Yarn for hair. Baby and regular rickrack.

DIRECTIONS: Enlarge patterns by copying on paper ruled in 1″ squares; complete all half-patterns indicated by long dash lines. Short dash lines on clothing patterns indicate seam and hem allowances.

To Make Doll Body: One 16″-square foam pad makes stuffing for two dolls. Cut two bodies and four arm pieces out of lightweight cardboard to make durable patterns. Place patterns on foam rubber padding; with ball-point pen, mark outlines on padding. Cut bodies and arms out of foam; trim away sharp edges.

For each doll, fold terrycloth in half crosswise. Place one body and two arm patterns on one folded terrycloth. Adding ½″ on all edges for seams, cut body and arms of terrycloth through both thicknesses. Make a tracing of face; pin on one terrycloth head as a guide. Using six strands of floss in needle, embroider features on head through tracing: noses and cheeks are satin stitch; mouths are outline stitch; eyes are straight stitch. For stitch details, see Contents. After embroidering, tear away tracing paper.

Place one foam body between two terrycloth bodies; turn in seam allowance and overcast cloth bodies together, making terrycloth cover fit snugly. Overcast two terrycloth arms together with foam arm between; repeat for second arm. Stitch finished arm to each side of body at point indicated on pattern by X's.

To Make Hair: For girl, cut 30 strands of yarn, each 12″ long. Beginning at center top of head, stitch center of each piece in parallel rows to halfway down back. Bring strands slightly across face and stitch flat in place at temples. Pull ends together at sides with 8″-long ribbon for each; tie bow. Trim ends of strands. For bangs, cut three strands, each 4″ long; stitch centers of strands at center top of head.

For boy, cut eight 8″ pieces of yarn. Place in a line across top of head and stitch down at sides and above one side to give effect of side part as shown. For back of head, cut 14 strands of yarn, each 6″ long. Fold each strand in half and stitch centers across top back of head. Tack ends at bottom.

To Make Clothes: Girl: Cut two tops and two pajama pants of dotted swiss. For lining, cut two tops

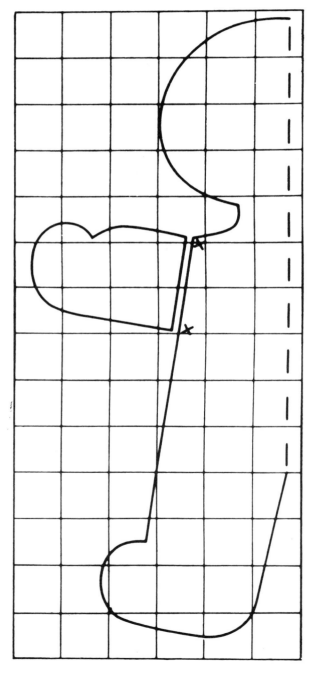

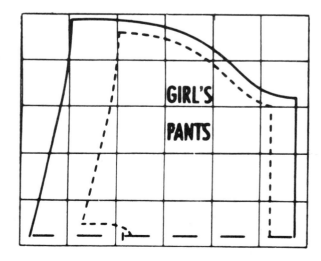

GIRL'S PANTS

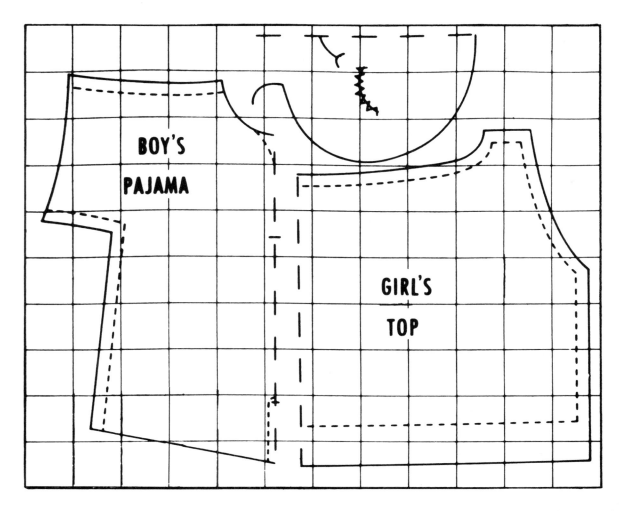

and two pants of plain white fabric. Place a lining and a dotted swiss piece together with right sides facing for fronts and backs of tops and pants. Stitch together at neckline and armholes and around legs. Turn to right side. Place backs and fronts together with right sides facing; stitch shoulders and sides of top and sides of pants together with $\frac{1}{4}''$ seams. Stitch $\frac{1}{4}''$ hems on lower edge of top and around waist of pants. Turn to right side. Stitch eyelet beading around neckline, top hem, and pant legs. Thread ribbon through eyelet on top hem; stitch ribbon ends together at seam. Thread long length of ribbon through each eyelet of pant leg and neckline with ends free at center front for gathering. Tie bows after dressing. **Boy:** Cut front and back of printed fabric. Slash at crotch up to cross-line. On front, slash at centers of neckline down to crossline and round top corners as indicated by short dash line on pattern. With right sides facing, sew shoulders, sides, and crotch together with $\frac{1}{4}''$ seams. Bind sleeves, legs, and neckline with bias tape. Make two large, loose cross-stitches of black floss at neck opening. After dressing boy, pull end of floss to tighten stitches. ◇

Cuddly Pup

Shown on page 113

EQUIPMENT: Paper for patterns. Pencil. Ruler. Scissors. Straight pins. Sewing needle.

MATERIALS: Acrylic pile fabric, 54" wide or less: $\frac{1}{2}$ yard tan, 8" × 9" white. Matching sewing thread. Batting. Felt: scraps of black, pink, white.

DIRECTIONS: Enlarge patterns on next page by copying on paper ruled in 1" squares. Add $\frac{1}{4}''$ for seam allowance all around fabric and felt pieces, except features. From doubled fabric, cut two bodies, four ears, eight legs and two tails; cut paw pads and features of felt; cut face area of white fabric. Before sewing bodies together, appliqué white area to one body (Read How to Appliqué; see Contents). Pin raw end of ears in place between crosslines on head to secure when sewing body seam.

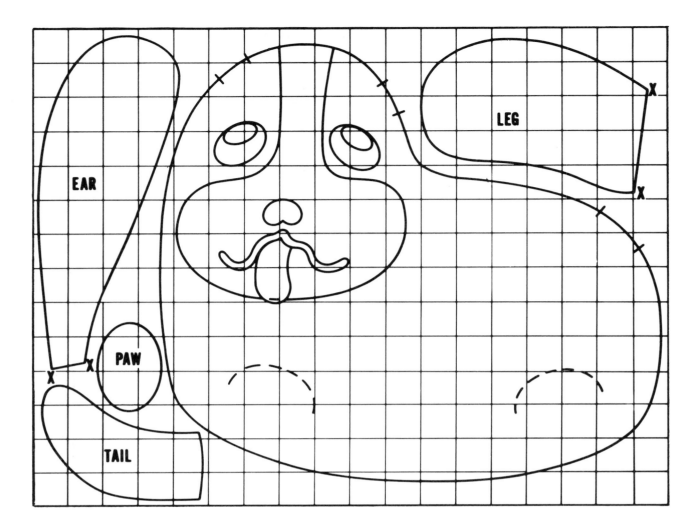

With right sides facing, pin two bodies together; sew with ¼" seams; leave open at stomach. Clip into seam allowance all around. Turn to right side; stuff fully. Turn raw edges in and slip-stitch closed. For each ear, sew two together with right sides facing, making ¼" seams; leave open between X's. Clip into seam allowance along curves; turn to right side. Do the same with each matching pair of legs, but before turning to right side, stitch paw pads to straight ends of legs, leaving an opening. Turn to right side; stuff fully. Slip-stitch opening closed; sew features in place. ◇

Sleepy Sock Doll

Shown on page 115

EQUIPMENT: Scissors. Pencil. Ruler. Tracing paper. Small, fine paintbrush. Fine sandpaper. Measuring spoon and cup. Jar lids about 2" diameter.

MATERIALS: Newspaper and flour. Small bead for shaping nose. Non-toxic enamel paint: pink, red, black, brown. One size 9 or 9½ pink sock. All-purpose glue. Flannel fabric for sleeper and blanket. Yarn for hair. Batting for stuffing. Vaseline.

DIRECTIONS: Trace patterns; complete half-patterns indicated by long dash lines.

Head: To make head, glue bead 1¼" from rim (this will be top edge) on front of jar lid; let dry. Cover jar lid and bead nose with vaseline. Make paste by mixing two tablespoons of flour with one cup of cold water; cook until thick. Use while still warm for best results. Moisten strips of newspaper with paste, using brush. Place layer after layer of moistened newspaper strips over top and side of jar lid and bead until covered and firm; shape nose over bead. Remove lid. Let dry; to hasten drying, place in oven set at 300° F. When dry, sand face smooth and paint with pink enamel. When enamel is dry, paint features: make eyelashes brown, mouth red, and nose dots black. Darken cheeks with pink paint mixed with a little red.

Body: Cut off ribbed top portion of sock. Cut small opening in sock about 1″ or smaller, around toe of sock for face to show through. Spread glue around edge of face and glue sock hole edge over edge of face; and let glue dry. Stuff head to round out back of head and secure sock under chin by winding thread around sock several times and knotting. Head should be about $2\frac{1}{2}$″ long. Stuff remainder of sock foot for body, making it about $3\frac{1}{2}$″ long; fold up heel flat against body and slip-stitch in place. Fold in raw bottom edges; overcast.

For arms and legs, cut down center of ribbed top to make two pieces for arms each $3\frac{1}{2}$″ long. Sew lengthwise edges of each together; stuff; turn in top and bottom ends and sew closed. Sew arm to side top of body. Wrap thread around end of arm to make wrist. Take a few stitches to shape chubby fingers. Make legs 4″ long in same manner, cut from top of other sock. Sew legs to bottom of body.

For hair, cut about 50 strands of fine pale yellow yarn, each about 8″ long; place across head from side to side and stitch along center. Trim. Glue some of bottom layer to head; leave the rest loose.

Sleeper: From flannel fabric, cut one sleeper top and two sleeper bottoms; cut two pieces for drop seat, each $2\frac{1}{8}$″ × 4″. Cut flannel strip for neckband, $\frac{3}{4}$″ × $4\frac{3}{4}$″. Fold sleeper top in half crosswise, with right sides facing along top half-pattern line; sew $\frac{1}{8}$″ underarm and side seams. Turn sleeve edges up $\frac{1}{4}$″

and tack. Cut down center back along half-pattern line. Cut slit for neck opening. Fold neckband in half lengthwise with wrong sides facing; turn long edges in and sew closed. Sew neckband around neck opening so seams will be on inside. Place top on doll; turn raw edges of center back in and sew closed, sewing ends of neckband closed. Hem bottom edge.

Place bottom pieces together with right sides facing. Sew $\frac{1}{8}$″ underleg seams and $\frac{1}{8}$″ back and front seams. Then cut back out, following dot-dash lines on pattern. Sew soles to ends of leg bottoms. Turn to right side. Put on doll; tack in place. Wrap thread around ankle; knot. Turn top edge of front down to make waistband; tack so that raw edges and ends do not show. For drop seat, place two pieces together with right sides facing and sew $\frac{1}{8}$″ seams all around, leaving small opening for turning. Turn to right side, and sew opening closed. Sew one long edge of drop seat to back top edge. Cut slits in each top corner for buttonholes. Work buttonhole stitch around slit. Sew buttons on each end of waistband for buttoning on drop seat. Sew two buttons on front as shown. For blanket, cut piece of flannel $3\frac{1}{2}$″ × 4″; overcast edges; sew to doll's hand. ◇

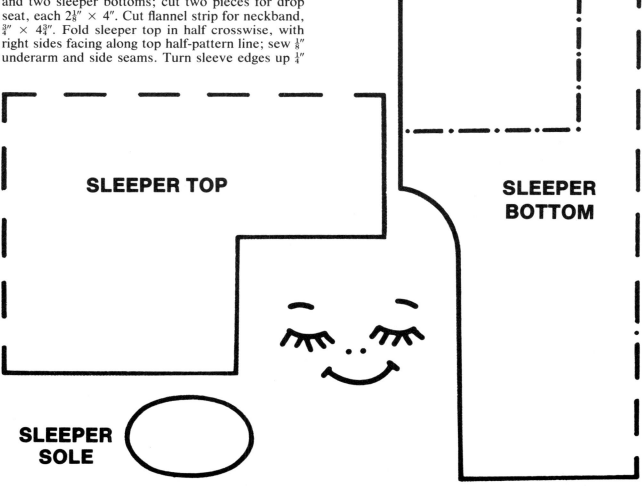

SLEEPER TOP

SLEEPER BOTTOM

SLEEPER SOLE

Fabric Transports

Shown on page 116

EQUIPMENT: Paper for patterns. Ruler. Compass. Pencil. Scissors. Straight pins. Sewing machine. Regular and large-eyed sewing needles. Iron.

MATERIALS: For each vehicle: Large scraps of cotton or cotton-blend fabrics in a solid, print and check of compatible colors. For car headlights: Small scrap of yellow-orange cotton. Sewing thread to match. Iron-on interfacing, medium weight, 18″ wide, 1 yard. Small amount of fusible web. Polyester fiberfill for stuffing. Small amount of six-strand embroidery floss in matching or contrasting colors.

GENERAL DIRECTIONS: Enlarge patterns by copying on paper ruled in 1″ squares; complete half-pattern of propeller indicated by long dash line. Heavy lines indicate cutting lines; short dash lines indicate position of appliquéd pieces. Fine lines on car in-dicate embroidery (see Table of Contents for stitch details).

Using patterns, cut out fabric pieces, adding $\frac{1}{4}$″ to all edges of each piece for seam allowances unless otherwise indicated. With right sides facing, sew pieces together, making $\frac{1}{4}$″ seams throughout.

For each piece, with the exception of appliquéd windows and hubcaps, cut interfacing the same size as pattern (omitting seam allowance). With shiny side of interfacing on wrong side of fabric, press with iron following package instructions.

Plane

Cut two side sections and one bottom from solid fabric. Cut out and press interfacing to each piece. Stitch bottom to each side of plane, matching A's

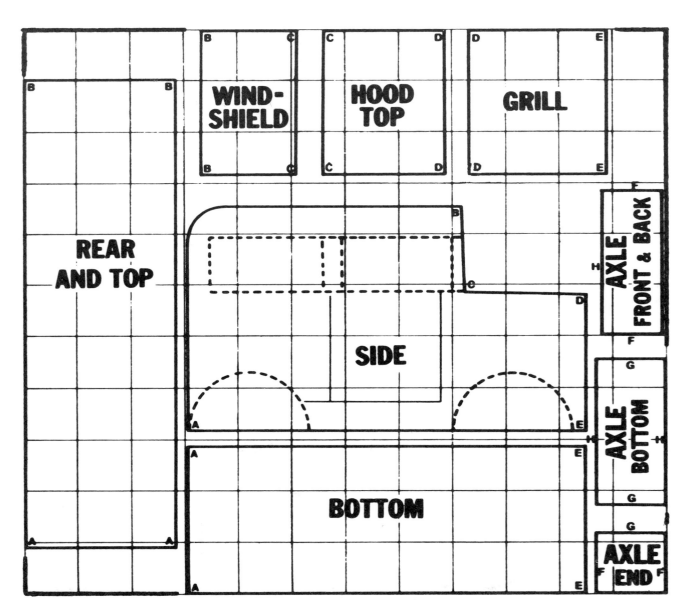

150

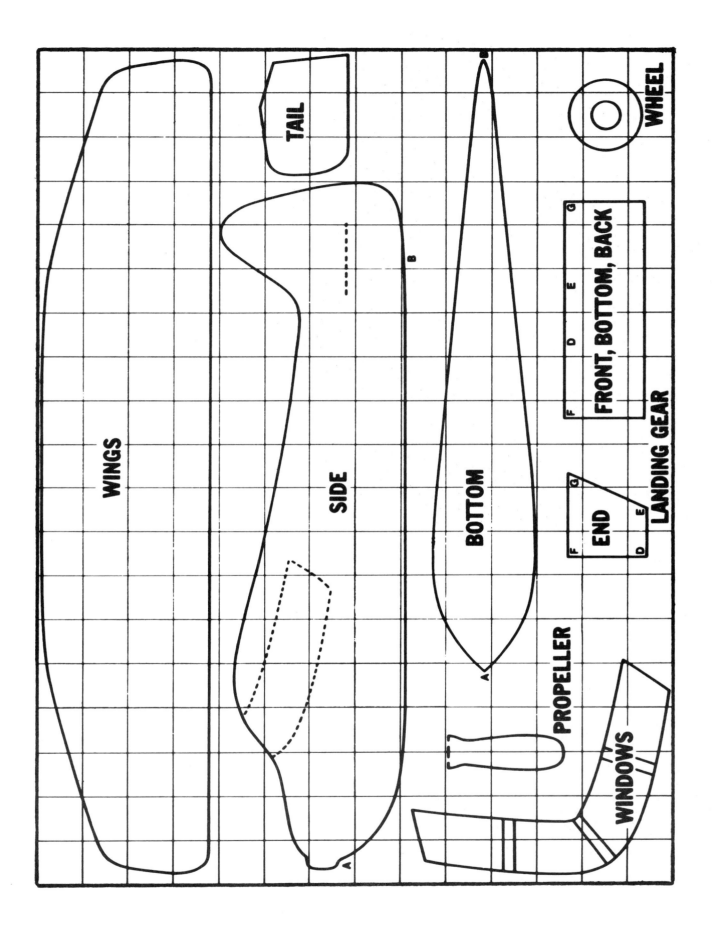

WINGS

TAIL

SIDE

BOTTOM

WHEEL

FRONT, BOTTOM, BACK

END

LANDING GEAR

PROPELLER

WINDOWS

and B's. Stitch plane sides together at top, leaving open at tail end. Clip into seam allowance at curves. Turn to right side; stuff and slip-stitch opening closed.

Cut windows from check fabric; cut strips for window framing from solid fabric. Turn raw edges under $\frac{1}{4}''$ on all pieces and appliqué strips in place (for appliqué details see Contents). Appliqué window in place on plane.

Cut one wing, two tail flaps and one propeller from check fabric; cut same pieces from print fabric. Cut interfacing for each piece and press to fabric. Stitch two corresponding pieces together, one check and one print; leave opening for turning. Clip into seam allowance at curves; turn and stuff each tail flap and wing fully; slip-stitch pieces closed.

For landing gear, cut two ends of solid, one bottom-front-back of check. Cut interfacing for each piece and press to fabric. Baste and sew each side of bottom to each end piece, matching letters on patterns. Turn to right side; stuff, turn edges under and stitch to plane bottom.

For each wheel, cut one of check, one of print. Cut and press on interfacing. Cut wheel center of check; press in place on print wheel with webbing. Embroider wheel center edge with line of outline stitch. Sew two wheels together; leave small opening in center of one side. Clip into seam allowance at curves. Turn to right side through opening; slip-stitch closed. Sew wheel to each side of landing gear.

Slip-stitch wings and tail flaps to plane following dash lines and illustration. Pinch center of propeller and tack; slip-stitch to nose of plane.

Car

Cut two car sides, one rear-top, one windshield, one hood, and one bottom from solid fabric. Cut grill from print.

Referring to pattern, mark lines for door on each side of car. Using one strand of embroidery floss in needle, embroider door in outline stitch.

Cut out and press interfacing to each piece. Matching letters, pin and stitch hood to windshield, windshield to one end of rear-top, rear-top to bottom, bottom to grill and grill to hood. Pin and stitch sides of car, matching corners carefully; leave 3″ opening along bottom for turning. Clip into seam allowances at curves and turn to right side. Stuff car fully and slip-stitch closed.

Cut one long strip for side and front windows $12\frac{3}{4}''$ × $1\frac{1}{2}''$ and a piece for back window $1\frac{3}{4}''$ × $2''$ from check fabric. Using pattern cut two separating strips from solid fabric; press edges under and appliqué one to each side of long window piece. Press all window edges under and appliqué to car.

Cut two separating strips $1\frac{1}{2}''$ × $1''$ from solid fabric. Fold in half lengthwise; press, then press under edges and appliqué to front window at sides (see illustration).

For each axle, from checked fabric, cut two axle ends, one bottom, and two front and back pieces. Stitch the five pieces together, matching letters, to form a rectangular shape open on one side. Stuff fully, turn raw edges under and slip-stitch open end in place across bottom about $\frac{1}{2}''$ from either end of the car.

To make wheels, cut five print and five check wheels, each 3″ in diameter. Cut out and press interfacing to wheels. For each wheel, stitch one check and one print together; leave opening for turning. Clip into seam allowances all around; turn to right side. Cut five 1″-wide circles from print and fusible web. Center a circle on checked side of each wheel with fusible web between and press with hot iron. Stuff wheels loosely. Slip-stitch closed. Tack wheels to car as illustrated.

For headlights, cut two circles from the solid car-body color and two circles from orange fabric, each 1″ in diameter. Assemble headlights in same manner as for wheels. Tack to front of car, with orange side facing out. ◇

Felt Set

Shown on page 116

EQUIPMENT: Paper for patterns. Ruler. Pencil. Scissors. Straight pins. Sewing needle. Sewing machine.

MATERIALS: Black felt ($\frac{1}{2}$ yard, 72″ wide will make all three). Medium rickrack: red (R), green (G), gold (Y), blue (B); one package of each color for tote, one package of each color for both bagette and eyeglass case. Foldover braid, 2 yards red, and one black snap fastener for bagette. Black lining and interlining materials. Thread to match fabric and rickrack.

GENERAL DIRECTIONS: Enlarge patterns on page 161 by copying on paper ruled in 1″ squares; complete half-patterns indicated by long dash lines.

Eyeglass Case

Using pattern, cut pieces from felt, interlining, and lining, adding $\frac{1}{4}''$ seam allowance all around. To trim, place felt piece flat. Following Diagram A, cut and pin rickrack to felt in colors indicated; have raw edges flush. Stitch a straight line down center of each with matching thread.

Baste interlining all around to wrong side of felt. With right sides facing, stitch felt to lining along top

Continued on page 161

Three boxes to cover in linen, embroider in satin-stitch blossoms. Choose 8″ × 8″, 7½″ × 2½″, or 7½″ round—or make all three. Directions for Covered Boxes are on page 202.

Woodland creatures and outdoor leaves —simply embroidered, simply quilted, simply lovely! What could be more natural than unbleached muslin decorated with squirrels, rabbits and delicate leaves cozying up to your favorite plants? The plant wrapper, worked by hand in an easy running stitch, fits a pot 13″ in diameter and 11″ high. Directions for Quilted Cover-Up are on page 207.

Portable desk top is great to use in the car, backyard, any-where. Of ¼″ wood, top is sturdy with plenty of storage under vinyl blotter. Add pencil box to match. Directions for Desk Set, page 200.

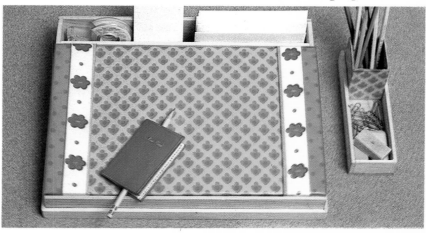

Now, about that person on your gift list who "has everything." We'll wager she doesn't have enough good-looking portfolios for those endless papers and bills and letters on her desk.

Wouldn't she love to have lots of fabric-lined folders in handsome end papers? You could make a whole dozen—one for every month—for very little money. Directions begin on page 206.

Candles, whether
store bought or
hand wrought,
can be stenciled
in gold paste
for Midas-touch
treasures.
Instructions
include how to
make the green
candle, plus
all stenciling.
Directions for
Candles are on
page 204.

1. Press only the freshest flowers. A telephone book, with its super-absorbent pages, works best.
2. When flowers are dry, touch up faded colors with watercolors.
3. Dilute a little white glue; coat back of flower with a cotton swab; apply to page, using a facial tissue to pat.
4. Cut out vase picture (museum catalogs are an excellent source); glue it over stem ends.

Directions for Pressed Flower Designs are on page 207

Pressed flowers hold the memory of a special summer garden or a quiet country walk. "Arranged" in a vase cut from a magazine, they become a delicate still life. Frame them, set them into a keepsake box lid, or make notes—they're sealed with a self-adhesive protective plastic covering to last a lifetime. Pressed flower designs by Irma Castelli.

Beautiful tulips and
tiger lilies will
never wilt—they're
made of silk fabric
and painted with water-
colors. Directions
for Silk Flowers are
on page 210.

158

Bazaar ideas to make a lady's day a bit nicer. Embroider a softly padded bouquet of French knots for a picture that's about 11″ square. French Knot Bouquet by Nancy Lemke. Try your hand at ''garden needlepoint'' with a sprightly array of little gifts—stitch slipcovers to make plain bookends beautiful; make a matching cushion (or sachet) for pretty pins; cover a juice can for a flowery pencil holder; needlepoint a tiny floral basket (3″ square) that's just the right size for a small spot on a desk or wall. Garden Needlepoint by Marilyn Clark.

Directions for Garden Stitchery begin on page 211.

159

Sew on a button—not to close a coat, but to create Floss Necklaces! Buttons, beads, small shells, miniature fruit, anything little and interesting can be sewn onto twisted embroidery cotton to make great necklaces and bracelets to show off summer fashions!

Embroidered Sun Pillow uses a variety of simple stitches; about $13\frac{1}{2}'' \times 14\frac{1}{2}''$. Satin-Stitch Rooster Pillow is worked completely in satin stitch, and measures about 15″ square, with zipper.

Tasseled Totes are perfect for cameras and combs, lipsticks and suntan lotions. Durable yet lightweight bags help keep things together at the beach, on a picnic, in the mountains—anywhere that warm, summer days might carry you! First make $10'' \times 10\frac{1}{2}''$ fabric bag, then glue on yarn braids to make designs. You decide how you want to carry it—with a convenient shoulder strap, or a drawstring to pull it closed. Directions for Floss Necklaces, page 217; Sun Pillow, page 220; Rooster Pillow, page 223; Tasseled Totes, page 217.

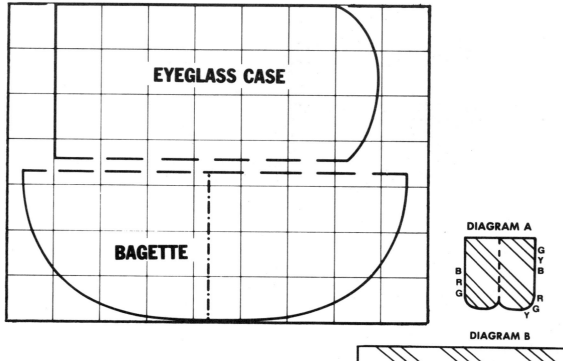

EYEGLASS CASE

BAGETTE

DIAGRAM A

G
Y
B
B
R
G
R
G
Y

DIAGRAM B

Y
G
R
B
Y
G

G Y B   R G Y   B R G   Y B R

Continued from page 152
straight edge with ¼″ seam. Turn to right side and
refold case with felt side inward; stitch together along
side and bottom with ¼″ seam. Turn.

Bagette

Using pattern, cut one complete piece (for back
and flap) and one half piece indicated by dot-dash
line (for front) from felt and lining. For trim, cut six
12″ pieces of rickrack in colors desired and interlock
into three pairs, hooking V's of two colors together
for each. Cut each interlocked strip into 8″ and 4″
lengths. Pin and stitch the 8″ interlocked strips down
center of large felt piece. Repeat with 4″ strips on
small piece, being sure colors will match flap when
large piece is folded down. Baste lining pieces to
wrong sides of matching felt pieces. Carefully pin
and baste foldover braid along top straight edge of
small piece; stitch across, securing both sides of
braid to felt and lining. Pin the large and small pieces
together, lining sides facing.

Pin one length of foldover braid around entire
edge. For strap, cut 40″ length of braid and stitch
open edge closed. Insert ends of braid into outer
braid, on lining side of piece and just above dot-
dash line.

Stitch braid around entire edge of purse, catching
in strap at same time. Fold purse flap down. Sew
on snap to fasten.

Tote

Cut pieces 30″ × 15″ each from felt, interlining,
and lining. Place felt piece out flat. Following Diagram B, pin and stitch rickrack diagonally across
felt in groups of three as for eyeglass case. Baste
interlining to wrong side of felt.

For two handles, cut four strips of felt each 16″
× 1¼″. Stitch two strips together on long edges for
each handle; stitch a row of red rickrack down center of each handle. Fold tote in half, felt side inward;
pin handle ends 3″ apart and centered along each
top edge of tote, raw edges flush. Stitch in place 1½″
from top edge. With right sides facing, stitch lining
and tote piece together along handle edge making ½″
seam. Pull lining up, refold piece with right sides
facing, and sew side edge of tote and lining piece
making ½″ seam.

Fold lining down over tote and continue folding
felt over about 1⅝″ to point where handles are stitched.
Trim lining fabric at bottom so edges are even. Stitch
tote and lining together along bottom edges with ½″
seam. Trim seam. Turn right side out. ◇

Rainbow Toys

Shown on page 116

EQUIPMENT: Tracing paper. Scissors. Pencil. Large-eyed sewing and embroidery needles. Sewing machine.

MATERIALS: *For Each Doll:* Rickrack in desired colors: jumbo, 6 yards; regular, one 2½-yard package. Small amounts of six-strand embroidery floss in colors desired for facial features. Discarded nylon stocking. *For Snake:* Jumbo rickrack in gold, red, green and blue, two 2½-yard packages each. Small amounts of felt in red, green, gold and black. All-purpose glue. *For Both:* Thread to match rickrack. Cotton balls for stuffing heads.

Doll

From jumbo rickrack, cut 1½ yards for body, 1½ yards for each leg, and ¾ yard for each arm. Cut 20″ length of thread, double it, and knot ends. Follow Figures 1-4 to make all parts of doll. Bring needle through edge of first point and insert into the edge of next point on opposite side (Fig. 1). Slide threaded points together, allowing rickrack to twist slightly, and insert needle in next point on opposite side (Fig. 2). Continue second step to end of piece, sliding rickrack tightly together on thread. To end thread, make knot. Stitch legs to one end of body piece, arms to other end.

From regular rickrack, cut ⅓ yard for each hand and ½ yard for each foot. Fold each piece in half and interlock V's together. Roll up piece, turning raw edge under. Tack to secure, then tack to end of limb.

For head, shape cotton into 1″-diameter ball. Place ball into stocking and twist tightly at base of ball. Stitch stocking closed. Cut excess stocking close to stitching; tack head to body. For hair, stitch regular rickrack around top of head, beginning at base of neck and wrapping around top; for old man, cut and stitch small length of regular silver rickrack around head from ear to ear. Using three strands of embroidery floss in needle, make small straight stitches for eyes and mouth in desired colors. To make glasses, use small backstitches and refer to color illustration. For stitch details, see Contents.

Snake

Unwind each package of the rickrack and cut length in half. Use three halves of each color for snake illustrated. Cut 70″ length of thread, double it, and knot 3″ from end. For snake's body, thread 12 sections of rickrack onto thread, repeating color sequence as shown and following Figs. 5 through 7 for each.

For first color section, bring needle in and out through rickrack points on one edge only; slide group to knotted end. Continue adding colors, twisting all groups in the same direction.

For head, trace actual-size patterns. From green felt, cut two heads, one mouth; from red felt, cut two mouths and one 3″ × ¼″ strip for tongue. For eyes, cut two small circles of black and two larger ones of gold felt. From green felt, cut one strip ½″ × 4½″ for tail; from gold felt, cut one strip ¼″ × 4″ for inner tail.

Machine-stitch top halves of head together from A to D. Stitch one red mouth to head; stuff head fully. Glue remaining red and green mouths together for lower jaw; add tongue to red felt side. Stitch lower jaw to head along sides from B to C. Insert one end of body through opening at neck; glue. For eyes, glue felt circles together; glue to head. Cut a V in tongue. Taper tail pieces to a point at one end. Glue gold tail to green tail; glue straight end of tail to body. ◊

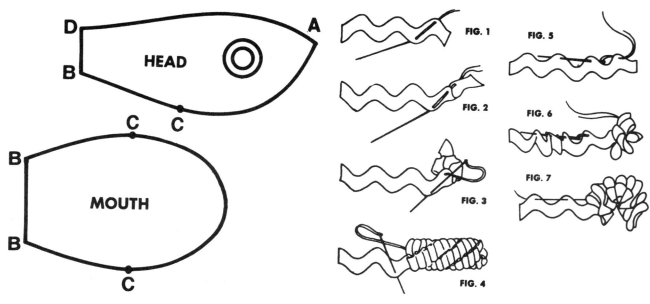

Little Miss Dolls

Shown on page 117

SIZE: About 20″ high.

EQUIPMENT: Pencil. Ruler. Paper for patterns. Tape measure. Dressmaker's tracing (carbon) paper. Dry ball-point pen. Embroidery and regular scissors. Straight pins. Embroidery and sewing needles. Knitting needle. Sewing machine with zig-zag attachment. Steam iron.

MATERIALS: *For Princess Lost Feather* (doll at top right): Gingham fabric 36″ wide, ½ yard tan. Homespun fabric 36″ wide: ⅜ yard print in desired color for dress; ⅛ yard coordinating color for panties. Felt: 9″ × 12″ sheet coordinating color for moccasins; scraps of black, orange. Trims to match dress fabric: Fringe 1″ wide, 2 yards; baby rickrack, 4 yards; jumbo rickrack, ½ yard; grosgrain ribbon 1″ wide, ½ yard; assorted threading beads ⅛″-³⁄₁₆″ diameter, about three dozen. White flat elastic ¼″ wide, piece 11″.

For Patience (blonde doll at top left): Cotton fabric 36″ wide: white, ¼ yard; pink gingham, ½ yard; green calico, 1 yard. Felt: 9″ × 12″ sheet green for shoes; scraps of navy blue, pink. Nylon net 36″ wide, ¼ yard white. Medium-weight fusible interfacing 18″ wide, ¼ yard white. White flat elastic ¼″ wide, piece 12″. White flat lace trim: ¾″ wide, piece 19″; 1″ wide, 1 yard; 1⅝″ wide, 1 yard. White satin ribbon ½″ wide, ¾ yard. Two round white buttons ½″ diameter. Miniature artificial flowers.

For Prudence (doll at bottom right): Cotton fabric 36″ wide: white, ¼ yard; brown gingham, ½ yard; red calico, ⅝ yard. Felt: 9″ × 12″ sheet red for shoes; scraps of black, pink. Nylon net 36″ wide, ¼ yard white. White flat elastic ¼″ wide, piece 12″. White flat lace trim: 1″ wide, ¾ yard; 1⅝″ wide, 2 yards. Two round white buttons ½″ diameter. Miniature artificial flowers.

For Each Doll: Sewing thread to match fabrics, felt, and trims. White heavy-duty sewing thread. Sport-weight yarn: three ounces desired color for hair; small amount same or coordinating color for bows. Six-strand cotton embroidery floss, one skein to match hair; small amount red. Two tiny hook-and-eye fasteners. Polyester fiberfill for stuffing.

GENERAL DIRECTIONS: Draw lines across patterns on next page, connecting grid lines. Enlarge patterns by copying on paper ruled in 1″ squares. Complete half-patterns indicated by heavy dash lines. Make separate patterns for eyes and cheeks. Use dressmaker's carbon and dry ball-point pen to transfer patterns to wrong side of fabrics, unless otherwise directed, placing them ½″ from fabric edges and ½″ apart; reverse for each second piece. Cut out ¼″ beyond marked lines for seam allowance, unless otherwise directed. When cutting pieces from felt or additional pieces without patterns, do not add seam allowance. Pin fabric pieces together with right sides facing and raw edges even; stitch on marked lines, making ¼″ seams. Stitch felt pieces to right side of fabric, using wide zigzag stitch. Clip into seam allowance at curves and across corners; turn piece to right side and poke out corners with knitting needle. Referring to color illustration, assemble and finish piece as directed below.

Dolls

For each: Read General Directions. From gingham fabric, cut two heads, one head center, two arms, and two bodies. **For Princess Lost Feather,** cut two rectangles for legs, each 5⅝″ × 9¾″. **For Patience and Prudence,** cut two gingham lower legs, each 5⅝″ × 5″, and two white upper legs, each 5⅝″ × 5¼″. From felt, cut the following pieces: **For Princess Lost Feather,** cut two black eyes, two orange cheeks, and two blue moccasins, transferring dots to one (right) side of moccasins. **For Patience,** cut two blue eyes, two pink creeks, and two green shoes. **For Prudence,** cut two black eyes, two pink cheeks, and two red shoes. Cut away toned area on each shoe.

Following original pattern for placement, stitch eyes and cheeks to one head piece (head front). Work red satin-stitch mouth, using two strands of floss in needle (see Contents for stitch details). Pin head center to head front and back with bottom straight edges even. Stitch around sides and top, leaving neck edge open. Fold neck ¼″ to wrong side; baste. Turn head to right side. Stuff firmly with fiberfill.

For Each Arm: Fold arm in half lengthwise, right side in. Stitch raw arm and hand edges, leaving top straight edge open. Turn; stuff firmly. Baste arm together ⅛″ from raw edges, enclosing stuffing.

For Each Leg: For Patience and Prudence, pin shoe to one 5⅝″ edge (bottom) of lower leg, matching bottom and side edges. Stitch all around shoe, including opening. Cut 10″ length from 1″-wide lace. Baste across top of lace, close to edge. Pull basting threads gently to gather lace to 5⅝″. Place lower leg face up on work surface with shoe pointing toward you. Place upper leg over lower leg, right sides facing, matching top and side edges. Sandwich lace between leg pieces with gathers at top, matching straight edges; pin. Stitch through all thicknesses. Open out leg; press lace toward shoe; press seam toward leg top. **For Princess Lost Feather,** pin and stitch moccasin, marked side up, to leg bottom as for shoe. For each doll, fold leg in half lengthwise, right side in; stitch long raw edges. Flatten leg so that seam is at center back; stitch across leg bottom. Turn and stuff. Baste leg top as for arm. **For Patience and Prudence,** sew a button to outer side edge of shoe opening.

For Princess Lost Feather, sew a large bead to moccasin at each large dot; sew on small beads at small dots.

On right side of fabric, pin arms to sides of one body piece ½″ down from shoulders, so that hands face in, thumbs point in same direction, and side edges are even; baste. Baste legs to body bottom in similar manner, so that shoes point toward shoulders and legs face up. Pin second body piece to first, sandwiching arms and legs between. Stitch around sides and bottom, leaving shoulder edges open. Turn and stuff. Turn raw edges $\frac{1}{4}''$ to inside; slip-stitch opening closed. Using heavy-duty thread, slip-stitch head, centered, over shoulders.

For Hair: For Patience and Princess Lost Feather, mark center part from front head seam to nape of neck. For braids, cut 120 30″ lengths of yarn. Working with groups of 10 strands at a time and all six strands of matching embroidery floss, stitch center of each group to part, working from front seam back. Divide yarn on each side into three sections and braid; tie each braid with 8″ length of yarn in same or coordinating color. Tack top of braids to head near cheeks to secure. **For Prudence,** mark center part on head center only. For long braids, cut 72 18″ lengths of black yarn. Working with groups of 12 strands at a time, stitch groups to center part, working from front seam back. Divide yarn on each side into six sections. Divide each section into thirds and braid; tie each braid with 6″ length of red yarn. Arrange braids evenly around head; tack bows to

head to secure. For braided bangs, cut nine 5″ lengths of black yarn. Stitch to front of part. Divide yarn into three sections and divide and braid each section; tie with red yarn. Do not tack down.

Clothes

Read General Directions. When transferring patterns for clothes, mark X's on wrong side of fabric; mark fine lines (placement lines) on right side. When assembling all clothes except Patience's bonnet, press seams open after stitching, unless otherwise directed.

To Bind Neck: From dress fabric, cut 2″-wide bias strip to size plus $\frac{1}{2}''$, piecing together as necessary. Press short edges and one long edge of strip $\frac{1}{4}''$ to wrong side. With right sides facing, stitch strip to neck, matching raw edges. Do not press seam open. Fold strip to inside of neck and slip-stitch in place.

For Princess Lost Feather: Panties: From solid color homespun fabric, cut two panties for front and back. Press waist edges $\frac{1}{4}''$ to wrong side. Cut elastic in half to form two $5\frac{1}{2}''$ lengths. Starting at one side edge of waist on each fabric piece with one end of elastic, pin length of elastic to wrong side of waist $\frac{1}{8}''$ from fold; stitch, using wide zigzag stitches. Reset

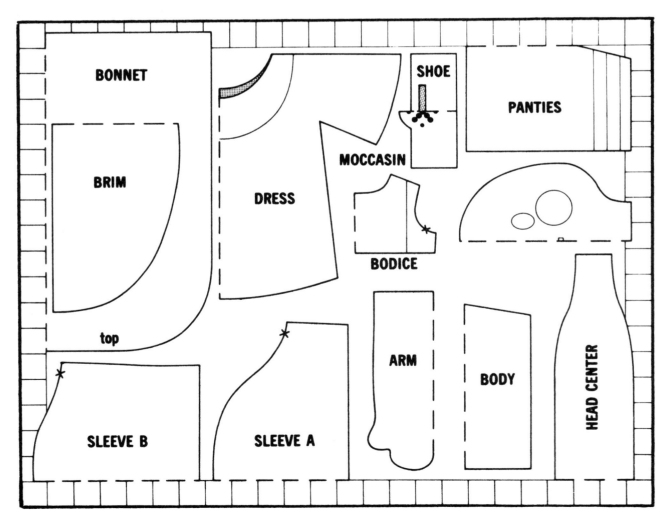

machine for straight stitch. Following markings for placement, stitch baby rickrack cut to size across top and bottom markings; stitch jumbo rickrack between. Stitch panties front and back together at sides and crotch. Fringe leg bottoms by pulling crosswise threads for $\frac{1}{2}''$.

Dress: From print homespun fabric, cut one dress front using complete pattern; cut away toned area. Also cut two backs, using half-pattern; transfer X to backs only. Stitch backs together at center back below X; press seam open. Above X, press edges under $\frac{1}{8}''$ twice; topstitch. Press sleeve bottoms $\frac{1}{8}''$ to inside twice; topstitch. Cut fringe to fit stitched edges. Cut two pieces baby rickrack same length as fringe. Pin fringe to each sleeve bottom on right side so it extends $\frac{1}{2}''$ beyond fold; stitch. Stitch baby rickrack to fringe along topstitching. For bodice trim, cut 21'' length each of fringe and baby rickrack. Starting at center front of bodice with center of fringe, pin fringe in place along marked lines; stitch. Attach rickrack as for sleeves. Bind neck, following directions above. Stitch each underarm and side in a continuous seam. For hem, press under $\frac{1}{8}''$ twice; stitch. Cut fringe and baby rickrack to fit hem, plus 1''. Trim hem, overlapping ends at center back. Sew hook-and-eye fasteners to opening at neck and center back.

Headband: Cut two pieces baby rickrack same length as grosgrain ribbon. Stitch to ribbon $\frac{1}{4}''$ from long edges. Test-fit band around doll's head; pin ends. Remove band and stitch ends together; press seam open. Turn ends under $\frac{1}{4}''$ twice; stitch. Sew beads around band, following color illustration.

For Prudence: Dress: From calico fabric, cut one bodice front using complete pattern, two backs using half-pattern, and two A sleeves; cut one 34'' × 9'' rectangle for skirt. From nylon net, cut two 34'' × $7\frac{1}{2}''$ rectangles for underskirt. Stitch bodice front and backs together at shoulders.

For each sleeve: Fold under bottom edge of sleeve $\frac{1}{8}''$ twice; topstitch. Cut $12\frac{1}{2}''$ length of $1\frac{5}{8}''$-wide lace. On right side of sleeve, pin lace over stitching, so that bottom edge extends $1\frac{1}{4}''$ beyond fold; stitch. Cut elastic in half to form two 6'' lengths. Starting at one side edge of sleeve with one end of elastic, pin elastic to sleeve bottom on wrong side $\frac{7}{8}''$ above top fold; stitch, using wide zigzag stitches. Reset machine for straight stitch. Machine-baste upper curved edge of sleeve between X's. Pin lower curved edges of sleeve to front and back armhole of dress below X's. Pull basting threads, gathering upper curved edge of sleeve to fit upper armhole; pin and stitch. Stitch underarm and side in a continuous seam; turn to right side.

For Pinafore: From white fabric, cut one $15\frac{1}{2}''$ apron, one 3'' × 4'' bib, and two $2\frac{1}{4}''$ × $6\frac{1}{2}''$ straps. Mark a line on one (wrong) side of bib halfway between 3'' edges. With 3'' edges at top and bottom, center bib on bodice front, right sides facing, with waist edges even; pin. Topstitch on marked line. Press bib top down over bottom, matching edges; baste $\frac{1}{8}''$ from waist. Cut two 11'' lengths from $1\frac{5}{8}''$-wide lace. Baste

and gather top edge of each to $6\frac{1}{2}''$. Pin lace to bodice front and back, gathers facing, following lines for placement (lace will extend beyond shoulders); baste. Press fabric straps in half lengthwise; baste over lace, matching raw edges; stitch. Press fabric straps toward center front, covering bib sides. Press under short side edges and one long (bottom) edge of apron $\frac{1}{8}''$ twice; stitch. Cut $15\frac{1}{2}''$ length of $1\frac{5}{8}''$-wide lace and trim apron bottom as for sleeves, except turning under lace ends before stitching. Stack net underskirt pieces on flat work surface with long edges at top and bottom. Place skirt, right side up, over underskirt, matching top (waist) and side edges. Center apron, right side up, on skirt with waist edges even; pin. Machine-baste waist close to edge through all thicknesses. Pull threads to gather waist of skirt and underskirt to fit bodice waist. Stitch assembled apron/skirt to bodice.

To Finish Dress: Press center back edges $\frac{1}{8}''$ to wrong side; topstitch. Starting at hem, stitch center backs together to 1'' below waist; press seam open. Above seam, press edges under $\frac{1}{8}''$; stitch. Turn dress to right side. Bind neck, following directions above, and hem skirt. Sew hook-and-eye fasteners to opening at neck and center back. Tack miniature flowers to waist front.

For Patience: Dress: From calico fabric, cut one bodice front using complete pattern, two backs using half pattern, and two B sleeves; cut one 34'' × 9'' rectangle for skirt. Assemble bodice and sleeves as for Prudence, trimming each sleeve with $9\frac{1}{2}''$ length of $\frac{3}{4}''$-wide lace. *For skirt and apron:* From white fabric, cut one $15\frac{1}{2}''$ × $6\frac{1}{2}''$ apron. From nylon net, cut two 34'' × $7\frac{1}{2}''$ rectangles for underskirt. Cut $15\frac{1}{2}''$ length from $1\frac{5}{8}''$-wide lace. Assemble as for Prudence's pinafore bottom; gather at waist and stitch to bodice. *To finish dress:* Finish back and neck as for Prudence. Tack miniature flowers to center of white ribbon. Place dress on doll; tie ribbon around waist with bow at center back.

Bonnet: From calico fabric, cut one bonnet, two brims, and two 2'' × 12'' ties. Cut two brims from fusible interfacing, omitting seam allowance. Fuse interfacing, centered, to wrong side of each brim, following manufacturer's directions. Baste and gather 1''-wide lace to fit curved edge of brim. Place brims together, right sides facing; sandwich lace between, so that gathers are even with straight edges; pin and stitch. Turn to right side (lace will extend beyond brim). Press raw edges $\frac{1}{4}''$ to inside. Baste curved edge of bonnet and gather to fit straight edge of brim. Insert gathered edge $\frac{1}{4}''$ into brim between layers and slip-stitch in place on each side. Press straight edge $\frac{1}{8}''$ to wrong side twice; hem. Baste $\frac{1}{8}''$ from hem; do not end off. Test-fit bonnet on doll and pull basting, gathering to fit head. Secure thread; end off. Remove bonnet from doll. Fold each tie in half lengthwise, right side in. Stitch raw edges, leaving opening in each long edge for turning; turn. Fold raw edges $\frac{1}{4}''$ to inside on each; slip-stitch openings closed; press. Tack ties to back edges of brim. ◇

Bean Bags

Shown on pages 118-119

EQUIPMENT: Paper for patterns. Pencil. Ruler. Tracing paper. Scissors. Embroidery needle. Sewing machine.

MATERIALS: Felt, large and small pieces in a variety of colors (see individual directions for colors). Dry beans. Glue. Thread to match fabric. Yarn and embroidery floss (see individual directions). Polyester fiberfill batting.

GENERAL DIRECTIONS: Trace full size patterns; on pages 166–170; complete half-patterns indicated by long dash lines; short dash lines show overlapping pieces. Trace individual parts of each pattern separately. For each bean bag, cut two complete body pieces, plus four arms and four legs, of color felt indicated in individual directions. Stitch arm and legs together with matching thread, leaving top end open, and stuff with fiberfill batting; stitch top end closed. Place bodies together; pin arms and legs in place between body pieces. Stitch around body with matching thread, $\frac{1}{8}''$ from edge, leaving a small area open. Stuff body with dry beans; stitch body closed. Cut features from felt and glue to body, following individual directions and referring to pattern.

Tomato

From felt, cut red bodies; olive green arms, legs, stem, eye centers, and lashes; pink mouth and cheeks; white eyes. Assemble bean bag, following General Directions.

Green Pepper

From felt, cut green bodies, arms and legs; white eyes and brown centers; red mouth and cheeks. Assemble bean bag, following General Directions.

Carrot

From felt, cut orange bodies; green arms and legs; white eyes and brown centers; red mouth. Cut 11 $1\frac{1}{2}''$ pieces of green yarn for beard and one 6" piece of orange yarn for stem. Assemble bean bag, following General Directions; insert beard and stem, following pattern.

Radish

From felt, cut red bodies; green arms and legs; white eyes and brown centers; pink mouth. Cut sixteen $1\frac{1}{2}''$ pieces of green yarn for beard and one 4" piece of red yarn for stem. Assemble bean bag, following General Directions; insert beard and stem, following pattern.

Strawberry

From felt, cut red bodies and legs; green stem and arms; pink mouth; white eyes and green centers. Assemble bean bag, following General Directions. Embroider lines on body with straight stitch, following pattern.

Lemon

From felt, cut yellow bodies; lime green arms, lashes and leaf; camel legs and eye centers; white eyes; red mouth. Assemble bean bag, following General Directions.

Lime

From felt, cut lime green bodies; green leaf and arms; brown legs and eye centers; white eyes, red mouth. Assemble bean bag, following General Directions.

Orange

From felt, cut orange bodies; green leaf, arms and eye centers; brown chin, legs and lashes; white eyes; red mouth. Assemble bean bag, following General Directions.

Apple

From felt, cut red bodies; green leaf and arms; brown legs, stem and eye centers; white eyes; pink cheeks and mouth. Assemble bean bag, following General Directions.

Pear

From felt, cut gold bodies; olive green leaf and arms; brown legs and eye centers; red cheeks and mouth; white eyes. Assemble bean bag, following General Directions.

Banana

From felt, cut yellow bodies; olive green arms; brown legs, spots and eye centers; white eyes; red mouth. Assemble bean bag, following General Directions.

Peapod

From felt, cut olive green bodies, legs and arms; green stem and peas; white eyes and brown centers; red mouth. Assemble bean bag, following General Directions. ◊

Giant Car

Shown on page 117

SIZE: 23″ long, 14″ tall.

EQUIPMENT: Pencil. Ruler. Paper for patterns. Scissors. Compass. Dressmaker's tracing (carbon) paper. Dry ball-point pen. Sewing needle. Sewing machine. Iron.

MATERIALS: Closely woven cotton fabric 45″ wide in compatible colors: solid, 1¾ yards; print, ½ yard; check, ⅜ yard; scrap of yellow. Sewing thread to match fabrics. Medium-weight fusible interfacing 18″ wide, 2 yards. Polyester fiberfill.

DIRECTIONS: Using pencil and ruler, draw lines across pattern on page 150, connecting grid lines. Enlarge patterns by copying on paper ruled in 3″ squares. Solid outlines indicate stitching lines, heavy dash lines indicate appliques, fine dash lines indicate placement lines, and fine solid lines indicate embroidery. Using compass, mark circles for additional patterns: 6½″ dia. for wheel, 3¼″ dia. for hubcap, and 2″ dia. for headlights.

Cut out the following pieces, using patterns and adding ¼″ seam allowance all around: From solid fabric, cut two sides, one rear/top, one windshield, one hood, one bottom, two axle bottoms, four axle sides, four axle ends, and two headlights. Cut one grill and 10 wheels from print fabric. Cut two headlights from yellow fabric. For each piece, cut a same-size piece of interfacing, omitting seam allowance, and press to wrong sides of fabric pieces.

Using dressmaker's carbon and dry ball-point pen, transfer embroidery and appliqué lines to fabric pieces. Using patterns and following directions for How to Appliqué (see Contents); cut windows from checked fabric and machine-appliqué to sides of car, windshield, and rear/top, setting sewing machine for close zigzag stitch (about ⅛″ wide); also, stitch embroidery lines on sides. Cut five hubcaps from solid fabric and applique to five wheels.

With right sides facing and edges even, and making ¼″ seams, pin and stitch pieces together as follows: Matching letters, pin and stitch hood to windshield, windshield to rear/top, rear/top to bottom, bottom to grill, and grill to hood. Pin and stitch sides of car, matching corners carefully; leave 6″ opening along bottom for turning. Clip into seam allowance at corners and turn. Stuff car with fiberfill; turn edge of opening ¼″ to inside; slip-stitch opening closed.

Make two axles: For each, stitch one bottom, two sides, and two ends together to form a rectangular box; turn and stuff. Place car with bottom up. Fold open edges of axle ¼″ to inside and slip-stitch to bottom of car along placement lines (see pattern). Pair appliqued wheels with remaining wheels and stitch together ¼″ from edge; leave 2″ opening for turning. Clip into seam allowance all around; turn. Loosely stuff wheels; turn openings ¼″ to inside and slip-stitch closed. Following placement lines on pattern, tack center of one wheel to rear of car; tack others to axle ends so that wheels rest on surface. Stitch headlights together as for wheels; tack to front of car, following placement lines (see pattern), with yellow side facing out. ◊

Foam Pillow Animals

Shown on page 120

EQUIPMENT: Scissors. Compass. Paper for patterns. Pencil. Ruler. Needle. Scrap of cardboard for Rabbit's tail.

MATERIALS (for each): Foam rubber, 1″ thick, 8″ × 10″. Fabric, such as velveteen, corduroy, polished or printed cotton, 12″ × 18″; matching sewing thread. For individual animals, you will need scraps of felt, fabric, yarn, ball fringe with matching sewing thread; small amount of cotton for stuffing; seed beads, buttons (see individual directions).

GENERAL DIRECTIONS: Enlarge patterns on next page by copying on paper ruled in 1″ squares; complete half-patterns indicated by long dash lines. Dotted lines indicate seam lines. Dot-dash lines indicate fold lines. Cut one body of foam. Using same pattern, cut two body pieces out of fabric, adding ¾″ all around for sides and seams. Cut out and make features and trims as directed below; tack in place as shown. Place fabric body pieces together, right sides facing, with legs, ears, tail, or beak in place between and ends or raw edges out. (If pieces are large, it may be helpful to baste them in place first.) Using matching sewing thread, stitch together all around, ¼″ from edge, leaving 4½″ opening on bottom. Clip seam all around. Turn to right side, stuff with foam body, turn in edges of opening and overcast closed. Follow individual directions for variations.

Mouse

Cut body of gray velveteen. Cut two ears of pink felt. For eyes, cut two black felt circles ⅜″ diameter; sew one to each body as shown with black seed bead in each center. For nose, use orange pompon with string, cut from ball fringe. For tail, cut six 16″ strands of pink yarn; knot at one end. Using double strands, braid yarn to 9″ long; knot at this end and trim. Fold ears almost in half. Stitch body pieces together, right sides facing, with pompon, ears, and tail between, ends facing out. Finish according to General Directions.

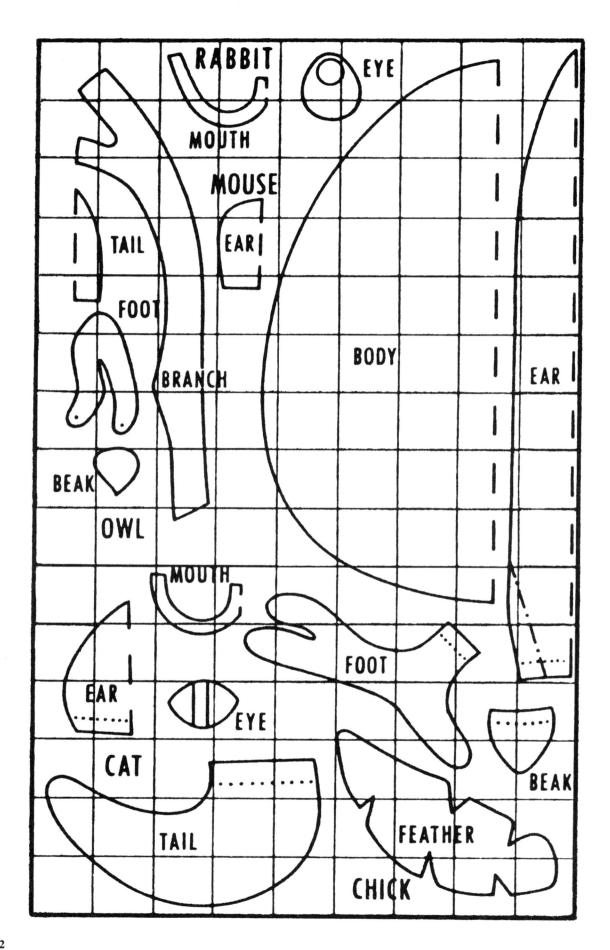

RABBIT

EYE

MOUTH

MOUSE

TAIL

EAR

FOOT

BRANCH

BODY

EAR

BEAK

OWL

MOUTH

FOOT

EAR

EYE

CAT

BEAK

TAIL

FEATHER

CHICK

Rabbit

Cut body of red print fabric. Cut two ears of same fabric and two ears of solid red fabric. Cut mouth of black felt, inner eyes of blue felt, outer eyes of white felt. Sew mouth to one body piece. Sew on eyes as shown. For nose, sew $\frac{5}{8}$"-diameter shiny black button above mouth. With right side of one solid and one print ear facing, sew together $\frac{1}{4}$" from edge, leaving bottom open; turn to right side; press. Make two ears. Baste three 2" red yarn loops to top edge of one body piece on right side with loops toward center. Fold bottoms of ears diagonally toward center as indicated on pattern and baste to body as for yarn loops. Stitch and stuff following General Directions. For tail, make pompon by wrapping red yarn around $3\frac{1}{2}$" piece of cardboard 60 times. Tie together at one side and cut through loops opposite tie; sew to back of Rabbit.

Chick

Cut body of bright yellow velveteen. Cut two beaks, four feet, and two feathers of bright orange felt. Cut two feathers of magenta and two of shocking pink felt. Cut two black felt circles $\frac{3}{8}$" diameter for eyes. Sew one of each color feather and an eye on right side of each body piece. Whip two feet together for each foot; stuff lightly up to seam line with cotton as you sew. Do the same for beak. Stitch and stuff following General Directions.

Owl

Cut body of chartreuse polished cotton. For outer eyes, cut two 2"-diameter circles of deep turquoise felt. Also cut one tail feather of turquoise. Cut two 1"-diameter circles for inner eyes, of black felt, and cut two branches of black felt. Cut two tail feathers of olive green felt. Cut two feet of yellow felt. Cut one beak of gold felt. Sew eyes and nose to one body piece. Sew only tops of feet in place as shown. Stitch and stuff following General Directions. Whip branches together, stuffing lightly with cotton as you sew; tack in place under feet, secure toes to body with French knots using black thread (for stitch detail, see Contents).

Cat (not shown)

Cut body of rose-red corduroy. Cut two ears, two tails, mouth, and two inner eyes of black felt. Cut two outer eyes of green felt. Whip edges of tail together, stuffing lightly up to seam line with cotton as you sew. Sew on mouth, eyes, and button nose as for Rabbit. For whiskers, make 8 or 9 French knots (for stitch detail, see Contents) with fine black wool, on each side of mouth area. Stitch and stuff following General Directions. ◇

Vegetable Pillows

Shown on page 133

EQUIPMENT: Paper for patterns. Pencil. Ruler. Scissors. Sewing needle. Large-eyed embroidery needle. Compass.

MATERIALS: Fabrics, sewing thread and tapestry yarn (see individual directions for colors). Polyester batting for stuffing.

DIRECTIONS: Enlarge patterns on next page by copying on paper ruled in 2" squares; complete half and quarter-patterns indicated by long dash lines. Fine lines indicate lines to be embroidered. Cut pieces out of fabric indicated in individual directions, adding $\frac{3}{8}$" all around for seam allowances. When sewing pieces together, make $\frac{3}{8}$" seams. Make pillows following individual directions. Refer to stitch details (see Contents) when doing all embroidery.

Squash

Out of white cotton, cut two complete scalloped shapes and one $12\frac{1}{2}$"-diameter circle. Place the scalloped pieces together with right sides facing. Sew together around edges, leaving two scallops open. Clip into seam at curves. Turn to right side. Fill shape with stuffing. Turn edges of opening in and slip-stitch the opening closed.

On center circle, lightly mark the center on right side, then mark 1", 3", and $8\frac{1}{2}$" diameter concentric circles. Following lines on pattern, mark lines dividing the 3" and $8\frac{1}{2}$" circles into 10 sections. Cut piece of lining fabric 9" diameter; place cotton and lining together with wrong sides facing; place a layer of stuffing between; baste the three thicknesses together. Work embroidery as indicated through the three thicknesses. Fill in the center 1" circle by couching gold-color yarn with yellow yarn around in spiral. Work the lines radiating out from center and lines of 3" and $8\frac{1}{2}$" circles with yellow yarn in running stitch. With gold yarn, fill in the spaces between the radiating lines at center with two short straight stitches on each side of a longer straight stitch. Clip into $\frac{3}{8}$" seam allowance of circle and press under. Place circle on top at center of scalloped piece; place a thick layer of stuffing between; pin edges in place. With yellow yarn, sew together at edges through all thicknesses with running stitches.

Cucumber

Out of green polished cotton, cut two basic pieces. On piece which will be front, mark lines for embroidery following pattern. With apple green yarn, embroider the lines at one end in long and short stitch, the long lines in outline stitch, and the dots in French knots.

Place the two cucumber pieces together, right sides facing; sew together around edges, leaving a 6" opening at side. Clip into seam at curves. Turn to right side. Stuff fully; turn edges of opening in and slip-stitch opening closed.

Carrot

Cut two pieces out of orange polished cotton. Lightly mark lines across on right side of one piece. With bright orange yarn, make running stitches along lines. For carrot top, cut 70 pieces of bright green yarn, each 10½″ long. Place yarn strands together and fold them all in half. Sew strands together across fold. With bright orange yarn, make 5″-long piece of twisted cord, following directions for making twisted cord (see Contents).

Place the two orange pieces together, right sides facing; insert and pin yarn carrot top between fabric (across top where indicated by double crosslines on pattern) with folded edge flush with seam. Insert about 4″ of twisted cord at bottom point. Sew together along edges, leaving a 6″ opening at side. Clip into seam at curves. Turn to right side. Stuff carrot. Turn edges of opening in and slip-stitch closed.

Eggplant

Cut two main pieces out of purple cotton; cut two stems out of green polished cotton. With right sides of purple pieces facing, sew together at edges; leave top completely open. Clip into seam at curves and turn to right side. Place the two stem pieces together with right sides facing; sew together around edges, leaving bottom completely open. Clip into seam at curves and turn to right side. Stuff purple piece fully, then stuff stem fully. Place stem over top of eggplant. Turn bottom edges of stem under ¼″ and slip-stitch to purple eggplant.

Lima Bean Pod

Cut two pod pieces out of apple green wool. Using pattern, mark embroidery lines on right side of one wool piece. With right sides facing, sew together along top and ends, leaving bottom open. Turn to right side. First fill entire pod with one layer of stuffing, then fill the bean area with thick pads of stuffing. With olive green yarn, make running stitches through all thicknesses, along lines for embroidery. Turn edges of opening in and slip-stitch closed. ◊

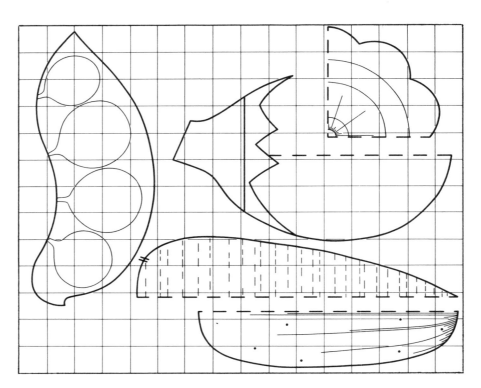

Switch Plate Dress-Ups

Shown on page 134

EQUIPMENT: Paper for patterns. Carbon paper. Pencil. Ruler. Masking tape. Coping saw. Drill with $\frac{3}{16}$″ bit. Sandpaper. Flat and pointed paintbrushes.

MATERIALS: Large scraps of wood ¼″ thick. Acrylic paints. Varnish.

DIRECTIONS: Trace actual size patterns on pages 175–176; complete half-patterns indicated by dash lines. Tape pattern on wood with carbon paper between. Go over pattern with pencil to transfer to wood. Saw design out of wood. Drill hole in center of shaded area; insert blade of saw through hole, then reattach blade to saw; cut out shaded rectangular area for switch. Drill holes for screws indicated by solid dots on pattern. Sand rough edges.

On one side, paint individual areas in colors as desired. With black, paint outline of entire piece, outline individual areas, fill in solid black areas on pattern, paint edges and backs. Let dry. Give switch plates two coats of varnish. ◊

Fabric Pets

Shown on page 136

EQUIPMENT: Tracing paper. Pencil. Ruler. Scissors. Straight pins. Sewing needle. Masking tape.

MATERIALS: Large scraps of cotton fabric. Sewing thread to match. Scraps of felt. Piece of foam padding, 1″ thick, enough for each body and each leg. Four white two-hole buttons, ½″ diameter for each. All-purpose glue. See any additional materials in individual directions on following pages.

GENERAL DIRECTIONS: Trace patterns on following pages.

For each animal, cut two bodies, four of each leg piece, four of each ear piece, and two of each tail piece out of fabric, adding ¼″ all around for seam allowance. Cut body and two of each leg out of foam, cutting about ⅛″ inside lines of patterns.

Place the two tail pieces together with right sides facing, sew ¼″ from edges all around, leaving straight end open. Clip into seam allowance at curves. Turn to right side. Place fabric bodies together, right sides facing; insert tail in place where indicated by crosslines on pattern, making raw edges flush. Pin pieces together, then sew, making ¼″ seam; leave open between X's. Clip into seam allowance on corners and curves. Turn body to right side. Insert foam body into fabric body. Foam piece will look larger than fabric piece; compress foam as you fit it into fabric; use pencil eraser to help work foam into corners and small spaces. Turn edges of opening in and sew opening closed. For each leg, pin two together with right sides facing; sew together ¼″ in from edges, leaving open between X's. Clip in seam allowance on corners and curves. Turn leg to right side; insert foam leg. Turn edges of opening in and sew opening closed. Using long double strand of thread, sew a button onto one leg where indicated by large dot on pattern; run thread through body where indicated by large dot on pattern, then through the other matching leg at dot, being sure legs are even. Put a button on the needle and sew it on through the leg only. Pull thread tight so legs stay straight enough for animal to stand. Wind thread around thread between leg and body; fasten well and cut thread. Repeat for other set of legs, making sure animal will be able to stand evenly.

For each ear, pin two ear pieces together with right sides facing. Sew ¼″ in from edge, leaving straight end open. Clip into seam allowance at corners and curves. Turn to right side. Turn in straight edges of ear ½″; sew closed. Sew an ear in place at straight end only, where indicated by short dash line on pattern, on each side of animal's head.

For each animal, cut two outer eyes, two pupils, and one mouth of felt. Glue a pupil to each outer eye; glue outer eyes in place on each side of animal where indicated by short dash lines. Glue mouth in place where indicated by short dash lines.

For additional instructions, follow individual directions for each animal.

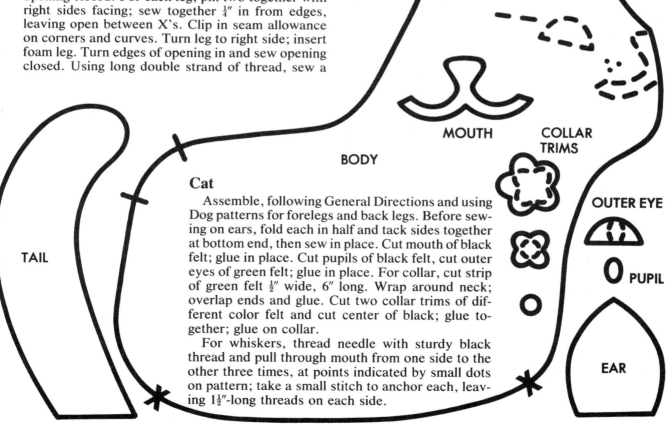

Cat

Assemble, following General Directions and using Dog patterns for forelegs and back legs. Before sewing on ears, fold each in half and tack sides together at bottom end, then sew in place. Cut mouth of black felt; glue in place. Cut pupils of black felt, cut outer eyes of green felt; glue in place. For collar, cut strip of green felt ½″ wide, 6″ long. Wrap around neck; overlap ends and glue. Cut two collar trims of different color felt and cut center of black; glue together; glue on collar.

For whiskers, thread needle with sturdy black thread and pull through mouth from one side to the other three times, at points indicated by small dots on pattern; take a small stitch to anchor each, leaving 1½″-long threads on each side.

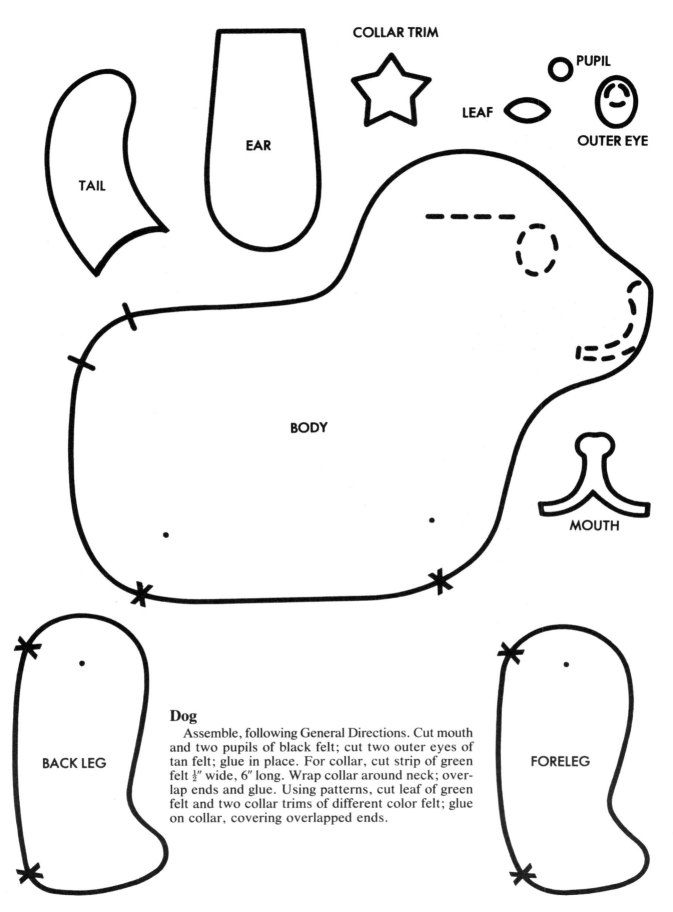

COLLAR TRIM

PUPIL

EAR

LEAF

OUTER EYE

TAIL

BODY

MOUTH

BACK LEG

Dog

Assemble, following General Directions. Cut mouth and two pupils of black felt; cut two outer eyes of tan felt; glue in place. For collar, cut strip of green felt $\frac{1}{2}$" wide, 6" long. Wrap collar around neck; overlap ends and glue. Using patterns, cut leaf of green felt and two collar trims of different color felt; glue on collar, covering overlapped ends.

FORELEG

Bunny

Assemble, following General Directions but omitting tail. For tail, cut circle of white terrycloth; with thread, gather around edges $\frac{1}{4}''$ in from edge. Stuff tail with cotton; pull gathering thread to form ball shape; knot thread. Sew tail to back of Bunny where indicated.

Before sewing ears in place, fold each in half and tack sides together at bottom end, then sew in place.

Cut mouth, two pupils, and two outer eyes of felt; glue in place.

Make four whiskers with blue thread on each side of mouth, where indicated by small dots on pattern, as for Cat.

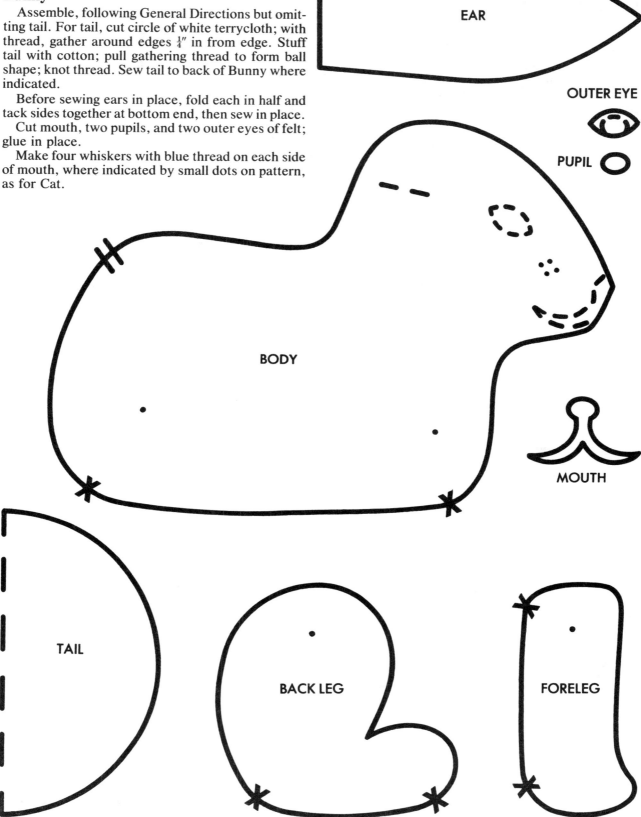

EAR

OUTER EYE

PUPIL

BODY

MOUTH

TAIL

BACK LEG

FORELEG

Elephant

Assemble, following General Directions, omitting tail. For tail, cut piece of fabric $\frac{3}{4}''$ wide and $2''$ long. Turn each end in $\frac{1}{4}''$ and then fold in half lengthwise; turn remaining edges in $\frac{1}{4}''$ and sew side and ends closed. Sew tail in place. Cut mouth of felt; glue in place. Cut two pupils and two outer eyes of two colors of felt; glue.

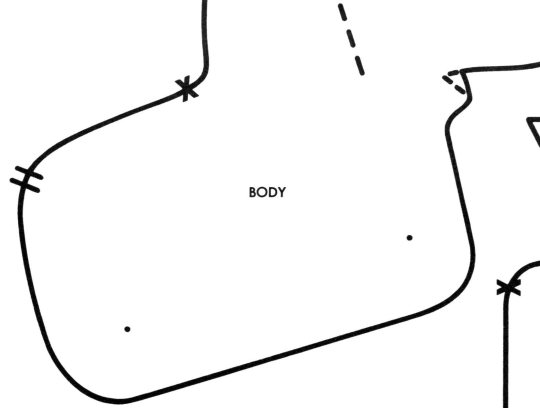

EAR

OUTER EYE

PUPIL

MOUTH

BODY

LEG

Giraffe

For tail, cut piece of fabric $\frac{1}{2}''$ wide, $2\frac{1}{2}''$ long. Turn ends in $\frac{1}{4}''$; fold in half lengthwise with wrong sides facing. Turn remaining edges in $\frac{1}{4}''$. Insert small amount of embroidery floss into one end; sew side and ends closed. Assemble, following General Directions.

For mane, wind embroidery floss into 25 1'' loops. Place tape over loops at one edge. Fold loops in half and stitch down untaped edge. Tack stitched edge of mane along neck where indicated between crosslines. Cut off tape and trim mane.

Before sewing ears in place, fold each in half and tack sides together at bottom end, then sew in place.

Cut two eyelids, two outer eyes, two pupils, and one mouth out of felt; glue in place. Cut four giraffe horns of felt. For each, glue two together, leaving straight ends unglued; spread these ends apart and glue to head where indicated by small square.

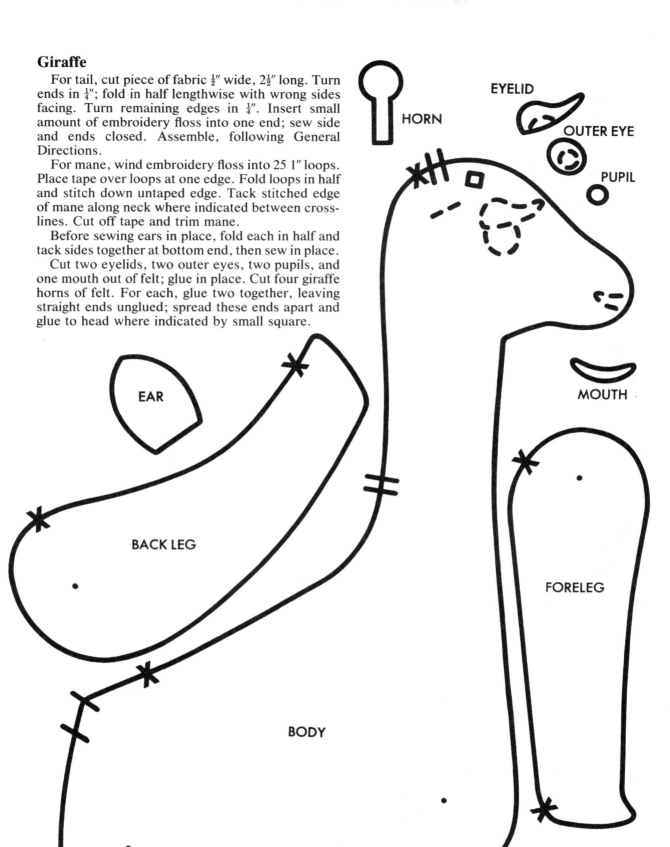

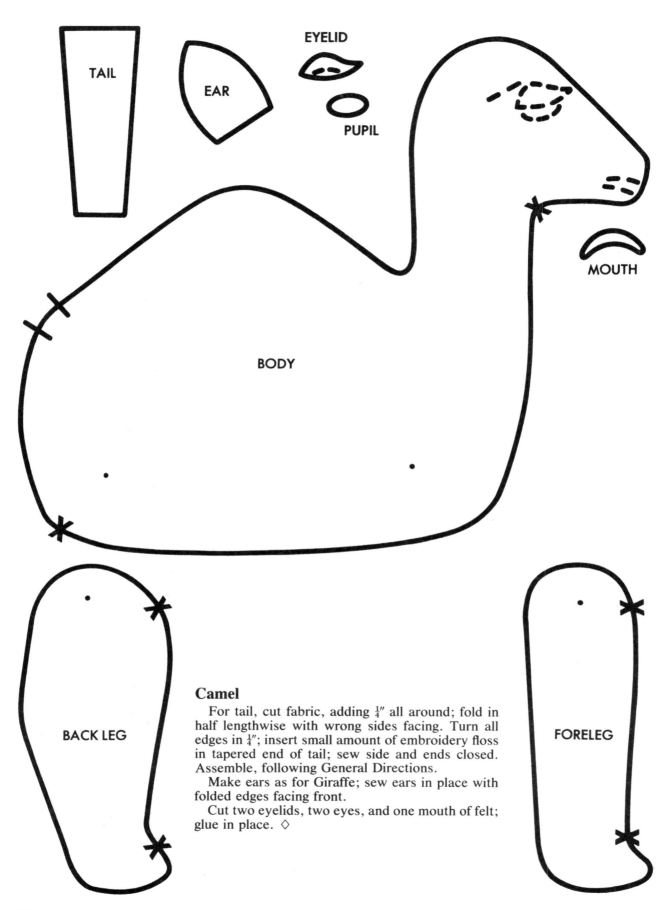

Camel

For tail, cut fabric, adding $\frac{1}{4}''$ all around; fold in half lengthwise with wrong sides facing. Turn all edges in $\frac{1}{4}''$; insert small amount of embroidery floss in tapered end of tail; sew side and ends closed. Assemble, following General Directions.

Make ears as for Giraffe; sew ears in place with folded edges facing front.

Cut two eyelids, two eyes, and one mouth of felt; glue in place. ◇

TAIL

EAR

EYELID

PUPIL

BODY

MOUTH

BACK LEG

FORELEG

A flutter of pretty ribbons adds new charm to any natural-colored basket with wide-open spaces. Simply weave ribbons and rickrack in and out, skipping holes at random or following the basket's own pattern. Fill with a bouquet of dried flowers or a leafy plant.

Springtime flowers bloom on a basket you can paint in a jiffy! First spray basket with flat white latex paint, then use acrylic paints (or fluorescent poster paints for the high-key colors) to paint fantasy flowers free-hand. It's easy—just one dab creates a petal or a bud! For a guide, select a floral fabric or gift-wrap paper that you like. Simplify the flowers, and place them to suit your own basket.

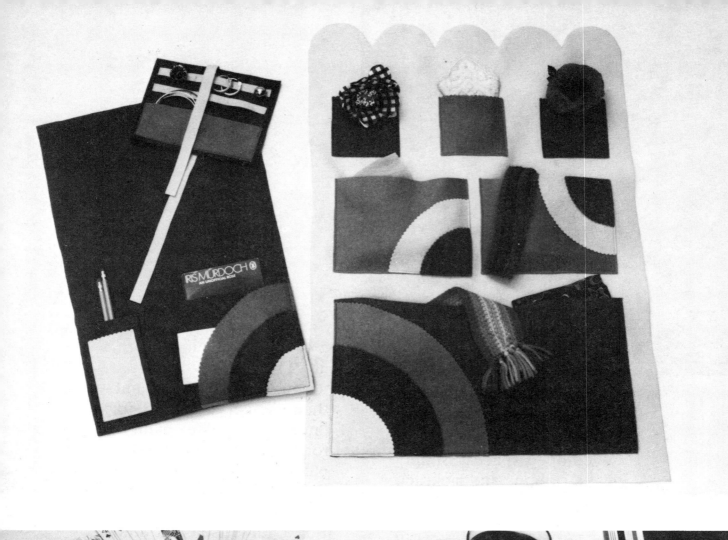

Bedside Organizer is a practical as well as decorative gift idea. Fill large wall hanging with belts, scarves, and lingerie. Book holder fits between bed-springs and mattress. Jewelry case completes the ensemble. All of felt; glue and machine-stitch. Dress up a cardtable with a ribbon-trimmed cloth; add double thick top-stitched coasters. Handy card tote holds a pair of decks; on its cover, a cutout symbol of each suit. Directions for Cardtable Companions, page 219; Bedside Organizer, page 223.

Cherished patchwork designs borrowed from favorite quilts are great for this year's greeting cards. With felt and glue, each is quickly finished, ready to carry good tidings to someone special. Designed by Constance Spates. Directions for Patchwork Cards are on page 224.

Perfect frames for treasured photographs are embroidered, then softly padded. Designed by Ellen Swendrowski Evett. Directions for Embroidered Frames are on page 225.

Sweet memories are charmingly depicted in four pictures that combine applique and embroidery. Delightful as singles or grouped as shown, each measures 6″ × 5″. Mats, covered in striped fabric, add a contemporary note to the old-fashioned subjects. Directions for Memory Pictures are on page 228.

Linen eyeglass cases, beaded in sprightly designs, are charming accessories. Motifs are worked by couching strung seed beads. Red ladybug leaves turquoise flight line on green background. Three circles of orange and gold accent white case. Dainty bouquet is "tied" with a yellow bow. Sunny blossom of yellow, orange, red is beaded spirally from center. Bright red cherries sparkle on blue background. From Constance Spates. For directions for Beaded Eyeglass Cases, see page 234.

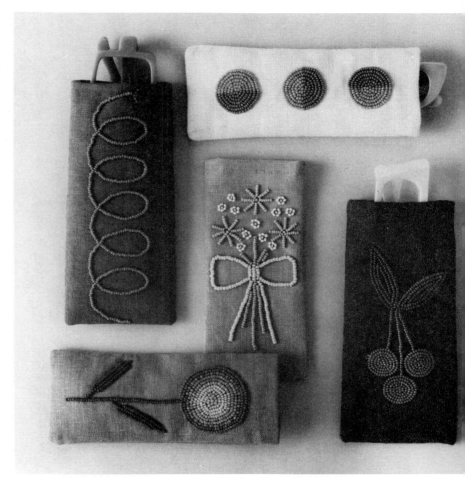

Blue and aqua duster has strands of rug yarn knotted on wire coat hanger. Winsome hangers, decorated with cardboard and papier-mâché, make it fun to hang up clothing. Pretty ring holder is clear pine adorned with a felt flower, gold braid. Wooden box is painted with felt-tipped pens in three contrasting colors. Embossed gift wrap, gold braid trim and "jewels" alter a six-pack carton. Colorful trivet is made of strips cut from magazines, folded, then linked, coiled. Make a coaster, too. Owl on store-bought mirror is of cardboard glued to papier-mâché base. Owl pin, $4\frac{1}{2}''$ high, is of papier-mâché, trimmed with cord, then painted. Small, plain box is embellished with paint, marbleized paper, gold paper trims, and tiny cards. Directions for all begin on page 228.

No two seashells are exactly alike and that's the fun in creating these items—their unique qualities depend on the shells you choose. Shells such as the cowry, olive, auger, snail, and turkey wing help shape some delightful, though somewhat unconventional, creatures. Directions for Shell Show-Offs are on page 235.

Fantasy Elephant

Shown on page 135

EQUIPMENT: Paper for patterns. Soft and hard-lead pencils. Ruler. Tracing paper. Dressmaker's tracing (carbon) paper. Straight pins. Scissors. Embroidery hoop. Embroidery and sewing needles.

MATERIALS: Orange cotton or linen fabric 36″ wide, ¾ yard. Six-strand embroidery floss: about three skeins each of yellow-gold, orange, magenta, shocking pink, medium blue, dark blue or colors desired. Orange sewing thread. Polyester fiberfill for stuffing.

DIRECTIONS: *To Make Patterns:* Enlarge patterns by copying on paper ruled in 1″ squares; complete half-pattern indicated by long dash lines. Trace

complete body and two ears (including fine lines for embroidery) and one separate underbody piece.

To Mark and Work Embroidery: Pin patterns to fabric (be sure to reverse patterns for second body and two ears); mark two complete elephant body outlines, allowing at least 1″ of fabric between; do the same for four ears, and one underbody.

Transfer lines for embroidery to two bodies and two opposite ears with dressmaker's carbon and hard-lead pencil.

Put fabric in hoop. Use three strands of floss in needle. Work all lines and fill in all areas with chain

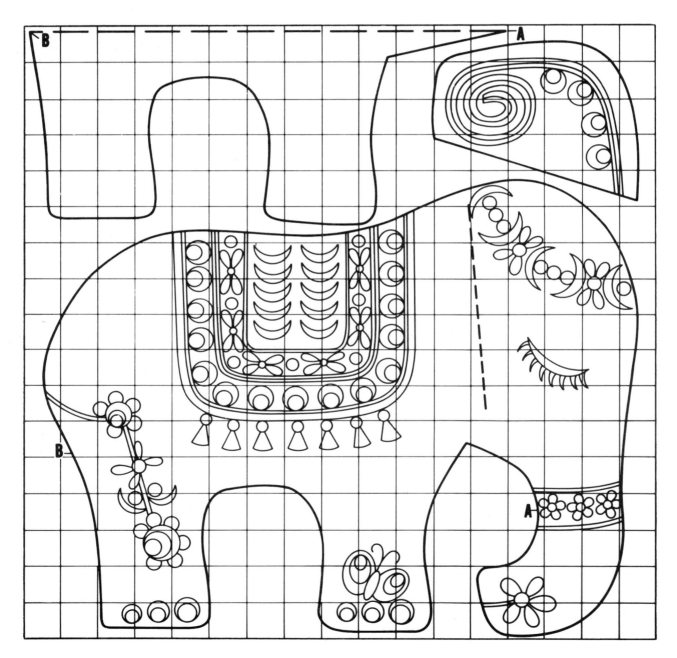

stitch (see Contents for stitch details), using desired colors.

To Assemble: Cut out the two bodies, four ears, and one underbody, adding ½" all around each for seam allowances. With right sides facing, pin one half of underbody to one elephant, matching letters; do the same with second body; stitch from A to B with ½" seams on each side of body, then continue stitching the two bodies together with ½" seams; leave about a 5" opening at front and back of elephant. Clip into seam allowance at curves. Turn body to right side. Stuff elephant through openings. When elephant is well stuffed, turn in edges of openings and slip-stitch closed.

For each ear, place together an embroidered and a plain ear with right sides facing; sew together all around making ½" seams, leaving straight edge open. Clip into seam allowance all around. Turn to right side. Press, if necessary. Turn edges of opening in and slip-stitch closed. With invisible stitches, sew straight edge of ear to each side of elephant (indicated by short dash lines). ◊

Square Dancers
Shown on page 137

EQUIPMENT: Tracing paper. Pencil. Ruler. Scissors. Dressmaker's carbon. Straight pins. Sewing and embroidery needles.

MATERIALS: *For each:* Pink cotton fabric ¼ yard, 36" wide for two. Sewing thread to match fabric, yarn, and felt. All-purpose glue.

For Cowboy: Brown, blue, and pink embroidery floss. Red knitting worsted. Cotton fabric: small amounts of blue denim, blue work-shirt fabric, red print, blue print. Light and dark beige felt. Yellow and gold narrow looped fringe. Three tiny white buttons. Small strip of leather ½" × 9". Small scrap of cardboard. Small scraps of lightweight aluminum foil. Black buttonhole twist.

For Gingham Girl: Red and brown embroidery floss. Rouge for cheeks. Brown knitting worsted. Cotton fabric: red-and-white-checked gingham ¼ yard, small amounts of plain white, dotted swiss, stretch white. White eyelet edging. White baby rickrack. Red felt. Two tiny white buttons. White narrow ribbon 2 yards.

GENERAL DIRECTIONS: Trace patterns on the following pages; complete half-patterns indicated by long dash lines. For each doll, cut two head-body pieces, four arms, and four legs (reversing patterns for two arms and two legs) out of pink fabric, adding ¼" on all edges for seam and hem allowances. Cut girl's legs at dot-dash line to make her shorter.

Using carbon, transfer features to one head. Using two strands of floss in needle, make noses, mouths, and eyebrows and outline eyes in outline stitch. Fill in eyes in satin stitch (shading indicates direction of satin stitches). For stitch details, see Contents.

With right sides facing, sew bodies together, leaving bottom open. With right sides facing, sew two legs and two arms together for each, leaving straight ends open. Clip all curves. Turn pieces to right sides. Stuff each. Turn in raw edges of openings and sew closed. Sew arms and legs in place, with leg seams at front and back centers.

Continue following individual directions. Add ¼" seam and hem allowances on all edges of all fabric pieces. Use sewing thread to match fabrics.

Cowboy

Embroider eyebrows, outlines of eyes, and nose in brown, mouth in pink, and pupils in blue floss.

Before sewing head-body pieces together, cut four ears of pink fabric. With right sides facing, sew two together for each along curved edges only. Turn each to right side. When sewing head together, insert ears between, where illustrated, with raw edges flush with raw edges of head.

For hair, cut about 40 strands of red yarn, each 8" long; fold each in half and tack at midpoint across back of head to cover; make second layer of hair to thicken. Cut about 50 strands of yarn about 6" long; place across top of head in two layers; stitch across top of head at one side to secure and to make part. Glue strands onto head at sides; trim strands in front.

For shirt, cut back (use pattern for front, using short dash line as half-pattern line and omit collar, cutting across at solid line) and two fronts of work-shirt fabric. With right sides facing, sew shoulder, sleeve, and side seams together. Hem sleeve ends. Turn shirt to right side and hem collar and neck edge on right side. Put shirt on doll. Fold front edges under; overlap right side with left; sew three buttons down front where indicated by X's on pattern. Turn collar down.

For pants, cut two of denim. Fold each in half with right sides facing and sew center front and center back seams (A to B). Then sew up crotch and leg seams (C to B to C). Hem waist. Turn pants to right side. Put on doll. Gather waist to fit.

For belt buckle, cut out of cardboard; cover with foil. Place leather strip for belt around waist and slip on buckle; glue. With buttonhole twist, make five loops around belt to hold belt in place. Cut 2" square of blue print fabric; hem edges. Fold and glue under belt at one side in back.

Cut scarf of red print fabric, hem edges, and tie around neck.

Continued on page 197

SQUARE DANCERS

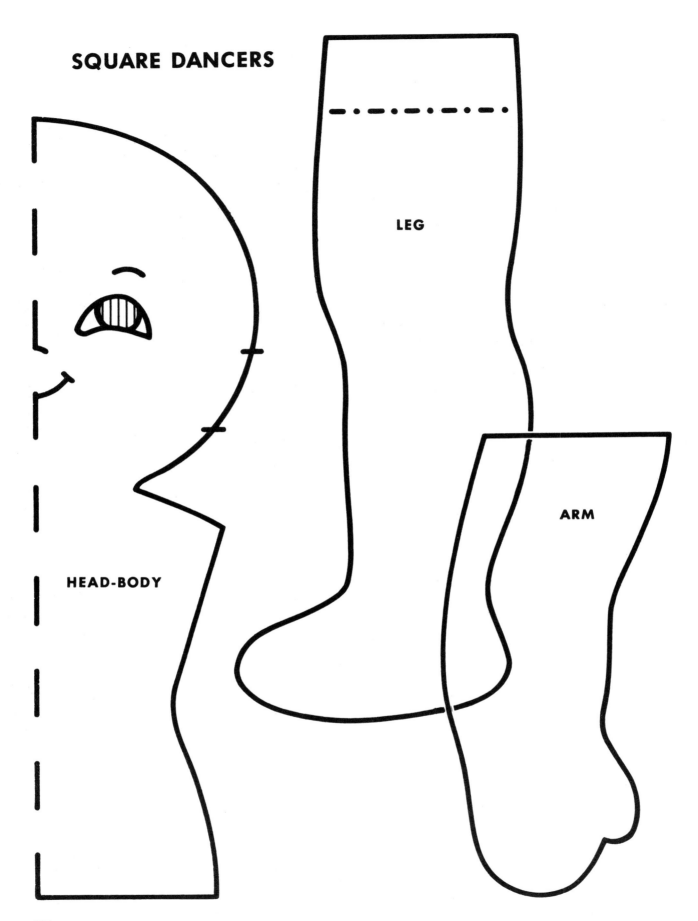

LEG

ARM

HEAD-BODY

COWBOY

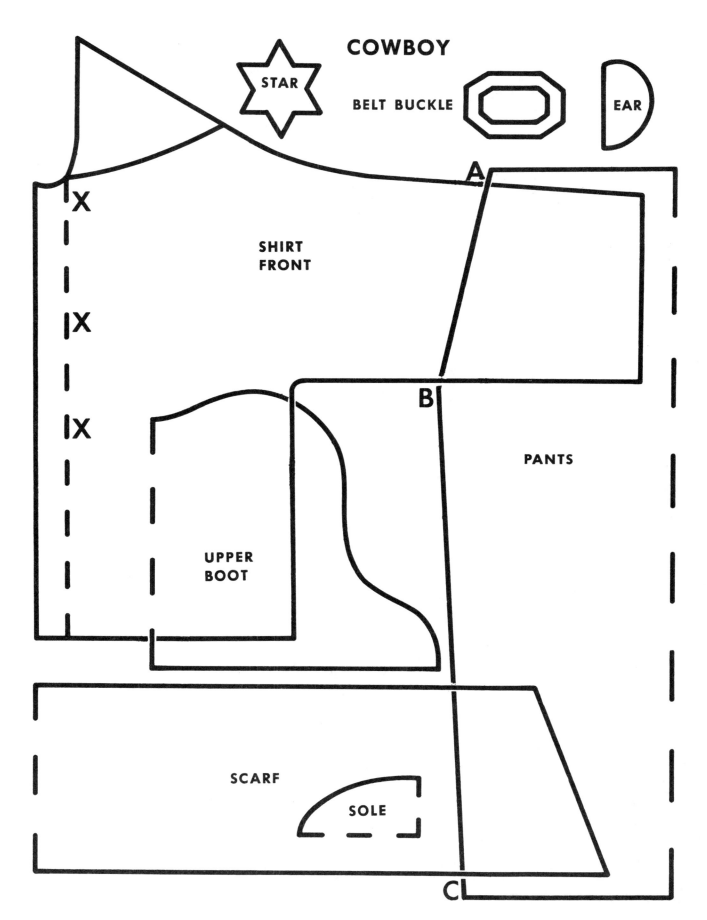

STAR

BELT BUCKLE

EAR

X

X

X

SHIRT
FRONT

A

B

PANTS

UPPER
BOOT

SCARF

SOLE

C

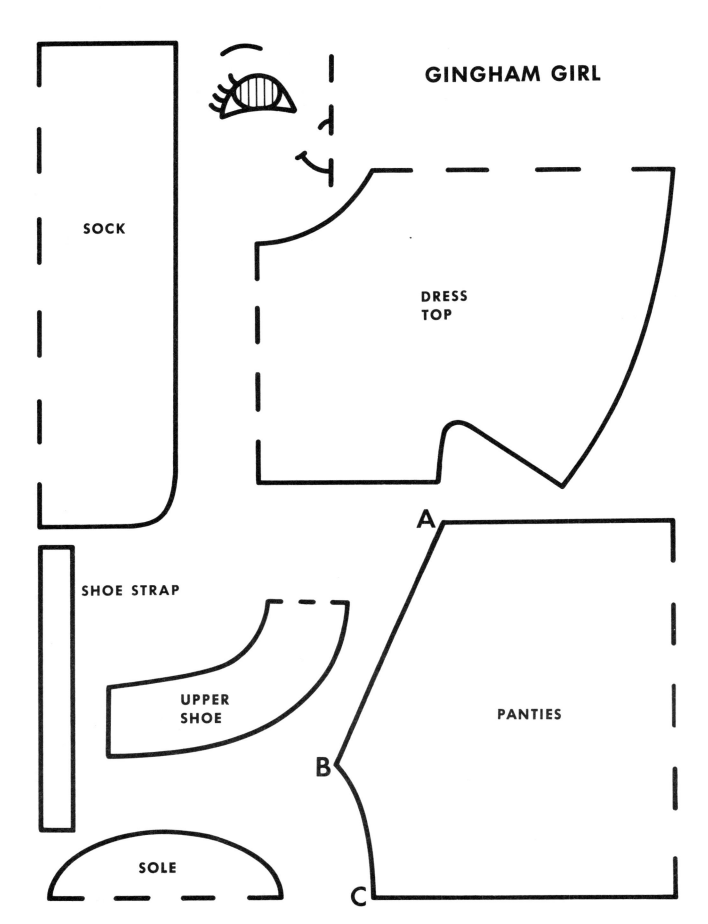

GINGHAM GIRL

SOCK

DRESS TOP

SHOE STRAP

UPPER SHOE

PANTIES

A

B

C

SOLE

Continued from page 193

For each boot, cut upper and sole of light beige felt. Fold upper in half and whip ends together; whip sole to upper. Turn boot to other side. Overcast top edges of each boot with matching sewing thread. Glue looped fringe around top edge. Cut two stars for each boot of darker beige felt. Glue star on each side of each boot. Put boots on doll.

Gingham Girl

Embroider mouth in red and rest of features in brown. Rouge cheeks.

For hair, cut about 30 strands of brown yarn, each about 21″ long. Arrange in two layers and across back of head, centering yarn strands at center of head. Stitch across yarn centers to secure yarn and to form a center part. Tack hair at each side on back of head; bring strands from one side over top of head and down opposite side; repeat with strands on other side. Arrange on top and front of head; sew across strands to continue part line to front. Gather strands at sides into bunches. Cut white ribbon in half; tie a piece around each bunch into bow.

For panties, cut two of plain white cotton. With right sides facing, sew center front and back seams (A to B). Then sew crotch seam (C to B to C). Hem each leg edge and waist. Turn to right side. Put on doll; gather at waist to fit; gather leg ends ½″ from edges.

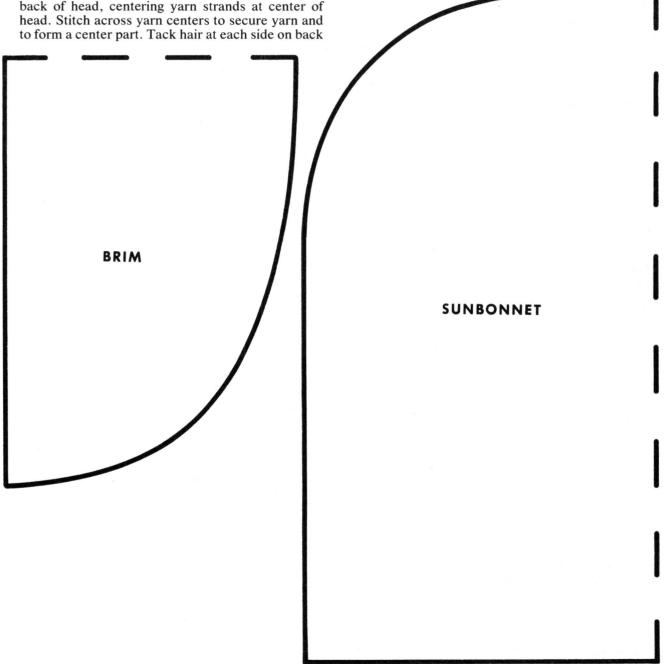

BRIM

SUNBONNET

For petticoat, cut dotted Swiss 3″ × 16″. Fold in half crosswise with right sides facing; sew ends together. Make hem at top and bottom. Turn to right side; sew eyelet edging around one (bottom) edge. Put on doll; gather waist to fit.

Cut dress top of gingham; fold in half at shoulder line with right sides facing. Sew underarm-side seams. Slash down one side (back) at half-pattern line. Hem neck and sleeve edges. Turn to right side. Sew two rows of rickrack all around neckline as shown. For dress skirt, cut gingham 5″ × 15″. Hem one long edge (bottom). For ruffle, cut gingham 1½″ × 36″. Hem long edges. Gather ¼″ from one edge to fit width of skirt and sew around bottom edge of skirt. Sew row of rickrack around skirt ¼″ above top edge of ruffle. Gather long raw edge of skirt to fit dress top and, with right sides facing, sew skirt and blouse together. Put dress on doll. Turn in back edges and sew closed. Gather sleeves ½″ from edge. For waistband, cut gingham strip 1″ × 6½″. With right sides facing, fold in half lengthwise and sew ends and long edge, leaving small opening. Turn to right side; sew opening closed. Tie band around waist, making bow in back.

For each sock, cut one of white stretch fabric. Fold in half with right sides facing; sew sides and bottom together. Turn to right side; put on foot; turn top edge under; tack to leg.

For each shoe, cut upper, sole, and strap of red felt. Fold upper in half and whip ends together; whip sole to upper. Turn shoe to other side. Put on foot. Tack strap ends on opposite sides of shoe front as shown. Sew button over outer strap end of each shoe.

Cut sunbonnet and two brims of gingham. With right sides of brims facing, sew curved edges together. Turn to right side. Hem straight edge of sunbonnet. Gather curved edge of sunbonnet to fit straight edge of brim. With right sides facing, sew gathered edge of sunbonnet to brim. For ties, sew length of ribbon to each side of sunbonnet. Place on head, tie under chin and then gather back bottom edge of sunbonnet to fit head. ◇

Block Clock
Shown on pages 138-139

EQUIPMENT: Paper for patterns. Tracing paper. Masking tape. Pencil. Ruler. Drill with 1″ and ¾″ bits. Handsaw and coping saw. Sandpaper. Compass. Small flat and pointed paintbrushes. Stencils for alphabet and letters, about ½″ to ¾″ tall and ½″ wide.

MATERIALS: Clear pine: 1¾″ × 7½″, 11″ long; ¾″ × 5″, 6″ long. Wooden dowels; ⅞″ diameter, 5½″ long; ⅝″ diameter, 2″ long. Medium-size can of gesso. Acrylic paints in tubes: light green, red, yellow, burnt umber, violet, blue, yellow oxide, black, white. Clear varnish for acrylic paints. All-purpose glue.

DIRECTIONS: Enlarge patterns by copying on paper ruled in 1″ squares; complete half-patterns and quarter-pattern indicated by long dash lines. Dotted lines indicate where pieces are to be cut. Trace patterns: trace each clock face separately; trace actual-size bird in place on clock pattern. Paint wood and dowels with two coats of gesso, drying between coats. Go over lines with pencil on wrong side of tracing. Place tracing (right side up) of one clock face on one surface of 1¾″-thick wood; tape paper to hold in place. Go over lines with pencil to transfer to wood. Remove tracing; go over lines on wood to darken if necessary. Do the same with other clock face and other surface of wood. Drill 1″-diameter hole in center where indicated by shaded area. With saw, cut wood into pieces where indicated by dotted lines; then cut top and bottom pieces in half along half-pattern line. For clock hands, transfer shapes and design lines to ¾″ wood and cut out as for clock. Drill 1″ hole in each piece of larger pair of hands; drill ¾″ hole in each piece of smaller pair of hands. For pins holding hands in place: cut a 1½″-diameter circle out of ¾″-thick wood; drill a ¾″ hole in center, ½″ deep. Cut a 3¾″ piece of ⅞″-diameter dowel; sand one end to taper, then insert and glue into hole in circle. This will be pin for larger hands. For smaller pin, drill ¾″ hole in one end of remaining piece of ⅞″ dowel, ¼″ deep. Insert and glue ⅝″ dowel piece into this hole.

Paint any edges which are not already painted with gesso; let dry. Paint cuckoo clock pieces as desired. For bold clock, clock face is green, clock face outline is violet, scrolls are white and background is yellow oxide. You can mix the colors given in materials to get various shades desired. Using any four colors of paint, paint the four edges of each of the five clock pieces a different color.

Divide each of the clock faces into 12 equal parts. With stencil, paint numbers in white on each surface, letting one side dry before turning to other side. Turn the five wooden pieces, with edges of same color up; paint alphabet on edges with black paint and stencil (see photograph). When dry, turn up all opposite edges and paint another alphabet in same manner. When dry, turn pieces to edges of one color and, with stencil, paint numbers 1 to 12 with white paint (see photograph). When dry, turn all pieces to remaining edges and paint numbers 13 to 24 in same manner. When dry, give each wooden piece a coat of clear varnish; let dry. ◇

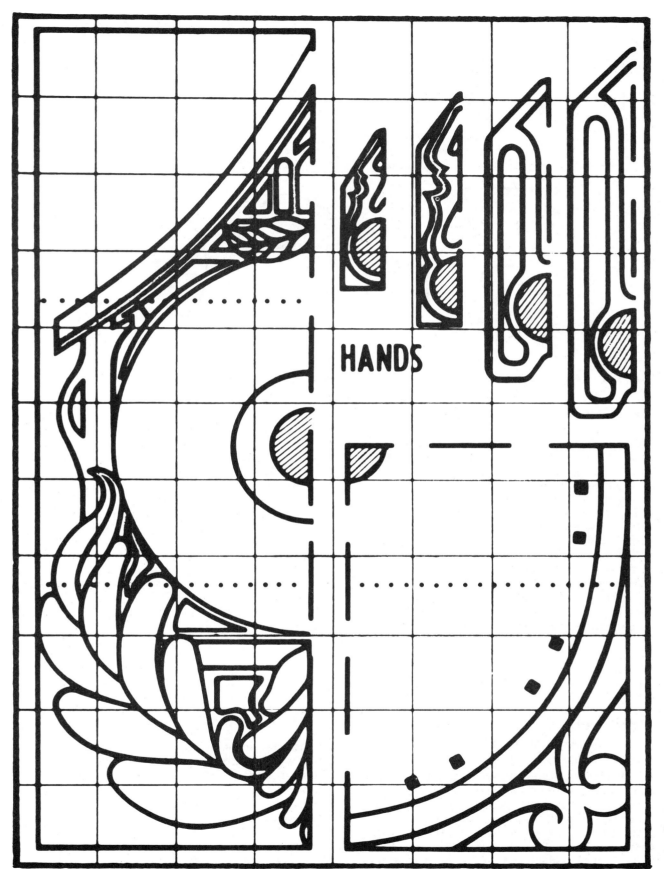

HANDS

Super Dominoes

Shown on page 140

EQUIPMENT: Tracing paper. Pencil. Ruler. Scissors. Sandpaper. Pointed and flat paintbrushes. Handsaw. Nail.

MATERIALS: Flat wood molding, $2\frac{1}{4}''$ wide $\times$ $\frac{1}{4}''$ thick, 10' long. Black felt-tipped marking pen. Acrylic paints in six colors. Gift-wrap paper and two complementary colors of acrylic paint. Clear acrylic spray. All-purpose glue.

DIRECTIONS: Trace patterns for numbers and complete half-pattern for the 0.

Saw molding into 28 pieces 4" long. Sand the edges of the wooden pieces. Score each piece with nail crosswise across center; mark line with fine, black felt-tipped pen. Trace numbers on the wooden pieces, each number facing the end. These are the number combinations needed: 0/0, 0/1, 0/2, 0/3, 0/4, 0/5, 0/6,

1/1, 1/2, 1/3, 1/4, 1/5, 1/6, 2/2, 2/3, 2/4, 2/5, 2/6, 3/3, 3/4, 3/5, 3/6, 4/4, 4/5, 4/6, 5/5, 5/6, 6/6. Paint the numbers in desired colors; use one color for the same numbers on all pieces. Let dry. Turn wooden pieces to other side. Paint this surface and all edges; paint 14 in one color and 14 in a contrasting color. Let dry. Cut rectangles out of wrapping paper $\frac{1}{4}''$ smaller all around than dominoes. Glue one on plain painted surface of each domino. Give all surfaces of each domino two coats of clear acrylic spray, drying between coats.

To play, turn dominoes so that numbers are face down; players select equal number of dominoes. Players try to match numbers end to end. If player cannot go, he loses turn. First player who uses up all his dominoes wins. ◊

Desk Set

Shown on page 153

SIZE: Desk: $15\frac{1}{2}'' \times 12\frac{1}{2}'' \times 2\frac{7}{8}''$.

EQUIPMENT: Ruler. Pencil. Coping saw. Hammer. Coarse and fine sandpaper. Flat brush, $\frac{1}{2}''$, for applying polyurethane. Single-edged razor blade. Miter box. Countersink (or large nail).

MATERIALS: Plywood $\frac{1}{4}''$ thick, $21\frac{1}{2}'' \times 15''$ sheet. Lattice stripping, $\frac{1}{4}''$ thick: $5'\frac{1}{2}''$ of $2\frac{5}{8}''$ wide, $1\frac{1}{4}'$ of $1\frac{5}{8}''$ wide, 2' of $1\frac{1}{8}''$ wide, and 5' of $\frac{7}{8}''$ wide. Two different but coordinating print vinyl fabrics, (one small, one bold), each 36" wide, $\frac{3}{8}$ yard. Compatible polka-dot

cotton fabric, 36" wide, $\frac{3}{8}$ yard, for lining. White felt, 36" wide, $\frac{3}{8}$ yard, for padding. Cardboard, $\frac{1}{16}''$ thick, one sheet 8" $\times$ 10". All-purpose glue. Spray adhesive. Matte-finish polyurethane. About 18 small-headed 1" nails. Four 1" brads. Plastic wood. Masking tape.

Desk

Cut the following pieces: From plywood, one bottom 12" $\times$ 15"; from $2\frac{5}{8}''$ stripping, two sides each $11\frac{1}{2}''$ long, one back 15" long, one divider $14\frac{1}{2}''$ long;

from $1\frac{5}{8}''$ stripping, one front 15″ long; from $\frac{7}{8}''$ stripping, four pieces of trim, two $15\frac{1}{2}''$ long and two $12\frac{1}{2}''$ long.

Following Diag. 1, measure and cut out side pieces. Starting at point A on one long side, cut away shaded area to point B. Following Diag. 2, miter ends of trim pieces 45°. Sand side pieces and trim.

To assemble desk, follow Diag. 3. First glue back and front piece to top of bottom piece, keeping outside edges flush. Glue side pieces to bottom between front and back pieces. *Note:* The wide end of side pieces will be flush with the back piece at top edges; the narrow end of side pieces will be $\frac{1}{4}''$ shorter than front piece, creating a lip across front of box. Using one brad at each end, nail front piece to sides. Using a countersink or point of large nail, drive the brad just below the wood surface; fill hole with plastic wood. Nail back to sides in same manner. Turn box bottom-side up. Using three nails evenly spaced for each side, nail bottom to back, front, and side pieces. Turn box right side up.

From dotted fabric, cut a piece $11\frac{1}{2}'' \times 14\frac{1}{2}''$. Spray wrong side with adhesive and press on inside bottom of box.

Following Diag. 4, glue trim pieces to outside of box with bottom edges flush; fill in mitered corners with plastic wood if necessary for a flush join; glue divider piece into place, $1\frac{5}{8}''$ in from back piece, lining ends up to points A on sides.

Sand outside of box, first with coarse sandpaper and then with fine. Brush away all sawdust residue. Apply two coats of polyurethane to outside of box; let dry between coats.

Blotter

(Desk top): Cut a $9\frac{3}{8}'' \times 15''$ piece from plywood. For sides, cut two $2\frac{1}{4}'' \times 9\frac{3}{8}''$ strips from $\frac{1}{16}''$-thick cardboard. For padding, cut one piece $9\frac{3}{8}'' \times 15''$ and two pieces $2\frac{1}{4}'' \times 9\frac{3}{8}''$ from felt. Glue felt to one surface of wood and cardboard pieces. For covering, cut one $12'' \times 18''$ piece from small-print vinyl; cut two pieces $4\frac{1}{2}'' \times 12\frac{1}{2}''$ from bold-print vinyl.

To cover, lay large piece of vinyl fabric wrong side up on work surface; spray fabric with adhesive; place plywood, padded side down, on center of fabric; fold fabric ends over plywood. Glue. For each blotter end, lay vinyl strip, wrong side up, on work surface; spray with adhesive; place cardboard, padded side down, on center of fabric. Fold over and glue only one long side (to be the inside edge of the finished blotter end). To attach ends to blotter, place one on either side of blotter top. Tape inside edge to hold in place (remove tape when blotter is complete). Turn blotter wrong side up; glue remaining fabric edges of blotter ends to bottom of plywood; miter and trim corners neatly. Cut 9″ × $14\frac{1}{2}''$ piece of dotted fabric; spray wrong side with adhesive and press onto bottom, covering all edges of vinyl fabric.

Tray

From $2\frac{5}{8}''$ stripping, cut one 8″-long piece for tray bottom. From $1\frac{1}{8}''$ stripping, cut two pieces 8″ long for sides and two pieces $2\frac{1}{8}''$ long for ends. Following assembly for desk, glue sides and ends to bottom. Sand and polyurethane as for desk.

Pencil Holder

Cut one 3″ × 9″ strip from cardboard. Using ruler and pencil, mark off strip into four sections as follows: Measure 2″ for first section, $2\frac{1}{2}''$ for second, and 2″ for third, leaving $2\frac{1}{2}''$ for the fourth. Score pencil lines with razor blade; fold strip on scored lines (with scoring to the outside) to form four sides of a bottomless box. Tape seam closed.

To cover, cut one $2\frac{3}{4}'' \times 9\frac{1}{2}''$ strip for inside and one $3\frac{1}{2}'' \times 9\frac{1}{2}''$ strip for outside from small-print vinyl fabric. Spray wrong side of wider strip with adhesive. Keeping bottom edges of fabric even with bottom edge of holder, press onto outside, overlapping seam edge. Clip corners of excess fabric at top of holder; fold and glue to inside. Spray narrower strip on wrong side with adhesive and press to inside of holder, keeping bottom edges even and overlapping seam. Place holder in tray. ◊

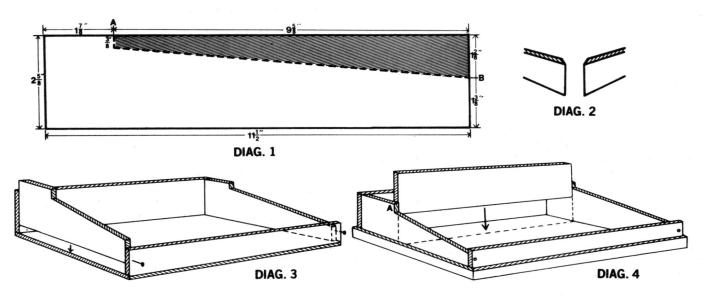

DIAG. 1

DIAG. 2

DIAG. 3

DIAG. 4

Covered Boxes

Shown on page 153

SIZE OF EMBROIDERED AREAS: Square, 8″ × 8″. Round, 7½″ diameter. Rectangle, 2½″ × 7½″.

EQUIPMENT: Pencil. Ruler. Tape measure. Scissors. Tracing paper. Dressmaker's tracing (carbon) paper. Dry ball-point pen. Crewel needle. Embroi-

dery hoop. Flat brush for spreading glue, ½″ wide. Padded ironing board. Steam iron.

MATERIALS: Cardboard boxes, larger than embroidered areas. Natural linen or linen-like fabric (see directions for measuring specific amounts). DMC

pearl cotton: size 5, 27-yard skeins: bright orange #946, three; yellow-orange #741, two; yellow #307, one; Size 8, one 95-yard ball brown #975. Batting. All-purpose glue. Light-weight cardboard. Adhesive-backed vinyl paper.

DIRECTIONS: Each box is covered with fabric, which has been carefully measured to fit. For each type of box, cut a piece of cardboard ⅛″ shorter and

⅛″ narrower than inside dimensions of box, for bottom insert. Cut another cardboard insert for lid, in same manner.

To Measure and Cut the Fabric: Square and Rectangular Boxes: For box lids, measure length and width of lid; add double the rim depth plus 1″ all around. Cut out fabric in one piece. For box bottom, measure perimeter of box and add ¾″ for length;

1 Bright Orange
2 Yellow Orange
3 Yellow

Fig. 1

Fig. 2

Fig. 3

measure the side depth, double it, and add 2" for width. Cut out fabric in one piece. For each insert, cut one piece of fabric the length and width plus $\frac{1}{4}$" all around.

Round Box: Place the box lid on fabric; trace around edge; add $\frac{1}{4}$" all around; cut out. For rim strip, measure the perimeter and add $\frac{1}{2}$" for length; measure the depth, double it, and add $\frac{3}{4}$" for width; cut out strip. For box bottom, measure and cut as for rim strip but add 1" for length and $1\frac{1}{4}$" for width. For each insert, cut one piece as for lid.

To Embroider: Trace patterns on pages 202 and 203; complete half and quarter patterns indicated by dash lines. (For round design, see color illustration and note placement of finials on the four main flowers.) Center tracing on right side of fabric cut for box lids, with dressmaker's carbon between. Transfer designs to fabric by tracing over lines of pattern with pencil or dry ball-point pen. Remove patterns and carbon. Insert fabric tautly in embroidery hoop, centering design area. Begin embroidery by leaving end of floss on back and working over it as you stitch to secure; end by running strand through stitches on back. Do not make knots. Using brown pearl cotton, work all stems in outline stitch, leaves in satin stitch, and tiny stem ends in straight stitch. Following color key, work flowers, buds, and berries in satin stitch. See Contents for stitch details. In round pattern, alternate the color of the finial at the top of each main flower, making two bright orange and two yellow-orange.

To block, place finished embroidery face down on padded board; steam.

To Cover the Boxes: Rectangular and Square Boxes: For box lid, cut a piece of batting the same size as top of lid and glue to the outside. Lay embroidered fabric, wrong side up, on work surface; center box lid, padding side down, on fabric: Following Fig. 1, slit sides of extending fabric on short dash lines; spread glue on sides. Fold fabric sides A and B over box rim first; smooth fabric around corners; clip where fabric meets underside of box lid, and press down flat. Fold sides C and D over rim, clip and glue in same manner as for A and B.

Center box lid insert on wrong side of fabric; fold edges over cardboard; clip and glue. Glue insert, covered side out to inside of box lid.

For box bottom, spread glue on sides, inside and out. With right side out, fold side piece in half lengthwise and, starting 1" before a box corner, drape folded strip over sides of box; smooth around corners and overlap seam; fold outside excess fabric under box bottom; clip corners and glue down. Do the same for inside excess fabric. Cover box bottom insert as for lid; glue in place. From adhesive-backed vinyl, cut a piece $\frac{1}{16}$" smaller all around than box bottom. Press onto outside of box bottom.

Round Box: For the box lid, cut a piece of batting the same size as top of lid; glue to the outside. Lay embroidered fabric wrong side up on work surface; center box lid, padding side down, on fabric. Clip edges $\frac{1}{4}$" in, about every 1". Spread glue on outside of rim and press fabric edges onto rim. Fold rim strip $\frac{1}{4}$" under to wrong side along one long edge; press. With right side out and folded edge flush with top edge of lid, glue strip to outside of rim, overlapping seam; fold fabric at rim edge to inside; glue to inside rim; clip excess every $\frac{1}{2}$" and glue to inside of box lid. Cover cardboard inserts and finish box as for other boxes.

To trim edge of lid, work herringbone stitch (Fig. 2) with bright orange pearl cotton and then work straight stitch over it (Fig. 3) with brown pearl cotton. ◇

Stenciled Candles

Shown on page 155

EQUIPMENT: *For Stenciling:* Paper for patterns. Pencil. Ruler. Tracing paper. Stencil paper. Rubber cement. Glass or other hard surface for cutting stencil. X-acto knife with #11 blade. Masking tape. Paint thinner and cotton swab. *For making large green candle:* Newspapers. Waxed paper. Metal candle mold 6" diameter, $6\frac{1}{2}$" high. Double boiler or large can and a larger sauce pan. Stick for stirring. Cooking oil. Candy thermometer.

MATERIALS: *For Blue, White, Orange, and Brown Candles:* Store-bought candles large enough to accommodate designs (see patterns): ours are 3" diamater, 6" and 9" tall; 4" diameter, $3\frac{3}{4}$" tall. *For green candle:* About $5\frac{1}{2}$ pounds paraffin wax. Dark green wax dye. Stearic acid. Candlewick. *For all:* Wax metallic color in Classic Treasure Gold.

DIRECTIONS: *Green Candle:* Cover work area with newspapers and waxed paper to catch spilled wax.

Melt all but $\frac{1}{4}$ pound of wax in top of double boiler or in large can set in pan of water. *Never melt wax over direct heat or leave unattended on a lit stove.*

Add stearic acid according to package instructions that come with mold. For color, gradually add pieces of candle dye to melted wax to get a very dark green color (darker than desired since color will lighten as wax solidifies).

Lightly coat inside of mold with oil. Prepare wicks, following instructions that come with mold.

Before pouring wax, make sure temperature of wax is about 150°F. Pour hot wax into mold to a height of 6". Let candle cool for about eight hours. As the wax hardens, a cavity will form in center. Melt the remaining wax without color dye and pour into cavity; cool thoroughly. Remove candle from mold as indicated in instructions that come with mold. Trim uneven edges with knife.

Continued on page 206

Continued from page 204

Stenciling: Trace full size patterns; complete half-patterns indicated by dash lines.

To Cut Stencils: Cement tracing at corners and edges onto stencil paper. Place stencil paper on glass surface. With knife, cut out design areas indicated by shading on pattern. When cutting, hold knife at slight angle, pointing toward cutout area to make slightly beveled edge. Cut all the way through in one stroke so edges will be clean. Turn stencil paper so that you always cut toward you. When design is completely cut out, remove tracing.

Although we give specific directions for these candles, you can plan designs and repeat motifs as desired.

Tape stencil in place on candle. Apply gold color with finger in a dabbing or stippling motion. When all areas have been colored, remove stencil carefully and let dry thoroughly. You can clean up edges with paint thinner and cotton swabs, if necessary.

Stencil design A vertically on brown candle and horizontally on white candle. Stencil design B on green candle. Stencil design C twice around top and bottom edges of blue candle. Stencil design D three times around orange candle.

To make bands of gold around top and bottom of candle if desired (see illustration), tape two strips of tape around candle, leaving $\frac{1}{4}''$ space between. Apply gold color between tape with finger. When dry, remove tape.

Because the gold color comes off easily, handle candles carefully. ◊

Paper Portfolios

Shown on page 154

SIZE: $9\frac{3}{4}'' \times 13''$.

EQUIPMENT: Pencil. Ruler. Scissors. Dressmaker's tracing (carbon) paper. Iron.

MATERIALS (for each portfolio): One sheet patterned end paper, at least $17'' \times 25''$. $\frac{1}{2}$ yard solid color linen or linen-textured fabric. $1\frac{1}{4}$ yards grosgrain ribbon, approximately $\frac{5}{8}''$ wide. $\frac{3}{4}$ yard fusible webbing, 21'' wide. White glue. Paper for pattern. Masking tape.

DIRECTIONS: Enlarge pattern shown in diagram onto paper ruled in 1'' squares. Mark $\frac{1}{4}''$ margins, fold lines, and $\frac{3}{4}''$-wide slash lines in Section 2. Cut out pattern and trace outline on wrong side of patterned end paper; cut along outline.

Use same pattern to cut fabric lining and fusible webbing. Using dressmaker's tracing paper and tracing wheel, trace fold lines and slash lines on right side of fabric. Trim $\frac{1}{4}''$ margins from fabric edges where marked on pattern. Center fabric over webbing, right side up, and pin in place. Trim edges of fusible webbing just inside edges of fabric.

Center fabric on wrong side of end paper, webbing side down, with $\frac{1}{4}''$ margins of paper extending beyond edges of fabric. Temporarily tape fabric to paper along margins, with four small pieces of tape. Pressing with steam or a wet cloth is usually recommended for fusing two fabrics together; *do not do so when fusing paper,* since dampness will cause most papers to buckle. Instead, press firmly with a hot, *dry* iron for a longer length of time than usual to fuse fabric to paper. When cool, cut through both thicknesses along slash lines. Clip into margins at two corners of Section 2 as indicated. Fold all margins of paper over edges of fabric and finger-press firmly, folding mitered corners; then glue to fabric, gluing side margins first and then margins at both ends.

With fabric side up, fold side edges of Section 1 towards center along solid lines, then fold outward

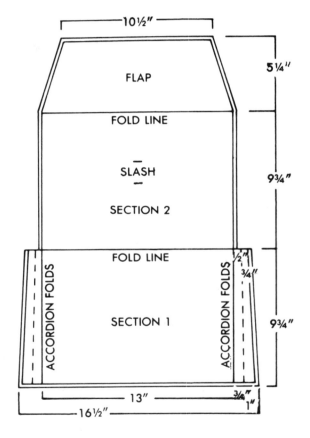

along broken lines to form accordion pleats. Press pleats down firmly with a cool dry iron and dry press cloth. Cover turned-in margins of Section 1 and Section 2 with glue. Fold Section 1 over Section 2 along fold line; with side edges even, press down firmly to glue edges together. Fold flap over Section 1 along fold line. Place several heavy books on top of envelope until glue is thoroughly dry. Draw ribbon through slash lines on back of portfolio and tie in front. ◊

Pressed Flower Designs

Shown on pages 156-157

EQUIPMENT: Telephone book. Paper towels. Boxes. Fine paintbrushes. Ruler. Pencil. Scissors. Fine curved scissors such as cuticle or decoupage scissors. Cotton swabs. Facial tissues. Iron.

MATERIALS: Small flowers, leaves and grasses. Watercolor paints. Magazines, catalogues, etc. with color photographs of vases. White or off-white heavy matt-finish paper, desired size. White glue. Clear self-adhesive protective plastic covering.

DIRECTIONS: *Drying Flowers and Leaves:* Gather flowers and leaves during midday when moisture has been dried by the sun. Never pick on cloudy days; stems have too much moisture and blossoms will wrinkle in drying. Pick only blossoms and leaves in perfect condition, in peak of bloom; if too mature, they will shatter in drying. Flowers with single layer of petals press more satisfactorily than blossoms with thick centers and many petals. Pick about twice as many flowers and leaves as you think you will need; press immediately to capture freshness.

Dry flowers and leaves in a telephone book, placing them carefully every eight or nine pages, face down. To curve some stems, gently shape by hand. Top with a light weight, such as a book. Keep in a dry, dark place (most basements are too damp). Allow to remain undisturbed for at least two weeks. When ready for use, carefully remove and place flowers and leaves on paper towels, layered in boxes.

Making Pictures: Paint any faded flowers with watercolors. Use only a small amount of paint; soaking will distort petals. Let dry.

With curved scissors, carefully cut out several vases in appropriate sizes from magazines or catalogues. Cut matt-finish paper to desired size. Plan flower arrangement on a separate piece of paper, keeping it light and airy; choose a vase to fit "bouquet."

Glue flowers and leaves, one at a time, to the cut paper, as follows: Dilute glue with a few drops of water to a consistency of medium cream. Coat back of flower or leaf with glue, using a cotton swab. Apply flower to paper, patting quickly with facial tissue to absorb excess glue; be careful that tissue doesn't stick. Place paper face down on a padded surface, such as an ironing board or table top covered with a towel. Press a cold iron on paper for a few minutes. Repeat gluing and pressing for each flower and leaf. Glue cut-out vase over stem ends in same manner. Let picture dry thoroughly.

Cut a piece of self-adhesive clear plastic covering, slightly larger than your picture; use it to seal arrangement, according to manufacturer's directions. Trim away excess. Finish piece as desired, to make notecards, bookmarks, place cards, framed pictures, etc. ◇

Woodland Creatures Plant Cover

Shown on page 153

SIZE: Cover measures 13½" diameter, 11½" high; fits pot 13" diameter, 11" high.

EQUIPMENT: Pencil. Ruler. Scissors. Dressmaker's carbon paper. Tracing paper. Tracing wheel or dry ball-point pen. Sewing and embroidery needles. Tailor's chalk. Sewing machine. Masking tape. Straight pins.

MATERIALS: Muslin, 45" wide, 1⅛ yards. Polyester batting. Six-strand embroidery floss, one skein brown and two skeins green.

DIRECTIONS: Cut three pieces of muslin, 11¾" × 42", one to be embroidered, one to back batting and one for lining. Cut one strip of muslin, 3½" × 42" for padded bottom edge roll. Cut one piece of batting, 11¾" × 42". Trace actual-size patterns. Transfer designs to one piece of muslin. *Note:* Place animals (two of each, alternately) 1¼" above lower long edge of muslin, 1½" in from short side edges, and 2" apart. Place foliage (seven clusters) ⅝" below upper long edge and ⅜" apart. See Placement Diagram. To transfer designs, place tracing on muslin with dressmaker's carbon paper between. Tape tracing and carbon to muslin to hold in place. Using dry ball-point pen, transfer all design lines to muslin. Remove tracing and carbon. Repeat until all multiple designs are transferred.

Pin the designed piece of muslin to a plain piece, with wrong sides facing and batting between. Baste the three pieces together ½" in from all edges. Using two strands of floss in needle, embroider design through all thickness with running stitch (see Contents for stitch details). Work animals in brown and foliage in green.

Fold 3½" × 42" strip of muslin in half lengthwise. Make a 1" diameter roll of batting to fit length of strip. Place batting into fold, pinning in place as you fill strip; baste 1¼" up from folded edge. When completed, machine stitch over basting.

Place padded strip on right side of quilted piece

with raw edge flush at bottom; pin lining piece of muslin on top. Fold short side edges of lining piece back $\frac{3}{4}''$ so that raw edge is facing front. Baste and sew through all thicknesses with $\frac{1}{2}''$ seams on two long sides, leaving short sides open for turning. Turn to right side. With embroidered side inward, sew short sides together $\frac{1}{2}''$ in from raw edges (do not catch folded edges of lining piece in this seam). Press seam open and tuck raw edges under folded edge of lining. Slip-stitch lining down. ◇

Silk Flowers

Shown on page 158

EQUIPMENT: Paper for pattern. Ruler. Pencil. Stiff, thin cardboard. Iron. Small containers for painting. Wire cutters. Scissors. *For dyeing:* Pan for dyeing silk. Old towels. Small and medium fine-pointed paintbrushes.

MATERIALS: White China silk 36″ wide, ½ yard makes six tulips or four lilies or about nine leaves. (Colored silk may be used instead of dyeing white fabric: lemon yellow for tulips, light orange for lilies, and green for leaves.) Inks for dyeing and painting: orange, yellow, emerald, sea green, red, brown, and fuchsia (watercolor paints may be used instead of inks). Florists' wire: white-covered fine and very fine; green-covered medium and heavy. Florists' tape. Small amount of absorbent cotton. Spray starch. All-purpose glue. Basket or bowl and plastic foam block to fit. Dried moss.

GENERAL DIRECTIONS: *To Dye Silk:* Add ink to pan of water to color intensity desired. Silk will dry a few shades lighter than dye solution. Dilute ink to pale colors for flower petals; light colors for leaves. Dip silk into diluted ink for several minutes; remove, do not wring. Press silk flat between towels until most of the moisture is absorbed. With iron set at silk setting, press silk dry, being careful not to scorch. Use spray starch to stiffen silk.

To Make Pattern: Trace full size patterns; complete half and quarter-patterns indicated by dash lines. Cut each pattern out and mark separately on piece of cardboard. Cut out cardboard patterns. Cut off tip straight across one end of each leaf; this will be bottom end.

Place cardboard patterns on the bias of silk, and mark outlines. You will need six petals for each flower, about ten leaves for tulip arrangement and about 25 leaves for lily arrangement.

Before cutting petals and leaves out of silk, paint them with inks or watercolors.

Painting with Ink: Dip brush in ink, let excess drip back into bottle and then, with quick even strokes, always in the same direction, brush color onto silk. Test paint on silk scraps before painting actual pieces. Do not let brush remain on any one spot too long, because ink will bleed. To darken areas, repaint. See individual directions for petal and leaf painting technique.

Painting with Watercolors: Brush silk with watercolors mixed with water to a pasty consistency. Follow directions above for painting.

To Assemble and Arrange: When ink or paint is completely dry, cut out petals and leaves. Cut a medium green wire, 17″ long, for each leaf. Glue wire along length of center back of each leaf, leaving 1½″ of silk at top. Cut fine white wire, 5″ long, and glue one to each petal as for leaf, but only 1″ from top petal edge. Refer to individual directions for specific assembling. Bend leaves down slightly for

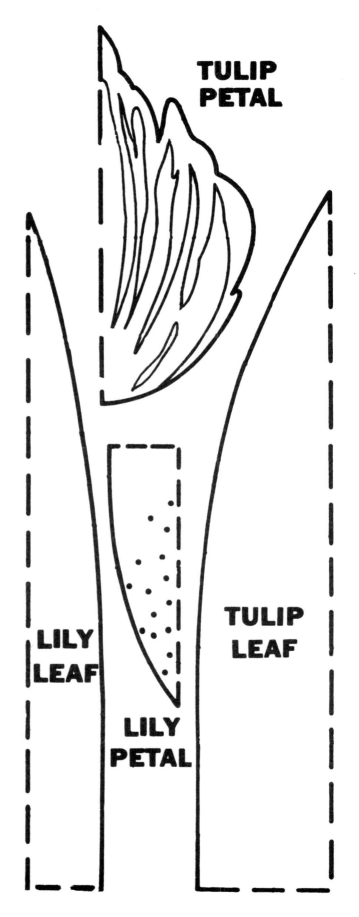

TULIP PETAL

LILY LEAF

TULIP LEAF

LILY PETAL

a more natural look. Insert flower wire stems into plastic foam in desired arrangement. Place plastic foam in basket and cover with dried moss.

Tulips

Dye silk for petals of all a pale yellow.

Painting: Using red, yellow, orange, or fuchsia, brush from center bottom toward petal edges and top. With a somewhat dry fine-pointed brush, paint vein lines indicated by fine line on pattern. Outline all edges of petals in same color.

Dye silk for leaves light sea green. With a medium brush, paint leaves with broad lengthwise strokes of full strength sea green.

To Make Center: Cut six 4½″ lengths of fine wire; paint all yellow. Apply small wads of cotton at end of each; glue and dip into brown ink or watercolor.

Tape to one end of heavy wire, cut 9″ long. Arrange six tulip petals around center with fine white wire veins on inside; tape. Bend petals inward. Wrap tape around entire stem.

Lilies

Dye silk pale orange.

Painting: Brush orange color along petal edges. Darken area around petal tip. With a fine-pointed brush, dot petal base and center with brown as indicated by dots on pattern. Dye leaves medium emerald green. Paint leaves with fine lengthwise strokes of full strength emerald green for shading.

To Make Center: Prepare one wire with cotton tip as for tulip. Cut six 4½″-long pieces of wire; paint yellow. Then paint 1½″ of one end of each brown. When dry, fold brown end down in thirds.

Gather these wires around the cotton-tipped wire; tape to the end of a heavy wire, cut 19″ long. Arrange six lily petals around center with fine white wire veins facing out; tape. Bend petals down slightly. Wrap tape around entire stem. ◊

French Knot Bouquet

Shown on page 159

SIZE: Embroidered circle, 8¼″ diameter; framed picture, 11″ square.

EQUIPMENT: Pencil. Ruler. Scissors. Tracing paper. Dressmaker's tracing (carbon) paper, yellow or white. Dry ball-point pen. Masking tape. Embroidery hoop, 10″. Embroidery needle. Compass. Mat knife. *For Blocking:* Softwood surface. Brown paper. Rustproof thumbtacks. Small tack hammer. Towel. T-square.

MATERIALS: Jade green brushed cotton fabric with herringbone twill pattern, 15″ square. Paternayan Persian yarn, one 8-yard skein of each color in key, unless otherwise indicated in parentheses. *For Mounting:* Illustration board, two 11″ squares. Vanilla closely woven cotton fabric, 15″ square. Batting, 9″-square piece. Ecru lace edging ¾″ wide, ⅞ yard. Glue. Masking tape. Two packages metal frame strips to make frame with 11″-square rabbet edge.

DIRECTIONS: Trace pattern on next page; heavy lines are straight or outline stitches; fine lines are fly stitches; open ovals are lazy daisy stitches. Symbols are French knots, keyed for color. Center pattern right side up on right side of green fabric with carbon between; tape both in place. Using dry ball-point pen, transfer all design lines to fabric. Remove tracing and carbon. Tape fabric edges to prevent raveling.

To Embroider: Place green fabric in embroidery hoop, centering design and keeping fabric smooth and taut. Separate strands of yarn and work with one strand in needle for lazy daisy and fly stitches; work with two strands for French knots and straight or outline stitches. See Contents for stitch details.

Begin first strand by leaving end on back, working over it to secure; end and begin subsequent strands by running strand through worked stitches on back.

Work all fly stitches with light olive then all straight or outline stitches with dark seafoam. Next, work lazy daisy stitches with aqua, pastel blue and yellow randomly, or following color photograph. Finally, work all French knots, following pattern and key for colors. When embroidery is complete, remove from hoop and block as directed below.

To Block: Cover softwood surface with brown paper; secure with thumbtacks. Draw a 15″ square on paper for guidelines, using square for corners. Place embroidery right side up on paper; stretch cloth to match guidelines and tack in place. Tack corners first, then the center of each side; continue placing tacks until there is a solid border of tacks around entire edge, dividing and subdividing spaces between thumbtacks already placed; hammer in tacks or they will pop out as fabric dries. Cover embroidery with damp towel; let dry.

To Mount: Find and mark the center point of one 11″-square illustration board by drawing vertical and horizontal lines between opposite sides; lines will cross at center point. Using center point and compass set for 4⅛″ radius, mark an 8¼″ circle. Using mat knife, cut out circle and discard. Center board on batting and mark outline of cut-out circle on batting; cut batting on marked line and set aside. Center board on fabric and lightly mark outline of cut-out circle on fabric; cut out circle at least ½″ inside marked line and discard. Place fabric wrong side up on work surface; center board on fabric and glue, making sure that fabric stays smooth. Fold excess fabric around circle to back of board, snipping edges to ease curves, and glue. Fold straight edges of fabric to back of board, cutting corners to lie flat, and glue. Trim right side of covered board by gluing ecru edging around cutout, with edges flush (see color illustration).

Place embroidery, right side down, on work sur-face; center batting on fabric. Cover batting with uncut illustration board, centered on fabric. Fold excess fabric to back of board, cutting corners to lie flat and pulling tautly; tape securely in place.

Assemble metal frame, following manufacturer's directions; place embroidery and trimmed board in frame so that padded stitched area is centered in opening. ◇

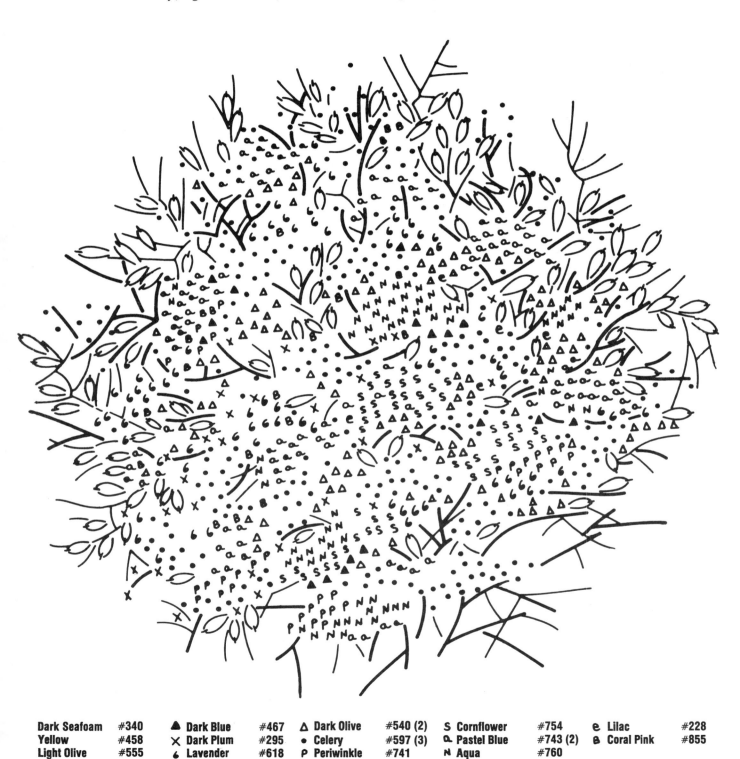

Dark Seafoam	#340	▲ Dark Blue	#467	△ Dark Olive	#540 (2)	S Cornflower	#754	e Lilac	#228
Yellow	#458	✕ Dark Plum	#295	• Celery	#597 (3)	ᴖ Pastel Blue	#743 (2)	ᴃ Coral Pink	#855
Light Olive	#555	ι Lavender	#618	ᴘ Periwinkle	#741	ᴎ Aqua	#760		

Garden Needlepoint

Shown on page 159

SIZES: Pillow, 6″ × 8½″. Pencil Holder, 2¾″ × 4⅞″. Bookend, 4⅝″ × 5½″. Picture, 3¼″ square.

EQUIPMENT: Masking tape. Scissors. Tapestry and sewing needles. Waterproof marking pen, pale color. *For Blocking:* Softwood surface. Brown paper. Rustproof thumbtacks. Square. Pencil.

MATERIALS: Mono needlepoint canvas. Persian 3-strand yarn. See individual directions for amounts and additional materials.

GENERAL DIRECTIONS: Tape edges of canvas to prevent raveling. Mark canvas as directed for each piece, using pale waterproof marking pen; there will be a 2″ margin all around finished piece.

To Work Needlepoint: Cut yarn into 18″ lengths. Separate the three strands of yarn and work with one or two strands in needle as directed. When starting first strand, leave 1″ of yarn on back of canvas and cover it as work proceeds; your first few stitches will anchor it in place. To end strand or begin a new one, run yarn under a few stitches on back of work; do not make knots. Keep yarn tension firm and even. Stitching tends to twist the working thread; now and then let yarn and needle hang straight down to untwist.

Follow chart and individual directions to work each design. Each square on chart equals one hole on canvas. Flowers are indicated on charts by circles. For each flower, work an eyelet variation, using one strand in needle: Working around a center hole, make 14–16 stitches, mostly over two meshes but occasionally over one or three meshes to vary the shape; pull stitches slightly to keep center hole open; see details. Shaded areas indicate variegated green foliage. Work flowers within each shaded area

first, varying size of each as desired, then fill in remaining area around flowers with greens: Using three shades of green yarn, separate strands of each then recombine in pairs, using two different greens in each pair; work foliage in plain needlepoint, using continental stitch; see details. Work open background areas in needlepoint. Work other design areas following individual directions. Begin each stitch in same mesh as a previous stitch, as shown on charts. For embroidery stitches, see Contents. When piece is finished, block if necessary.

To Block: Cover wooden surface with brown paper. Mark canvas outline on paper for guide, making sure corners are square. Mark horizontal and vertical center lines of marked outline on paper and on canvas. Place canvas, right side down, over paper guide, matching center lines on canvas with those on paper. Fasten canvas with tacks along canvas edges, stretching canvas to match guide. Wet with cold water; let dry.

Finish piece, following individual directions.

Pillow

Canvas: 13 mesh-to-the-inch, 10″ × 12½″. Yarn: 2 skeins white; 1 skein each pale gray-green, three other soft greens, pink, peach, lavender, blue, light yellow. Fabric for backing, 7″ × 9½″. Fiberfill. Coral twisted cord, 30″.

Read General Directions. Work all stitches (except eyelet flowers) with two strands of yarn in needle. Chart shows upper right quarter of complete design. Work flowers-and-foliage center area first, then borders. Mark off center area, 72 meshes wide by 48

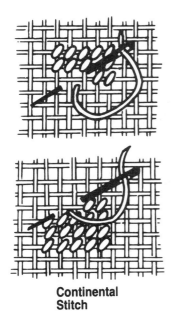

Continental Stitch

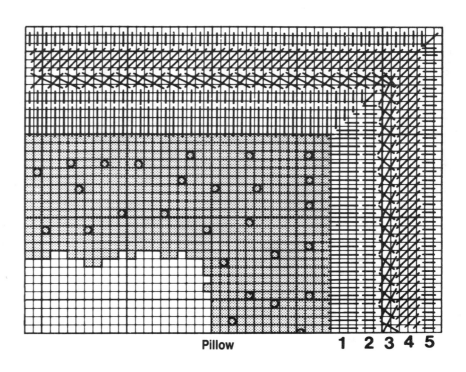

Pillow   **1 2 3 4 5**

meshes deep, leaving margin about 3″ wide all around. In upper right quarter of marked area, work an eyelet flower for each circle on chart, using pink, peach, lavender, blue and yellow as desired. Work flowers in three remaining quarters, reversing chart or placing them at random. Starting in upper right corner of marked area, fill in center with needlepoint: Mix soft greens for variegated tones in shaded area, working around flowers; use white for unshaded center; reverse chart for upper left quarter, then work bottom half in reverse of top.

Borders: Work borders from center out to edge, in order given. Use white for Borders 1, 3 and 4 and gray-green for Borders 2 and 5. For Border 1, work right edge first, turning canvas so right edge is at top and stitching from left to right; work each edge of border in same manner, turning canvas each time. Work Borders 2 and 3 in same manner; for Border 3, see detail for Long-Legged Cross-Stitch. For Border 4, begin at center of top edge with short stitches as shown, then work across to top right corner and down to center of right edge, ending with short stitches for a complete quarter. From this point, work second quarter of border to center of bottom edge,

reversing slant of stitches. Work third and fourth quarters, reversing slant each time; see color illustration. Work Border 5 as for first three. Block piece if necessary.

Assembling: Trim canvas margins to ½″. Place pillow top and backing together, right sides facing. Stitch all around with ½″ seam, leaving large opening in one long side. Trim corners. Turn pillow to right side, stuff fully with fiberfill, turn in seam allowance, and slip-stitch closed. Slip-stitch twisted cord around edge.

Pencil Holder

Canvas: 13 mesh-to-the inch, 9″ × 13″. Yarn: 2 skeins each white and light blue; 1 skein each yellow-green, dark olive and blue-green, plus light and bright yellow, orange and pink. Plastic juice can, 12 oz. White sewing thread.

Read General Directions. On canvas, mark outline of piece 4⅞″ × 9″, or size to fit around can; leave equal margins all around. Work all stitches (except eyelet flowers) with two strands of yarn in needle. Chart shows right half of design. In right half of marked area, work an eyelet flower for each circle,

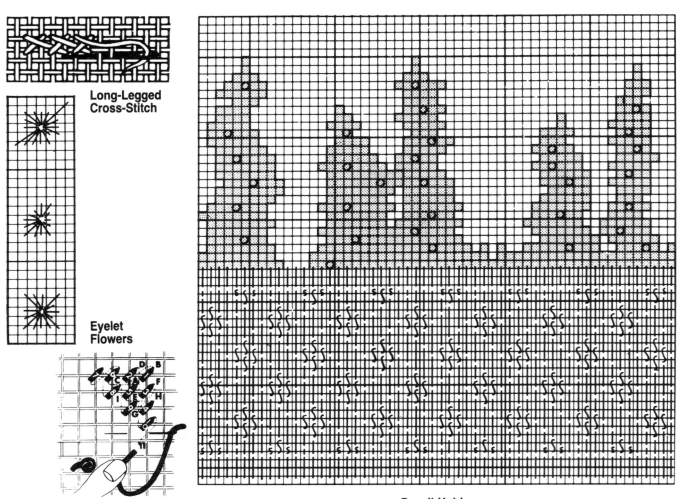

Long-Legged Cross-Stitch

Eyelet Flowers

Diagonal Stitch

Pencil Holder

using light and bright shades of yellow, pink or orange within each stalk. Repeat in left half. Starting in upper right corner, work upper half of design in needlepoint, using blue in empty area; mix the greens for variegated tones in shaded areas and work around flowers.

Work lower half of design with vertical stitches, following chart and repeating pattern to fill area; straight lines indicate white, curving lines indicate variegated greens. Block piece if necessary.

Assembling: Trim margins to $\frac{1}{2}''$. Turn top margin to back and, using blue yarn, whip through top two meshes of unworked canvas for a finished edge, going through first row of needlepoint. Turn bottom and one side margin to back and whip in place with sewing thread. Wrap piece around juice can, overlapping canvas margin with folded margin on side; slip-stitch in place.

Bookend

Canvas: 13 mesh-to-the-inch, $8\frac{1}{2}'' \times 9\frac{1}{2}''$. Yarn: 2 skeins each white and mint green; 1 skein each yellow-green, pale green, dark green, light blue, lavender, bright blue, plus light and bright orange, pink and yellow. White fabric for backing $5\frac{1}{2}'' \times 6\frac{1}{2}''$. Coral twisted cord, 16″. Metal bookend, $4\frac{5}{8}''$ wide $\times 5\frac{1}{2}''$ high.

Read General Directions. Work all stitches (except eyelet flowers and yellow circle) with two strands of yarn in needle. Chart shows complete design. With mint green, work cross-stitches in background first, indicated on chart by X's. For first stitch, measure 2″ down from top edge of canvas and $2\frac{1}{2}''$ in from left edge; make complete cross-stitch, going over one mesh in both directions. Working to right, make a cross-stitch over every fourth mesh as shown, for first row. Work remaining rows of cross-stitches.

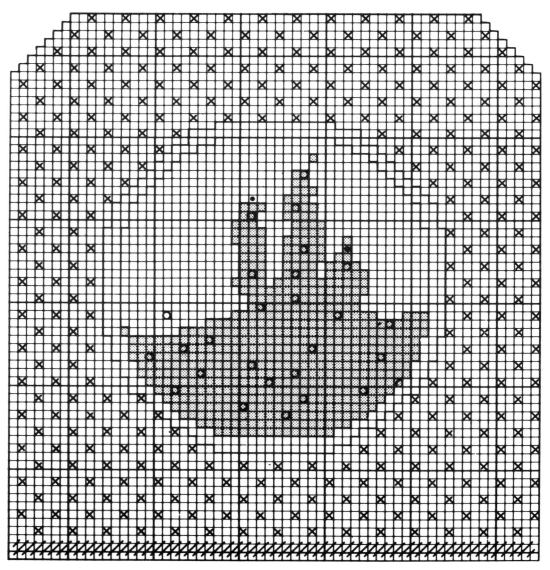

Bookend

Using white yarn, fill in background around cross-stitches with needlepoint, following chart and working up to outer circle. With mint green, work slanting stitches across bottom.

In center area, work an eyelet flower for each circle on chart, using bright blue, lavender, oranges, pinks and yellows at random. Fill in background with needlepoint, using light blue for empty area and mixing other greens for variegated tones in shaded area; work around flowers. Add French knots where shown by dots, using flower colors. Fill in circle between center and background with embroidery: With one strand of yellow, work outline stitch around center. With two strands of mint green, work split stitch or chain stitch around outline stitch. Block piece if necessary.

Finishing: Trim canvas margins to ½". Place needlepoint and backing pieces together, right sides facing, and stitch around sides and top of piece, rounding corners at top. Trim fabric to match canvas edges. Turn up excess canvas and fabric at bottom; slip-stitch in place. Turn piece to right side. Slip-stitch twisted cord around sides and top, turning ends to inside. Slip cover over bookend.

Picture

Canvas: 18 mesh-to-the-inch, 7¼" square. Yarn: 1 skein each pale, light, medium and dark green, plus chartreuse, beige, red, orange, and magenta. Light brown six-strand embroidery floss. Easelback frame, 3½" rabbet size. Lightweight cardboard, 3⅜" square. Tape.

Read General Directions. Work all stitches with one strand of yarn in needle. Chart shows overall design, but with border only partially worked. Mark design area on canvas, 59 meshes square. Starting in upper left corner of marked area, work outer border with slanted straight stitches, alternating pale and light greens for checkerboard pattern; work two rows across top as shown. Work border down right side, continuing pattern to bottom edge of chart. Return to upper left side and work border down left side and across bottom in same manner.

Return to upper left to begin inner border. With chartreuse yarn, work cross-stitches across top, starting at left and working to right with underneath stitches then returning to left with top stitches; note that first and last stitches in row are square and remaining stitches are widened. Work boxes around

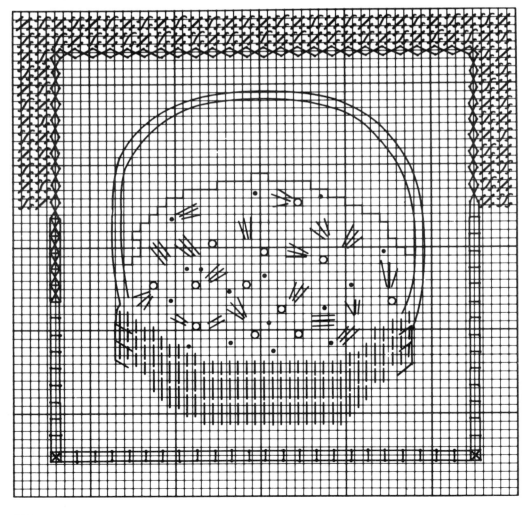

Picture

each cross-stitch; see chart. Work inner border on right side, turning canvas so right side is at top. Work bottom and left side in same manner, turning canvas each time.

With beige yarn, work basket in three rows of vertical stitches as shown. Following chart, draw curved basket handle on canvas. Work an eyelet flower for each circle on chart, using red, orange, and magenta at random. Work leaves in straight stitches with medium green. Fill in flower area with dark green needlepoint stitch, working around flowers and leaves and down to rim. Add chartreuse French knots where indicated by dots.

Work basket handle with beige split stitch. Fill picture background with pale green needlepoint stitch. Using two strands of embroidery floss in needle, work inner and outer outline of basket handle and basket tiers in outline stitch.

Finishing: Block piece if necessary. Trim canvas margins to ½″. Center work over cardboard; fold excess unworked canvas to back and tape in place. Remove easel back and glass (if any) from frame; discard glass. Place needlework in frame and slide easel back in place. ◊

Floss Necklaces

Shown on page 160

EQUIPMENT: Scissors. Embroidery and sewing needles. Steel crochet hook size 3 or 4.
MATERIALS: *For Each:* Pearl cotton size 5 (27.3-yard skein): two skeins for necklace, one-half skein same or contrasting color for ends and ties. Four to six small buttons, beads, or miniature fruit. Matching sewing thread.
DIRECTIONS: Open up two skeins of cotton. Place them together and twist one end for about 1″. With strand from third skein, wrap ends together tightly and closely for 1″, working over beginning of strand;

leave ¼″ at tip unwrapped. Cut strand and thread in embroidery needle; run strand through wrapped end to secure. Continue twisting the two skeins together, making 18 twists. Wrap other end in same way.

At center of necklace open a twist; make an overhand knot, going through the opening with one end. Pull tightly.

For each tie, cut a two-yard strand and make a twisted cord (see Contents). Pull folded end through tip of necklace with crochet hook; knot securely. Tie overhand knot at othe end and trim.

Add decorations as shown in color illustration. ◊

Tasseled Totes

Shown on page 160

BAG SIZES: Bird 10″ × 10½″; Fishes: 10″ × 10½″; Cat: 12¼″ × 13″.
EQUIPMENT: Pencil. Colored pencil. Scissors. Ruler. Paper for patterns. Dressmaker's tracing (carbon) paper. Tracing wheel or dry ball-point pen. Sewing machine. Crochet hook, size G. Tapestry needle. Two safety pins.
MATERIALS: Heavy textured woven ecru cotton fabric 36″ wide, ½ yard for each bag. Scraps of knitting worsted-weight yarn for applied decoration and tassels (see illustration for colors). 1½ yards of ¼″-thick cotton cord for drawstring. Thread to match fabric. All-purpose glue.
DIRECTIONS: Directions are for 10″ × 10½″ bag. Changes for larger bag (12¼″ × 13″) are in parentheses. Each bag can be made with either shoulder strap or drawstring.
To Make Bag: From fabric, cut an 11″ × 25″ (13¼″ × 30½″) piece. Fold both short ends over 2″ (2¼″) to

right side, for top-edge "cuff." Turn raw edges under ¼″ and topstitch. Fold fabric in half, widthwise, wrong side inward; fold forms bag bottom. Turn raw side edges in ½″ and topstitch, making ⅜″ seams.
For Shoulder Strap: Cut fabric strip 4⅛″ × 30″. Fold strip in half lengthwise, wrong side inward. Turn lower long raw edge in ½″; turn upper long raw edge in ⅝″; keeping edges uneven, baste. Turn strap over and topstitch both long edges ⅜″ from fold. With underside inward, pin strap ends to inside of bag at side seams, 1″ below upper edge of bag. Topstitch strap in place.
For Drawstring: Cut two 27″ lengths of cord. Make eight holes through the outside layer of bag "cuff," as follows: With blunt end of crochet hook or dry ball-point pen, poke two holes ¼″ in from each side seam, one ½″ above the other. Using safety pin at each end, insert ends of one cord through lower set of holes on one side of bag; pull cord through "cuff," across bag to opposite side, and out through holes.

Insert ends of other cord through upper set of holes on other side of bag in same manner. Sew ends of each cord together.

To Decorate Bag: With colored pencil, draw lines across patterns, connecting grid lines; enlarge by copying on paper ruled in 1″ squares. Transfer pattern to bag by placing pattern right side up on bag front with carbon between. Go over lines with tracing wheel or dry ball-point pen. Remove pattern and carbon.

Following color illustration for yarn colors, crochet chains or braid yarns into lengths that correspond to unbroken lines of design. Glue (or slip-stitch if desired) to front of bag over pattern lines. For Cat, add double border. For bags with shoulder strap, decorate front "cuff" and outside of strap with chains or braids laid down in a zigzag pattern. (See color illustration.)

For Tassels: To make tassels at cord ends of drawstring, cut a piece of cardboard 3½″ wide; following directions for How To Make a Tassel (see Contents), wind yarn around cardboard, tie at top and clip. Before wrapping below top, pass half the tassel through loop of sewn cord and wrap tassel encasing cord in "top knot." Make same size tassels for bag bottoms; stitch to bag. ◇

Cardtable Companions

Shown on page 184

EQUIPMENT: Pencil. Scissors. Ruler. Paper for patterns. Straight pins. Sewing machine.

MATERIALS: Felt 72" wide, 1½ yds. white. Two pieces of felt 9" × 12", one red and one black. Red, white, and black striped grosgrain ribbon about 1½" wide, 173" (5 yds). White and red sewing thread. Red shank button. All-purpose glue.

TABLECLOTH: Cut white felt piece 44" square.

Starting at a corner, lay ribbon all around square ½" from edges, pinning in place; fold at corners in right angles for mitred effect. Machine-stitch very close to both edges of ribbon with matching thread. Remove pins.

COASTERS: Trace full size patterns; complete half-patterns indicated by dash lines. Cut out patterns around the larger outlines of the four designs. From

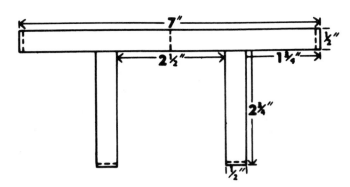

Diagram for Inside Cardholder

red felt cut two hearts and two diamonds; from black felt cut two spades and two clubs. Pin identical pieces together. Machine-stitch together with white thread $\frac{1}{8}''$ from edge. Stitch a second line $\frac{1}{8}''$ inside first line and a third line $\frac{1}{8}''$ inside second line.

CARDHOLDER: From black felt cut piece 6" × 8½". From white felt cut piece 5½" × 8". Cut out patterns around smaller outlines. Place patterns on white felt piece, a red and a black shape at each end, and mark around. Carefully cut out shapes. Glue red felt pieces behind diamond and heart shapes. Center white piece onto black piece and glue together.

For closing strap cut black felt piece $2\frac{3}{4}''$ × $\frac{3}{4}''$. Clip corners from one end to form a center point. Cut lengthwise slit for buttonhole in same end. Sew straight end of strap onto black border of cardholder cover centered on one short side. Sew red button to opposite side of cover, close to edge of white piece.

For holding straps inside case, cut double "T" piece from red felt, following dimensions in diagram. Place inside cardholder, on same half as closing strap with stems of "T's" near short end; adjust top of "T's" to accommodate packs of cards. Stitch in place following lines on diagram. ◇

Embroidered Sun Pillow

Shown on page 160

SIZE: $13\frac{1}{2}''$ × $14\frac{1}{2}''$.

EQUIPMENT: Scissors. Pencil. Colored pencil. Paper for pattern. Tracing paper. Dressmaker's tracing (carbon) paper. Dry ball-point pen. Large-eyed embroidery needle. Sewing needle. Masking tape. Embroidery hoop. Cardboard.

For Blocking: Iron. Padded surface. Straight pins. Pressing cloth.

MATERIALS: Loosely woven, bright yellow wool fabric 36" wide, $\frac{1}{2}$ yard. Persian yarn (8.8 yd. skeins), 1 skein (or less) of each color listed in color key. Yellow sewing thread. Muslin for inner pillow 36" wide, $\frac{1}{2}$ yard. Fiberfill for stuffing.

DIRECTIONS: Using sharp, colored pencil, draw lines across pattern, connecting grid lines. Enlarge pattern by copying on paper ruled in 1" squares. Trace design.

From yellow wool fabric, cut two pieces $14\frac{1}{2}''$ × $15\frac{1}{2}''$. On one piece (top), center tracing on right side, with carbon between. Go over lines of design with dry ball-point pen to transfer to fabric. Tape edges of piece, then place in hoop, centering area to be embroidered.

To embroider design, follow color and stitch keys; see Contents for stitch details. Arrows indicate stitch direction. Separate the strands of yarn and work with one two-ply strand in needle, cut to about 18".

(*Note:* Work deep pink straight stitches around sun face with three two-ply strands.) Do not make knots. Begin by leaving an end of yarn on back and working over it to secure; finish (and begin subsequent strands) by running yarn under stitches on back.

Blocking: Pin embroidered fabric face down on padded surface, being sure corners are square. Cover with damp cloth and press lightly with iron at warm temperature setting.

Pillow: Place the two yellow wool pieces together, right sides facing. Making $\frac{1}{2}''$ seams, stitch around sides, leaving opening in one side for inner pillow. Trim corners. Turn to right side.

For inner pillow, cut two pieces of muslin $15\frac{1}{2}''$ × $16\frac{1}{2}''$. Assemble in same manner as pillow, making $\frac{1}{2}''$ seams and leaving an opening for stuffing. Turn to right side, stuff fully, and slip-stitch opening closed.

Insert inner pillow in embroidered cover, adding extra stuffing in corners if necessary. Slip-stitch opening closed.

Tassels: Cut selvages from remaining piece of yellow wool. Pull out long strands to ravel fabric. Use the resulting yarn to make four tassels; see Contents for directions. Cut cardboard $2\frac{1}{2}''$ wide, and wind yarn around it about 150 times for each tassel, starting all new strands at one edge. Sew a tassel to each corner, using the yarn for thread. ◇

COLOR KEY

O - ORANGE
R - RED
P - LT. PINK
DP - DEEP PINK
W - WHITE
C - CELERY
V - VIOLET
F - FUCHSIA
G - BRT. GREEN

STITCH KEY

1 - OUTLINE
2 - SATIN
3 - CHAIN
4 - STRAIGHT
5 - FLAT
6 - CRETAN
7 - BUTTONHOLE

COLOR KEY

M - MUSTARD
B - BEIGE
DB - DARK BROWN
Y - YELLOW
W - WHITE
O - ORANGE
V - VARIEGATED

Satin Stitch Rooster Pillow

Shown on page 160

SIZE: 15″ square.

EQUIPMENT: See Sun Pillow, page 220.

MATERIALS: Heavy, closely woven dark orange cotton or linen fabric 36″ wide, ½ yard. Tapestry yarn (8-yd. skeins): For embroidery, 2 skeins mustard, 1 skein each beige, dark brown, yellow, white, and orange; scraps of pale yellow, black, shades of brown and tan; for tassels, 4 skeins orange. Muslin for inner pillow 36″ wide, ½ yard. Fiberfill for stuffing. Zipper, 12″ long (optional). Orange sewing thread.

DIRECTIONS: Using sharp, colored pencil, draw lines across pattern by connecting grid lines. Enlarge pattern by copying on 1″ squares. Trace design.

From dark orange fabric, cut two pieces 16″ square. On one piece (top), center tracing on right side, with carbon between. Go over lines of design with dry ball-point pen to transfer to fabric. Tape edges of piece, then place in hoop, centering area to be embroidered.

Embroider with one strand of yarn in needle, cut to 24″ length. Do not make knots. Begin by leaving an end of yarn on back and working over it to secure; finish (and begin subsequent strands) by running yarn under stitches on back.

To embroider design, follow color key. (For variegated areas, use black, browns, tans, mustard, and pale yellow in various combinations, shading from darks to lights; see color illustration.) Use satin stitch throughout; see Contents for stitch detail. In working each color area, stitch in direction of arrows, gradually shifting direction as indicated. Use a double satin stitch across wide areas: rooster's head, neck, and breast; crests of the orange, white, and beige tail feathers; see detail.

Blocking: See Embroidered Sun Pillow.

Pillow: Make in same manner as for Sun Pillow, inserting a 12″ zipper in one side if desired. Cut muslin for inner pillow 17″ square.

Tassels: Make four tassels: Cut cardboard 2½″ wide and wind yarn around it about 60 times for each tassel (see Contents for tassel directions). Sew tassels to corners. ◊

Bedside Organizer

Shown on page 184

EQUIPMENT: Pencil. Ruler. Scissors. Tape measure. String. Thumbtack. Scalloping shears. Sewing machine.

MATERIALS: Felt 36″ wide: yellow and blue, 1 yd. each; green, ½ yd. Sewing thread to match felt colors. All-purpose glue.

Large Accessory Organizer

From yellow felt cut piece 20″ × 29½″. Trace scallop pattern; complete half-pattern indicated by dash lines. Along one 20″ side of yellow felt, draw around pattern five times; cut out for scalloped edge. Cut a yellow strip 20″ × 3⅜″. Use pattern to scallop along one 20″ edge in same manner. Match scalloped edges of the two pieces. Machine-stitch together around scallops ⅛″ from edges. Turn other side out, for top edge of organizer.

For large blue pocket at bottom, cut piece 17″ × 9″. To make curved corner trim, mark a 4″ square, 6½″ square, and a 9″ square on yellow, blue, and green felt respectively; do not cut out. For yellow curve, make a compass by placing a thumbtack and a piece of string in one corner of the yellow felt square. Tie a pencil to the other end of the string; between tack and pencil string should measure exactly 3½″. Swing pencil in an arc to draw curve; cut on pencil line. Scallop curved edge with shears. Repeat procedure with 6½″ and 9″ squares, making curves

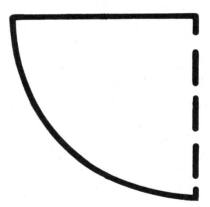

about ½″ less than side of square. (*Note:* Compass may be used for the smaller trims.)

Curves serve as pockets on organizer. Place in corner of blue piece, overlapping as shown in illustration. Glue down only those curves you do not wish to use as pockets; pin others in place.

Center blue pocket 1⅝″ up from bottom edge of organizer. Machine-stitch on three sides ⅛″ all around, leaving top edge open.

For green pockets, cut two felt pieces 8″ × 6″. Mark two pieces 5″ square on yellow felt and two pieces 3½″ square on blue felt. Mark and cut yellow and blue pieces into curves as for blue pocket trim. Scallop curved edge and place on green pieces, referring to photograph. Place green pockets 1⅝″ up from top edge of blue pocket. Machine-stitch around three sides as before.

For three small pockets, cut one green and two

blue pieces $4\frac{1}{8}''$ square. Scallop one edge for tops. Place $1\frac{5}{8}''$ up from top edge of green pockets and machine-stitch on three sides.

Book Holder

From blue felt cut piece $20'' \times 12\frac{1}{2}''$. Cut second blue piece for pocket $12\frac{1}{2}'' \times 6\frac{1}{2}''$. From yellow felt cut piece measuring $2\frac{3}{4}'' \times 5''$; scallop one $2\frac{3}{4}''$ edge for top. Place yellow pocket $\frac{1}{2}''$ in from left shorter side and $\frac{3}{4}''$ up from bottom edge of blue pocket. Machine-stitch $\frac{1}{4}''$ in from edges on two sides and bottom.

Mark pieces $2\frac{3}{4}''$, $5''$, and $6\frac{1}{2}''$ square on yellow, blue, and green felt respectively. Curve, cut, and scallop as before; pin in place in right corner of pocket.

Place blue pocket on large blue felt piece matching sides and bottom. Machine-stitch around three sides, $\frac{1}{4}''$ in from edges leaving top open. To divide pocket in two sections, sew up from the bottom to the top edge of the pocket $\frac{3}{8}''$ away from yellow oblong pocket.

Jewelry Case

Cut two pieces of blue felt $8'' \times 6''$. For outside trim, mark pieces $1\frac{1}{2}''$, $2\frac{1}{2}''$, and $3\frac{3}{4}''$ on yellow, blue, and green felt respectively. Curve, cut, and scallop. Pin curves in place on a corner of one large blue piece. Fold blue piece in half lengthwise so curves are showing on the outside of one of the halves. Clip top of green curve to match centerfold line. Glue all curves in place. For outside tie, cut yellow strip $\frac{3}{4}'' \times 26''$. Tack middle of strip crosswise, on centerfold line.

For inside of case, cut green felt piece $2\frac{1}{2}'' \times 7\frac{1}{2}''$. Place green piece on second blue piece, $\frac{1}{4}''$ in from three edges, and machine-stitch in place, $\frac{1}{8}''$ in from green edges.

Cut two yellow strips $7\frac{1}{2}'' \times \frac{1}{2}''$. Place on other half of inner blue piece and machine-stitch ends down, referring to photograph. With a pencil, divide each strip into three equal parts; sew at these points.

To complete case, sew the two blue pieces together, $\frac{1}{8}''$ from edges. ◇

Patchwork Cards

Shown on page 185

SIZE: Each card, 6″ square.

EQUIPMENT: Pencil. Ruler. Scissors. Tracing paper. Thin, stiff cardboard.

MATERIALS: Lightweight white cardboard, $12'' \times 36''$ for all cards. Small amounts of felt in desired colors or as suggested in individual directions. Fabric glue.

GENERAL DIRECTIONS: Trace actual-size patterns; complete quarter-patterns indicated by dash lines for Tulip (A), Feathered Star (B), and Mariner's Compass (C); complete half-pattern for tree trunk (D). Using cardboard, make a separate pattern for each part of design. Cut design pieces from felt.

For each card, cut a piece of lightweight cardboard $6'' \times 12''$; fold in half crosswise to measure 6″ square. Cut an additional piece 6″ square; glue design to square; glue square to front of card.

Tulip

Cut from felt: dark green center leaves and stem in one piece, eight light green leaves, four red tulips, four yellow border strips $\frac{1}{2}'' \times 5''$, four dark green corner pieces $\frac{1}{2}''$ square.

Lightly mark horizontal and vertical center lines on cardboard. Glue dark green center in place with leaves running horizontally and vertically (see photograph). Glue red tulips at ends of flower stems; glue light green leaves in place. Glue corners in place; glue yellow border strips between corner blocks around edge of cardboard.

Pine Tree

Cut from felt: light green tree trunk, 30 dark green tree triangles, two red border strips $\frac{1}{2}'' \times 6''$.

Mark a vertical center line on cardboard. Glue tree trunk along marked line $\frac{5}{8}''$ up from bottom of cardboard. Glue on tree triangles as follows: Starting at top of tree trunk, glue two rows of three triangles each along marked center line with right angles touching at lines (see photograph). Glue four additional rows (three triangles per row) on each side of the two center rows, working from center out and matching angles as shown. Add red border strips to side edges of cardboard.

Mariner's Compass

Cut one red center (1) from felt. Cut felt star points as follows: four dark green (2), four yellow (3), eight red (4), and sixteen pink (5). Cut four green border strips $\frac{3}{4}''$ wide, two 6″ long and two 5″ long.

Lightly mark horizontal and vertical center lines on cardboard. Glue pieces as follows: Glue red center in place first; glue dark green points around center, matching tips to marked lines. Glue yellow points between green points. Glue red points between yellow and green points. Glue a pink point between red, yellow, and green points. Glue dark green border strips in place; glue two long strips to top and bottom of cardboard and two shorter strips to sides.

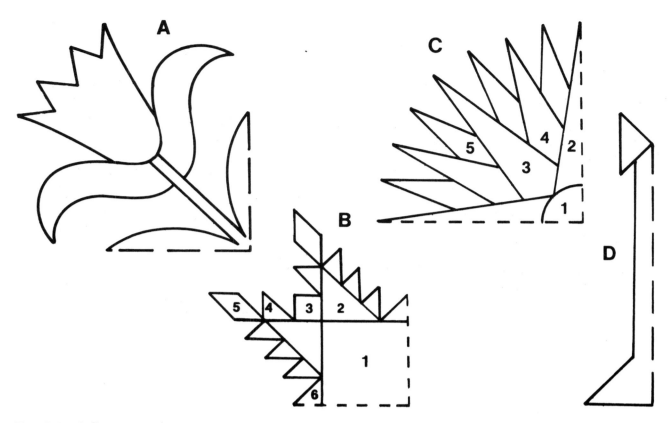

Feathered Star

Cut from felt: one large yellow center square (1), eight red triangles (2); four blue squares (3), 32 small blue triangles (4), eight blue diamonds (5), four large blue triangles (6) plus four blue $\frac{1}{2}'' \times 5''$ border strips and four yellow $\frac{1}{2}''$ corner squares.

With pencil, lightly mark two corner-to-corner diagonal lines on cardboard. Glue large yellow square to cardboard, centering it by matching corners to lines. Glue on red triangles, matching right angles at yellow corners as shown. Glue on large blue triangles between red triangles, matching long side of each triangle to a yellow side. Glue on a blue square at each yellow corner, between right angle formed by red triangles. Glue four small blue triangles around sides of each red triangle; see photograph. Glue a blue diamond to tip of each red triangle.

Glue yellow corner squares in place; glue blue border strips to edges of cardboard, between corner squares. ◊

Embroidered Picture Frames

Shown on page 186

SIZES: Small, $5\frac{1}{4}''$ square; medium, $6'' \times 7\frac{1}{2}''$; large, $7\frac{1}{4}'' \times 8\frac{1}{2}''$.

EQUIPMENT: Pencil. Colored pencil. Ruler. Scissors. Paper for patterns. Dressmaker's tracing (carbon) paper. Hard lead pencil or dry ball-point pen. Matte knife. Embroidery hoop. Embroidery needle. Iron.

MATERIALS: White linen or linen-like fabric 45" wide, $\frac{1}{2}$ yard for small frame; $\frac{5}{8}$ yard for medium frame; $\frac{3}{4}$ yard for large frame. Six-strand embroidery floss, one skein each: light pink, medium pink for small frame; light blue, medium blue, dark blue, pale green for medium frame; white, gray, beige for large frame. Batting. Heavy matte cardboard, $\frac{1}{8}''$ thick: 29" square for small; 35" × 48" for medium; 40" × 55" for large. Ribbon, $\frac{1}{4}''$ wide, 2" long for each. Clear glass, $\frac{1}{8}''$ thick: $2\frac{1}{4}''$ square for small; $3\frac{1}{2}'' \times 4\frac{1}{2}''$ for medium; $3\frac{1}{2}'' \times 4\frac{1}{2}''$ for large. All-purpose glue. Contact paper. Masking tape.

GENERAL DIRECTIONS: *To Embroider:* Using sharp colored pencil, trace full size patterns; complete quarter-patterns indicated by dash lines.

Cut out linen piece 4" wider and longer than desired-size frame. Place dressmaker's tracing paper over right side of fabric; center pattern over tracing paper, leaving 2" margin of fabric all around. With

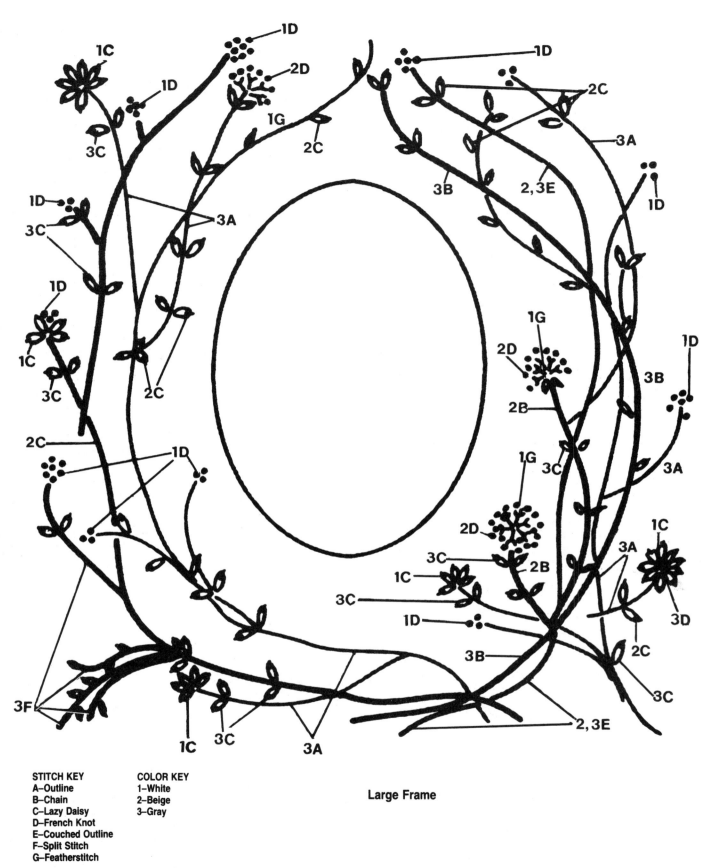

STITCH KEY
A–Outline
B–Chain
C–Lazy Daisy
D–French Knot
E–Couched Outline
F–Split Stitch
G–Featherstitch

COLOR KEY
1–White
2–Beige
3–Gray

Large Frame

226

hard lead pencil or dry ball-point pen, trace outlines of pattern to transfer design to fabric. Remove pattern and tracing paper; bind raw edges of fabric with masking tape to prevent raveling. Insert fabric in embroidery hoop to keep fabric taut. Embroider design, following individual directions; for stitch details, see Contents.

To block, cut away taped edges of finished embroidery, leaving 1″ allowance around all edges. Place embroidery face down on padded ironing board. Steam-press gently.

To Mount: Draw pieces for picture frame on cardboard, following diagrams and sizes given in individual directions; mark all pieces by letter. Cut out pieces, including centers, using matte knife; cut two of pieces A and C. Round corners of A and B pieces slightly. Place pieces A, B, E, and F on contact paper and trace outlines; cut out contact paper along marked lines. Glue the two A pieces together. Glue layer of batting to one side of A. Place embroidered fabric, wrong side up on flat surface. Center padded A piece, batting side down, on embroidered fabric. Carefully clip center section of embroidered fabric to marked line, clipping all around on oval-center frames and just at corners on square-center frame. Turn and tape inner edges to back of cardboard, smoothing fabric and arranging batting to achieve rounded edge. Glue A contact piece to back of cardboard piece, covering raw edges of fabric in center. Glue B piece to back of A piece, matching outside edges. Wrap excess fabric to back of cardboard, keeping fabric taut and making sure design is centered in front. Arrange batting and fold fabric at

corners to achieve smooth, rounded edges; tape edges of fabric to back of cardboard. Trim ½″ from outer edges of B contact piece; glue to back of frame, matching inner edges of cardboard B and covering outer raw edges of fabric.

To make frame for stand, glue two C pieces together with edges flush. Glue C to D with outer edges even; let dry. Place D piece on fabric and carefully trace outline; cut fabric, adding 1″ around all edges. Smooth fabric over D, mitering corners and keeping fabric taut; glue fabric to D. Fold 1″ allowance to back and over C pieces; glue. Glue wrong side of covered C-D piece to back of embroidered frame, inverting the U so base is at top of frame and centering U to cover edges of contact paper on back of embroidered frame; let dry. Slide glass through channel made, and insert in pocket formed by B piece.

To make stand, place E and F pieces on fabric and trace outlines; cut fabric pieces, adding 1″ allowance around all edges. Glue fabric to cardboard pieces, keeping fabric smooth and taut and mitering corners. Fold raw edges to back of cardboard and glue in place. Glue ½″ end of ribbon slightly below center of F. Place contact paper over F and make ¼″ slit in paper to indicate position of ribbon. Cover back of F with contact paper, drawing ribbon through slit. Mark line 1″ below narrow top edge of F; run matte knife along marked line to score, being careful not to cut through fabric. With bottom edges even, glue scored section of F to fabric side of E. Make ¼″-wide slit below center of E, and draw other end of ribbon through slit for ½″; glue to back of E. Cover

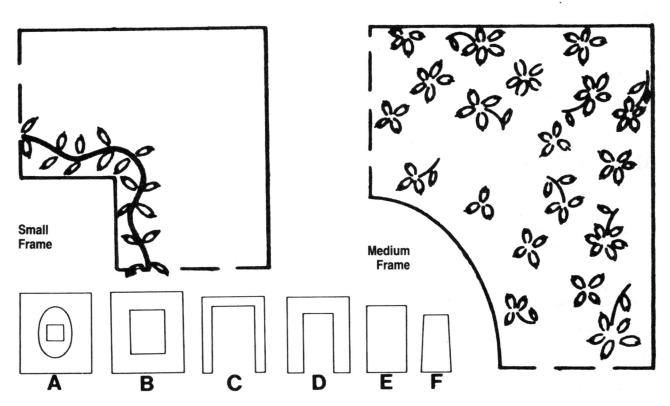

Small Frame

Medium Frame

A   **B**   **C**   **D**   **E**   **F**

back of E with contact paper. Slide stand into channel of frame.

Small Frame

To Embroider: Cut fabric 9¼″ square. Using two strands of medium pink embroidery floss in needle, embroider the curving line in chain stitch; add backstitches to chain, using two strands of light pink. Using three strands of light pink, embroider leaves in lazy daisy stitch.

Frame: Draw pieces on cardboard as follows: A, 5¼″ square, using embroidery pattern to mark center square; B, 5¼″ square, with 2¼″ square removed from center; C, 4½″ square cut into U-shape with 1″ wide bridge and arms; D, 4½″ square cut into U-shape with 2″-wide bridge and 1¼″-wide arms; E, 2½″ × 3½″; F, piece 3″ high, 1½″ wide at top, and 1⅞″ wide at base.

Medium Frame

To Embroider: Cut fabric 10″ × 11½″. Using two strands of floss in needle throughout, embroider flowers in lazy daisy stitch: inner flowers in light blue, center flowers in medium blue, and outer flowers in dark blue. With pale green, embroider leaves in lazy daisy stitch and stems in outline stitch.

For Frame: Draw pieces on cardboard as follows: A, 6″ × 7½″, use embroidery pattern to mark center oval; B, 6″ × 7½″, with 3½″ × 4½″ piece removed from center; C, 5½″ × 6⅞″ piece cut into U-shape with ¾″-wide bridge and arms; D, 5½″ × 6⅞″ piece cut into U-shape with 1⅜″-wide bridge and arms; E, 3¾″ × 6″; F, piece 5¼″ high, 1⅞″ wide at top, 2¾″ wide at base.

Large Frame

To Embroider: Embroider design following chart, and color and stitch keys. Use two strands of floss throughout, except for French Knots, which take three strands.

For Frame: Draw pieces on cardboard as follows: A, 7¼″ × 8½″, use embroidery pattern to mark center oval; B, 7¼″ × 8½″, with 3½″ × 4½″ piece removed from center; C, 6¼″ × 8″ cut into U-shape with 1″-wide bridge and arms; D, 6¼″ × 8″ piece cut into U-shape with 1¾″-wide bridge and 1⅝″-wide arms; E, 4″ × 7″; F, piece 6″ high, 2½″ wide at top, 3″ wide at base. ◇

Fringe Duster

Shown on page 188

EQUIPMENT: Scissors. Ruler.

MATERIALS: Wire coat hanger. Rug yarn, one skein each pale aqua and royal blue. Glue.

DIRECTIONS: Cover hook part of hanger by wrapping it with royal blue yarn, applying glue as you wrap. Let dry.

Remainder of hanger is covered with fringe, as follows: Cut 4″ strand of yarn; fold in half. Place behind wire hanger, with loop at top. Insert two ends through loop, and pull to tighten. Repeat, cutting strands of yarn as you go. Push knots very close together and alternate the colors until remainder of hanger is covered. Grasp sides of hanger and bring them toward each other, bending middle bar up toward hook. ◇

Memory Pictures

Shown on page 187

SIZE: Matted, 6″ × 5″.

EQUIPMENT: Ruler. Hard-lead pencil. Tracing paper. Dressmaker's tracing (carbon) paper. Scissors. Straight pins. Sewing and embroidery needles. Iron. X-acto knife. Metal-edged ruler.

MATERIALS (For each): White smooth-weave fabric, piece 8″ × 7″. Stiff cardboard, two pieces 6″ × 5″ (one for mounting, one for mat). Scraps of fabric, sewing thread to match, and embroidery floss in desired colors. Scraps of tightly woven fabric to cover mat in color desired or striped, as shown. Frame with rabbet size 6″ × 5″. Masking tape. All-purpose glue. Fine-tipped pen. Small brads.

DIRECTIONS: Read How to Appliqué (see Contents). Patterns are actual size; heavier lines indicate cutting lines for appliqué pieces; short dash lines indicate where pieces are overlapped; finer lines indicate embroidery lines. Trace a separate pattern for each part, including embroidery lines. Cut pattern pieces from appropriate fabric for appliqués, adding ¼″ all around for turning under.

Tape edges of white background fabric to prevent raveling. Prepare appliqué pieces; center and pin appliqués in place on white background fabric following pattern. Slip-stitch in place.

Using tracing paper and carbon, copy remaining embroidery design lines, then transfer all embroi-

dery design lines onto picture. Complete pictures by working embroidery with two strands of floss in needle as follows (see Contents for stitch details): all single fine lines are outline stitch; areas such as hands, feet, hats, collars are filled in with satin stitch; wedding scene flowers are outline stitch with French knot centers and lazy daisy leaves; wedding gown is outlined in outline stitch; eyes and mouths are tiny straight stitches. Write "Just Married" on fabric with pen.

Press completed picture.

Center embroidery over one cardboard; bring edges to back and tape in place.

To Make Mat: On second cardboard measure and mark a rectangle $4\frac{1}{2}'' \times 3\frac{1}{2}''$, having an even border all around. Using metal-edged ruler as guide, cut out inner rectangle with knife. Cut two strips of fabric $6'' \times 1\frac{3}{4}''$ and two strips $5'' \times 1\frac{3}{4}''$. Apply thin coat of glue to front surface of mat and smooth on fabric strips one at a time, having excess fabric at inner edges and mitering corners by marking, then cutting with knife. Be sure mitered corners are glued securely to prevent raveling. Fold excess fabric to back and glue.

Place mat in frame with picture behind. Use tiny brads to hold in place. ◇

Ring Holder

Shown on page 188

EQUIPMENT: Tracing paper. Pencil. Scissors. Drill with ½" bit. Sandpaper. Brush for shellac.

MATERIALS: Clear pine, ¾" thick, 2¼" square. Dowel, ½" diameter, 2" long. Walnut stain. Shellac. Small amounts of felt in bright colors and green. Gold metallic braid trim, ½" wide, 9". All-purpose glue.

DIRECTIONS: Taper one end of dowel slightly with sandpaper. Drill hole in center of pine block at a 45° angle (do not go all the way through the wood). Apply glue to inside of hole, and insert untapered end of dowel; let dry. Sand wood smooth. Stain and shellac all wood surfaces; let dry. Trace flower and leaf patterns; complete half and quarter-patterns indicated by dash lines. Using patterns, cut one flower of felt and one pair of leaves of green felt; cut out circle at center of flower to fit dowel. Glue leaves to block diagonally; then glue flower on top of leaves.

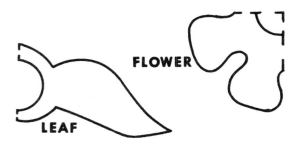

For flower center, cut a 1" circle in a contrasting felt color; cut circle out of center to fit dowel. Cut ⅛" notches or fringe in outer edge of flower center; glue in place over flower. Cut a 2¼" square of felt to match flower color; glue to bottom of pine block. Glue gold braid around edge. ◇

Letter Holder

Shown on page 188

EQUIPMENT: Scissors. Ruler.

MATERIALS: Soft drink or beer "six-pack" cardboard carton, preferably without partitions. Fancy embossed gift-wrap paper. Metallic gold braid trim, ¼" wide, at least 2½ feet. Artificial jewels in various shapes and colors. Rubber cement. All-purpose glue. Felt cut to fit bottom of carton.

DIRECTIONS: If carton has partitions, cut to separate from inside wall and glue down flat to outer wall in order to avoid weakening the construction. Cover inside and outside surfaces of carton with gift wrap, cutting separate pieces to fit each section; secure with rubber cement. Glue gold trim around front and handle front edges. Glue artificial jewels to front and handle. Glue felt piece to bottom. ◇

Decorated Hangers

Shown on page 188

EQUIPMENT: Paper for patterns. Pencil. Ruler. Bowl for mixing glue. Scissors. Paintbrushes: small flat and pointed.

MATERIALS: Wire coat hangers. Paper toweling or newspaper. Heavyweight cardboard. White glue. Liquid gesso. Tempera or acrylic paints in royal blue, light blue, green, flesh-color, yellow, fluorescent pink, black, brown, and orange, or as desired. Polyurethane varnish.

DIRECTIONS: Tear paper toweling into ½"-wide strips. Mix equal parts of glue and water in bowl. Cover hanger with strips which have been dipped, one at a time, in glue mixture; run strip through your fingers to remove excess moisture before wrapping strip around hanger. Use one or two layers to cover hanger completely.

Trace full size patterns on page 231. Using patterns, cut from cardboard: one girl front, one back, and two flower designs. Place one design on front of hanger and one on back. Cover the cardboard designs on each side with paper strips, as before, securing them together and to the hanger. Let hanger dry completely.

Coat entire hanger with gesso; let dry. Paint flower hanger royal blue. Paint flower petals light blue and center yellow with orange shading. Paint leaves green. With small pointed brush and black paint, outline petals and leaves and paint leaf veins.

Paint girl hanger black. Paint girl's face flesh-color, paint hair auburn (orange mixed with brown). Paint scarf pink with orange and blue polka dots. Paint blue eyes, brown freckles, pink lips, and brown eyelashes and eyebrows. Use black paint and fine pointed brush for remaining features and for outlining details.

When paint is dry, cover entire hanger with two coats of varnish; let dry. ◇

Spiral Trivet

Shown on page 188

EQUIPMENT: Scissors. Pencil. Ruler.

MATERIALS: Magazine with glossy coated color illustrations. All-purpose glue.

DIRECTIONS: To start, cut magazine pages into about two hundred 1″ × 2¾″ strips. Fold each strip in half lengthwise, and then in half lengthwise again. Fold in half crosswise, and then fold each end inward, to center fold. Following diagrams below, form a chain from the two hundred links. Make sure second lengthwise fold always faces direction from which next link is inserted. This will make it easier to insert next link between folded ends.

Steps 1-3: Insert folded ends of link B into folded ends of link A as shown. *Step 4:* Insert link C into folded ends of link B in same manner. *Step 5 (not shown):* Insert next link in link C in same manner and direction as link B is inserted in link A. Continue in this manner, alternating links C and B, until all links are used up.

Wind chain in a tight, flat coil; begin with first link at center of coil and glue as you wind. Leave about 6″ of chain unglued; let dry. Meanwhile, cut and fold an additional two hundred links. When coil is dry, add links to the end of chain and glue added part of chain to coil. Continue making and adding links, until trivet is size desired. Let dry thoroughly. ◇

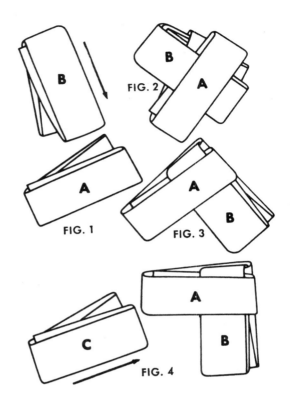

FIG. 1 FIG. 2 FIG. 3 FIG. 4

Trinket Box

Shown on page 188

EQUIPMENT: Pencil. Graph paper. Tracing paper.

MATERIALS: O-P Craft octagonal wooden box #1342 (4¾″ × 6″ × 3⅜″) or other small wooden box. Permanent marking pens: black, orange, and white for accents (or similar contrasting colors). Clear acrylic spray.

DIRECTIONS: On graph paper, mark outline of each facet of box separately. Plan geometric designs which can be repeated and lend themselves to size of each facet of box. Mark designs on graph paper for each facet, then trace designs. Place tracings, penciled side down, on appropriate facet and go over lines of design to transfer to wood. Using orange (or lightest color pen) first, carefully ink in design on all facets of box. Add touches of white on orange (or lightest color). Let ink dry completely. When dry, spray box with two or three coats of clear acrylic, drying thoroughly between coats. ◇

"Decoupage" Box

Shown on page 188

EQUIPMENT: Flat paintbrush. Single-edged razor blade.

MATERIALS: O.P. Craft recessed top basswood box #1300 (4″ × 5⅝″ × 2¼″), or other small wooden box with recessed top. Tempera or acrylic paint in yellow. Marbleized paper 4¼″ × 2¼″. Decorative gold embossed paper: keyhole; ⅛″ wide strip, 14½″; ½″-diameter stars, 4. Miniature playing cards, 6. Black felt, 4″ × 5⅝″. Black felt-tipped pen. All-purpose glue.

DIRECTIONS: Paint outside surfaces of box yellow; let dry.

Glue marbleized paper, gold strips, stars, and playing cards to recessed area of lid, as shown. Glue a playing card and star to one side as shown; reverse positions of star and card for other side; slit cards with razor blade to allow for opening. Glue keyhole to center front; color in hole with felt-tipped pen. Glue felt to underside of box to protect surfaces.

Owl Mirror

Shown on page 188

EQUIPMENT: Paper for pattern. Pencil. Ruler. Small bowl for glue. Scissors. Small pointed and flat paintbrushes.

MATERIALS: Small hand mirror about 4″ diameter. Newspaper. Lightweight cardboard. All-purpose glue. Thin twine. Liquid gesso. Dark brown, green, and black tempera paints. Clear lacquer or varnish for final coating.

DIRECTIONS: Trace full size pattern. Cut newspaper into small strips. Thin glue slightly in a bowl with water. Dip strips into glue and apply to mirror frame and handle on front and back until it is well covered with overlapping layers of glued strips; let dry.

From cardboard, cut one complete owl shape (including tail); cut two separate wings (cut into wings along solid lines on pattern); cut one complete head, one separate crest, two eyes, and two feet. Glue pieces to mirror back in same order as given for cutting, overlapping head on wings slightly. Use twine for branch; glue twine below body and overlap it with feet; let dry thoroughly.

Coat mirror frame completely with gesso; let dry. Paint frame brown on front and back. Lighten brown paint with water and paint crest, wings, and branch. Paint line around outer eyes, feather marks on crest and chest, lines on feet, and eyelashes with brown paint. With pointed brush, dab brown paint all around edges of white area of head to make feathery appearance. Paint eye centers green, then make circle of black in center. Make tiny dot of gesso in top left corner of each eye for highlights. Let paint dry. Coat front and back with lacquer or varnish; let dry. ◊

Owl Pin

Shown on page 188

EQUIPMENT: Paper for pattern. Pencil. Ruler. Scissors. Small, pointed and flat paintbrushes. Heavy weight.

MATERIALS: Piece of cardboard, 4″ × 5″. Newspaper. All-purpose glue. Medium-weight string or cord. Gesso. Polymer paints and gloss medium. Pin back.

DIRECTIONS: Trace full size pattern; complete half-pattern indicated by dash lines. Cut newspaper into twelve 4″ × 5″ pieces. Mark outline of owl on one newspaper piece. Glue this piece to five more newspaper squares, using flat brush to spread glue between each piece of paper. Repeat procedure with six remaining newspaper pieces. Cut owl outline out of pieces while paper is still wet; save glued paper scraps. Mark outline of owl on piece of cardboard; cut out. Glue a glued-paper owl shape to each surface of cardboard shape. Apply a thin line of glue around edges of owl and press string or cord onto

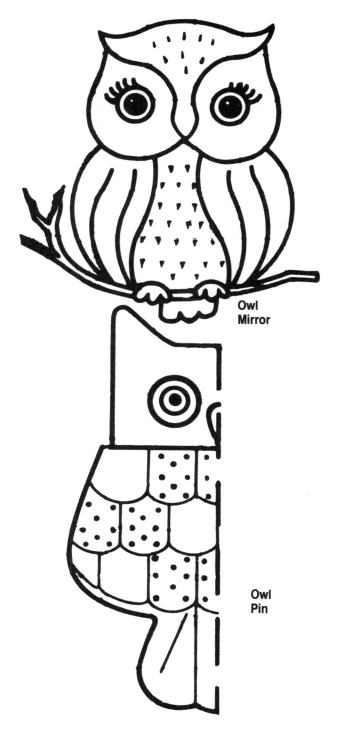

Owl Mirror

Owl Pin

glue line; hold until secure. From scraps of glued paper, cut out middle eye section (finer eye circle) and glue in place on owl. Place owl under heavy weight until dry. From remaining scraps of glued paper, cut strip $\frac{1}{2}″ \times 1\frac{1}{2}″$. Glue pin back to what will be back of owl; press strip with glue over back as if it were tape to secure.

Paint completely with gesso; let dry. Paint entire owl and cord one color. When dry, paint head and tail areas and lines (indicated on pattern by finer lines) in contrasting colors as desired. When dry, paint with gloss medium. ◊

Beaded Eyeglass Cases

Shown on page 189

EQUIPMENT: Scissors. Pencil. Tracing paper. Compass. Sewing needle. Beading needle. Ruler. Dressmaker's carbon. Embroidery hoop.

MATERIALS (For each): Linen fabric about 7" square. Iron-on interfacing, lightweight, 7" square. Lining fabric 7" square. Seed beads in colors given in individual directions. Thread to match beads and linen.

GENERAL DIRECTIONS: Mark two $3\frac{1}{4}'' \times 6\frac{3}{4}''$ rectangles on linen; do not cut out. Trace design and transfer to linen rectangle for front of case, using dressmaker's carbon. Place linen in embroidery hoop. The beading is done in the manner of couching. Thread needle with thread to match beads being used. Attach thread at a starting place of design. String about a $\frac{1}{2}''$ length of beads onto thread, pushing them close together. Holding threaded beads over line of design, insert needle through fabric to back at end of beads; keeping thread taut, bring needle up between first two beads of line. Take a small stitch over bead thread between first two beads and bring needle up between next two beads. Make a small couching stitch in this manner between all beads. String on more beads and work following individual directions.

When beading is complete, cut front and back from linen on marked outline. Cut two pieces of interfacing $3\frac{1}{4}'' \times 6\frac{3}{4}''$ and press one piece to back of each linen piece. With right sides of linen pieces facing, stitch around sides and bottom with $\frac{1}{4}''$ seams; for narrower case, make $\frac{3}{8}''$ seams; turn right side out. Turn in top edges $\frac{3}{8}''$. Cut two pieces of lining fabric $3\frac{1}{4}'' \times 6\frac{3}{8}''$. Stitch together as for case. Insert inside case; turn in $\frac{1}{2}''$ at top; slip-stitch lining to linen.

Ladybug

Use green linen for case. Transfer design, continuing looping ladybug flight to make five loops. Make flight line of turquoise beads; make ladybug red with four black beads on body, two for head.

Circles

With compass, mark three 1"-diameter circles on white linen. Mark a line dividing each circle in half as shown in photograph. Sew tan beads on one half and orange on other half of each. Work from center out in semicircular lines of touching beads.

Sunny Blossom

Use aqua linen; transfer design, completing flower; add another leaf near bottom of stem on other side. Starting at center of flower, work in circles of touch-

234

ing beads outward. Start with white for one round, then white and yellow, then two rounds of yellow, a round of yellow and orange, two rounds of orange, a round of orange and red, and two rounds of red. Make stem and leaves of medium-green beads.

Bouquet

Use blue linen; transfer design, completing other half. Make star flowers pink with yellow center; small flowers white with chartreuse center; bow with two streamers yellow; stems in chartreuse beads.

Cherries

Use medium blue linen; work leaves in medium-green beads, starting with outline. Following leaf shape, make two more rows of beads within, in same leaf. Make stems green. For cherries, start at center; work rounds of touching beads in red. ◊

Shell Show-offs

Shown on pages 190 and 191

EQUIPMENT: Tweezers. Scissors.
MATERIALS: Assorted seashells. All-purpose glue. *For Animals:* Items such as plastic eyes, seed beads, ink marker, sewing thread, pipe cleaners, wire, and ribbons for features and trims.
For Flowers: Florist's wire and green tape for stems. Absorbent cotton. Plastic calyxes (available at hobby shops that sell flower parts).
DIRECTIONS: The shape of the shells you have on hand may suggest any number of creatures or uses as in our illustrations. Shells such as olives, volutes, and tulips are especially good for bodies; augers make good tails; tiny clams are good for ears, beaks, and wings; snails are good for heads. Clamshells make good bases for creatures, and for ashtrays which are trimmed and footed with smaller shells. Glue shell pieces together, using tweezers to apply smaller shells.

Pipe cleaner pieces may be used for feet; wire for some tails; seed beads for eyes and noses; or mark eyes, noses, and mouths with ink.

For the carnation-like flowers, use small fluted shells called kitten's paws. For the stem, make a loop at the end of a length of florist's wire. Bend loop at right angle to stem. Glue a wad of cotton over loop. Glue the larger shells around cotton for bottom petals, with fluted side up for fully opened flowers, or fluted side down for partially closed flowers. Then glue overlapping rows of smaller shells around with fluted side down, using the smallest in the center, slanting the shells progressively until center cluster is erect. Slip plastic calyx on wire up to bottom of flower; then wrap base of calyx and stem with tape. ◊

GENERAL DIRECTIONS

Quilting

Making the Quilt Top

PATTERNS: In making a pieced (patchwork) or appliquéd quilt top, you will need a stiff pattern, also called a template, for each separate part of the design. Use thin but firm cardboard for your pattern, such as shirt lining. Some prefer heavy sandpaper, which does not slip on fabric. If the pattern is to be used many times, make duplicates and discard each as its edges become frayed from continued use. Or, cut your pattern from sheet plastic, preferably transparent. Whatever the material, make your stiff pattern with one of the following three methods, as directed for each project: 1) Trace actual-size pattern given; glue tracing to cardboard; let dry; then cut out. 2) If our pattern is given on squares, you must enlarge it to its actual size. Draw a grid on a sheet of paper with the same number of squares as in our grid, but making each square of your grid the size directed (usually 1″); the grid can be easily drawn on graph paper. Then copy design onto your grid, square by square. Glue to cardboard and cut on lines of design, ignoring the grid lines. An easier procedure is to have the design enlarged by photostat, if such a service is available in your area. 3) For very simple geometric shapes, such as squares, rectangles, and circles, you simply make the pattern yourself, following dimensions given.

It is essential that patch patterns be accurate. If the patterns are not perfect, neither will be the patches, and they may be impossible to piece together properly. To aid in making good patterns, you should have good tools, made of metal or plastic; a ruler with a perfect edge, a triangle, a T-square, and a compass. After you have made your patterns, test their accuracy before cutting any patches. If there is a Piecing Diagram, fit patterns together as shown or draw around them on paper. If piecing a large eight-pointed star with diamond patches, place (or draw) eight diamonds together with points meeting in center, to create a small eight-pointed star; there should be no gaps between or overlapping of the diamond segments. If making a design entirely from hexagons, make sure that six hexagons will fit neatly around the six sides of a center hexagon.

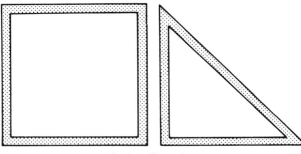

Window Templates

Window Templates: Our patterns are made the size of the finished patch piece, that is, what shows when the quilt top is assembled. The seam allowance is not included in the pattern, but is added when patches are cut. If you wish to cut your seam allowance with perfectly even edges, you may want to make a window template. Draw pattern shape as before, then draw another line around it exactly $\frac{1}{4}$″ away. Cut on both lines, leaving a frame. The window template is more difficult and time consuming to make, but it will make patches easier to cut. It is also advisable for using with certain prints, when placement of motifs is important.

PATCH PIECES: Use fabrics that are closely woven, so seams will hold and edges will not fray. The fabric should be fairly soft, but should not be so thin that seam allowances will show through. Before cutting patches, wash new fabrics to preshrink and remove sizing. Wash scraps in a net bag. Press all fabrics smooth. Lay fabric out flat, wrong side up for patch pieces. See How to Appliqué (refer to Contents) for how to cut appliqué pieces. Lay pattern on fabric, placing it so as many straight sides of pattern as possible are with the crosswise and lengthwise grain of fabric. If necessary, pull threads in both directions to determine grain. Using a sharp, hard pencil (light-colored for dark fabrics, dark-colored for light fabrics), draw around pattern; hold pencil at an outward angle, so that point is firmly against edge of pattern. Reposition pattern $\frac{1}{2}$″ away and draw around as before. Continue marking patterns $\frac{1}{2}$″ apart; do not cut fabric until all the patterns of one color are marked.

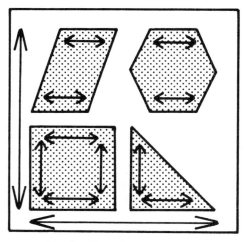

Placing Templates on Fabric

(Note: If large border pieces are to be cut later from the same fabric, be sure to consider their dimensions when marking smaller pieces; you may wish to mark your patches in vertical rows. Do not, however, cut out the border pieces before cutting patches).

When all patches of one color have been marked, cut out each patch, $\frac{1}{4}''$ away from marked line, which will be the stitching line. Cut the $\frac{1}{4}''$ seam allowance as accurately as you can, to make piecing easier. To keep patches of same shape and color together, put them in a pile and run a thread through center with a knot in one end; lift off each patch as needed.

PIECING: Several patch pieces will be joined to create a new unit, such as a larger patch or a block. Before sewing, lay out all pieces needed for the block. Begin by joining smallest pieces first, then joining the larger pieces made into rows, then joining rows for completed block.

By Hand: If duplicating one of the antique quilts in this book, you will find it easier to join the small patch pieces by hand. Hand piecing is also advised for patches with curves and sharp angles.

To join two patch pieces, place them together, right sides facing. If pieces are very small, hold firmly to sew. Larger pieces can be pin-basted, matching angles first, then marked lines between. Pin curved pieces together from center out to each corner. For piecing, use #7 to #10 sharp needle, threaded with an 18″ length of mercerized cotton or cotton-wrapped polyester thread. Begin with a small knot, then stitch along marked seam line with tiny running stitches, ending with a few backstitches; if seam is long, take a tiny backstitch every few stitches. Try to make 8 to 10 running stitches per inch, evenly spaced. If thread tends to knot or fray as you sew, run it over a cake of beeswax. If sewing two bias edges together, keep thread just taut enough to prevent fabric from stretching. As you join pieces, press seams to one side, unless otherwise indicated; open seams tend to weaken construction. Try to press seams all in the same direction, although darker fabrics should not fall under lighter ones, lest they show through.

As you piece and press, clip into seams of curves and other pieces where necessary, so they will lie flat. Clip away excess fabric, to avoid bunching. Be sure a seam is pressed flat before you cross it with another; take a small backstitch over the crossing.

Joining Diamonds: Diamonds may be pieced together in same manner as for other patches. When joining diamonds to form a row, stitch patches together along sides cut on straight of goods. Stitch from the wide-angled corner toward the pointed end. Trim seam at points as you piece. If piecing a star design, join the rows together to make a diamond-shaped section, matching corners carefully. When joining rows, you will be stitching along the bias edges; keep thread slightly taut.

However, it may prove difficult when piecing diamonds to keep angles sharp and seams precise. If so, prepare a paper liner for each diamond as follows: Cut a firm paper pattern from wrapping or shelf paper the exact size of cardboard pattern. Fit paper liner within pencil outline on wrong side of patch. Hold patch with liner uppermost. Fold seam allowance over each side, and tack to the paper with one stitch on each side, allowing the thread to cross corners; finish by taking an extra stitch on the first side. Cut thread, leaving about $\frac{1}{4}''$. To make removal of tacking easier, do not knot thread or make any backstitches. Press lightly. Hold prepared patches right sides together, matching the edges to be seamed exactly. Whip together with fine, even stitches (about 16 to the inch), avoiding the paper as much as possible. The liners may remain in place until the quilt top is completed. To remove liners, snip tacking thread once on each patch and withdraw thread.

Joining Hexagons: You may find it easier to join hexagons by using a paper liner, as for diamonds. Join hexagons in circular fashion, starting with six hexagons around a center patch. Whipstitch edges together as for diamonds, back-stitching where corners meet.

By Machine: Quilts of newer design are more apt to be made with larger patches and you might wish to piece them by machine. Set machine for 10 stitches to the inch, unless working with very heavy fabrics, and use needle #14. Use mercerized cotton thread #50 or cotton-wrapped polyester. Follow the same procedures as for hand piecing: Pin-baste, stitch, clip seams, and press. You need not, however, begin and end your thread with each patch; let thread run on for a continuous chain of patches. Patches will be snipped apart and their seams anchored by cross-seams.

ASSEMBLING QUILT TOP: As you construct your quilt top, building from patches to blocks to rows of blocks to borders, etc., it is important to measure each unit as you make it. Blocks to be joined should be of equal size. It is also important to compare your measurements with those given in the directions and make any necessary adjustments in the size of following pieces. Our measurements are strictly mathematical and do not allow for the variance that may easily result from multiple piecing. For example: We may have calculated that the pieced center of a quilt top should measure 79½" on the sides and we instruct you to cut side border pieces 79½" long. If your piece measures 80", naturally you will want to cut border pieces 80" long. You may need to adjust size of lining and edging strips as well. That is why we do not recommend cutting the larger pieces of a quilt top before the smaller units are assembled.

A Mitered Corner

To Miter Border Corners: Sew border pieces to quilt top, with an equal amount extending at each end, for the corners of quilt. Lay quilt top flat, right side down. Hold adjacent ends of border pieces together at corners with right sides facing. Keeping border flat, lift up inner corners and pin strips together diagonally from inner corners to outer corners; baste, then stitch on basting line. Cut off excess fabric to make ¼" seam; press seam open.

Preparing to Quilt

LINING AND BATTING: Cut or piece lining and batting as directed. If they are to be same size as the quilt top, you may want to make them a little larger to start with, such as 1" all around, and trim after basting or quilting. For comfortable hand quilting, the lining fabric should be soft; sheets, for example, are too densely woven for the needle to pass through easily.

In planning the batting, consider the style of the quilt and its intended use. Antique quilts with their close, ornate quilting designs usually were made with only a very thin filler. If you wish to duplicate the effect, use a split layer of polyester batting. The thinner the layer of batting, the easier and finer the quilting will be. For simpler quilting designs, or where more loft or warmth is desirable, use one or two full layers of polyester batting. Polyester is generally preferable to cotton batting, as it holds together, does not lump, and will dry quickly if the quilt is washed. If using cotton batting, be sure your lines of quilting are no more than 2" apart.

BASTING: After quilting design has been marked on the quilt top, assemble top, batting, and lining: Place lining, wrong side up, on large, flat surface. Place batting on top of lining and smooth out any bumps or wrinkles. Before adding quilt top, baste batting to lining by taking two long stitches in a cross. Place quilt top on batting, right side up. Pin all layers together to hold temporarily, using large

safety pins. Baste generously through all thicknesses, using a sturdy thread and a large needle. To prevent shifting, first baste on the lengthwise and crosswise grain of fabric. Then baste diagonally across in two directions and around sides, top, and bottom. If quilting is to be done with a quilting hoop or on the machine, extra care must be taken to keep basting stitches close, so they will hold in place as you work.

Quilting

BY HAND: When quilting by hand, the quilt may be stretched on a frame or in a quilting hoop. If the quilting design is especially ornate, it is best to use the frame; the hoop, on the other hand, is portable and more easily managed. If using neither hoop nor frame, you can quilt in your lap, working over a small area at a time.

Quilting Frame: Sew top and bottom edges of lining to the fabric strips attached to the long parallel bars of frame. Using strong thread so that quilt will not pull away from frame when stretched taut, sew securely with several rows of stitches. After quilt is secured in frame, start quilting midway between the long parallel bars of frame and sew toward you.

Quilting Hoop: Pull quilt taut in hoop and move any extra fullness toward the edges. Start quilting in the center and work toward edges. If necessary, cut basting thread as work progresses. As your quilting comes close to the edge, substitute smaller embroidery hoops for the larger quilting hoop, so that fabric will always remain taut.

Needle and Thread: Use a short, strong needle, between #7 and #10; experienced quilters may prefer a longer needle. If you can find it, use quilting thread, which has a silicone coating. If you can't, choose a strong (#50 to #30) cotton mercerized or a cotton-covered polyester thread. If thread knots, frays, or breaks as you quilt, try running each strand across a cake of beeswax.

Quilting Stitch: Cut 18" strand of thread. Knot one end. Bring needle up from lining through quilt top; give a little tug to thread so that knot passes through lining only and lies buried in batting. Sew on marked line with running stitch, in two separate motions:

Quilting Stitch

Push needle straight down through the three layers with one hand, take needle with other hand, pull thread through and push up close to the first stitch. An experienced quilter may be able to take two or three stitches before pulling needle through, holding quilt down at quilting line with thumb of other hand; do not try this method unless using a frame. Depending on thickness of fabric and batting, make stitches as small and close as you can (5 to 10 per inch); the longer the stitch, the less durable the quilting. Space stitches evenly, so they are the same length on both sides of quilt. From time to time, look underneath to check your stitches. To end off, backstitch and take a long stitch through the top and batting only; take another backstitch and clip thread at surface; the thread end will sink into batting. If you are a beginner, practice first on a small piece in an embroidery hoop, to find the easiest and best working method for you.

Start in the middle of the quilt and stitch toward you; shift your position as you work, so that the quilting progresses fairly evenly on all sides toward the outside of the quilt.

BY MACHINE: Quilting can be done on the machine, with or without a quilting foot. When working on a machine, the best quilting patterns to use are those sewn on the diagonal or on the bias. Fabric gives a little when on the bias, making it easier to keep work flat.

As a rule, machine quilting is done with a straight stitch. Set stitch length from 6 to 12 per inch. Adjust pressure so that it is slightly heavier than for medium-weight fabrics, with the bobbin thread a little loose. If you are using a scroll or floral design, it is best to use the short open toe of the quilting foot. This allows you to follow the curved lines with ease and accuracy.

To begin, roll up half of quilt and place to right of needle. Begin stitching in center of quilt and work to the right, unrolling quilt as you go. Repeat for remaining half. ◇

Macrame

EQUIPMENT: T-pins. Scissors. Working surface such as a homosote or wooden board, a foam rubber slab or foam pillow form (the size will depend upon the size of the project; see individual directions). Rubber bands. Tape measure.

MATERIALS: Cord or yarn as indicated in individual directions.

Note: Practice making the knots on a sample first to become familiar with the technique. The working surface may be placed on a table, set upright, or held in the lap. Some pieces may be easier to work on if suspended from a hook.

Preparing and Mounting Cords

A mounting cord to start the macrame piece is pinned horizontally across working surface. To do this, cut a length of the cord being used, about 6″ longer than the width of planned macrame piece. Knot both ends with an overhand knot (Fig. 4) and pin knots to working surface to hold cord taut; place pins along length of cord if necessary. For some projects the ends of the mounting cord are to be used as working cords; in such a case, cut the cord as long as the other working cords. The working cords are tied onto the mounting cord, and the macrame knots are tied with these cords to form the design.

To figure the length to cut required working cords, allow about 4 times the length of the finished macrame piece for each cord (if mounting cord singly). If cords are to be folded in half, the length of each cord should be about 8 times the length of the finished piece. The simpler the knots and the finer the cord, the less cord you will need; the more intricate the design and the heavier the cord, the more cord you will need.

Fold each cord in half and tie doubled cord on mounting cord as shown in Fig. 1A (Lark's Head Knot) or Fig. 1B (reverse Lark's Head Knot). Hold doubled cord in front of mounting cord, fold over to back and pull ends through loop, tightening knot. Mount required working cords close together.

To make working with long cords easier, wind each cord up, leaving about 15″ free below work; fasten each cord with a rubber band. As work progresses, unfasten rubber band and release more cord.

Knots

Most macrame designs are formed using two knots—the half hitch and the square knot—in various ways.

Square Knot: This knot is usually made with four cords. Keeping the two center cords straight, tie knot with the two outer cords as shown in Figs. 2A-2D. Always hold center cords taut and tighten knot

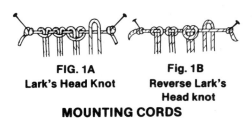

FIG. 1A
Lark's Head Knot

Fig. 1B
**Reverse Lark's
Head knot**

MOUNTING CORDS

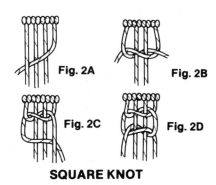

Fig. 2A

Fig. 2B

Fig. 2C

Fig. 2D

SQUARE KNOT

by pulling the two outer cords up into place. Some square knots are made with two outer cords tied over one center cord. Gathering square knots can be made with as many as 24 cords in the center. A simple square knot may also be made with just two strands, eliminating the center strands.

Alternate Rows of Square Knots: Make first row of square knots, using four cords for each. For second row, leave two cords at each side free and redivide

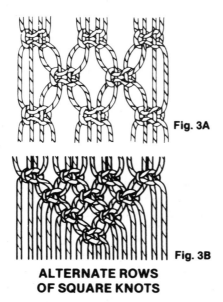

Fig. 3A

Fig. 3B

ALTERNATE ROWS OF SQUARE KNOTS

cords into groups of four, using two cords from adjacent knots of first row. Tie square knots across row, spacing row evenly across below and between knots of the first row. For third row, use all cords and make the same as first row (Fig. 3A). To form a pointed shape, work first two rows as above. Continue making each row narrower than last in same manner (Fig. 3B). Rows may be increased by adding two more cords on each side.

Sennits: Long lines called sennits can be made by repeating the first half of the square knot on four cords, which will twist the line as it grows. By repeating the complete square knot on four cords, you will get a flat sennit. Sennits can also be made with half hitch knots.

Overhand Knot: A small knot is sometimes used to bring cords together (Fig. 4). Mounting cord, if not used as working cord, is also knotted at both ends with an overhand knot.

Fig. 4

OVERHAND KNOT

Half Hitch Bars: The half hitch is used to make bars as in Figs. 5A-7C and for mounting cords with a picot edge. Bars are made over an end working cord, called a knot bearer. Always keep the knot

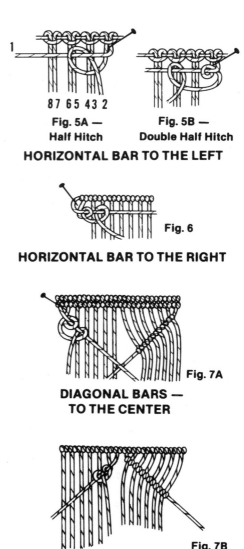

**Fig. 5A —
Half Hitch**

**Fig. 5B —
Double Half Hitch**

HORIZONTAL BAR TO THE LEFT

Fig. 6

HORIZONTAL BAR TO THE RIGHT

Fig. 7A

DIAGONAL BARS — TO THE CENTER

Fig. 7B

DIAGONAL BARS TO THE OUTSIDE

Fig. 7C

DOUBLE DIAGONAL BARS

bearer taut, and form the knot with another working cord over the knot bearer. Use pins to hold knot bearer in place whenever necessary (see Fig. 5A). With each working strand, make a half hitch as shown in Fig. 5A, then repeat, making a double half hitch as shown in Fig. 5B. Work bars from right to left or from left to right (Fig. 6). Fig. 6 shows a double bar being made. Work second bar close to first.

Diagonal Bars: These are made in same manner as horizontal bars with double half hitches, but the knot bearer is held diagonally downward to either right or left (Fig. 7A and Fig. 7B). For double diagonal bars, use end cords as knot bearers. Work double half hitches over outside cord for each bar, making second bar directly below first diagonal bar.

Instead of always using the outside cord as knot bearer when making double diagonal bars, work as in Fig. 7C. For first bar, use second cord as knot bearer working to right; then use first cord as knot bearer for second bar. Going to the left, use seventh cord as first knot bearer and outside eighth cord as knot bearer for second bar.

Vertical Double Half Hitch: Use one working cord, held vertically, as knot bearer. Work double half hitches over vertical knot bearer as shown in Fig. 8. Knot is made the same as for horizontal bar.

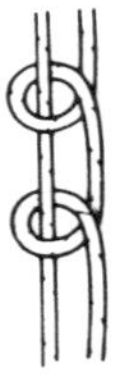

VERTICAL DOUBLE HALF HITCH

Fig. 8

REVERSED DOUBLE HALF HITCH

Fig. 9

Reversed Double Half Hitch: Make first half hitch by bringing working cord under knot bearer, around and over knot bearer, then under itself, Fig. 9. Make second half hitch by bringing working cord around and over knot bearer, then over itself.

Alternate Half Hitches: Work first double half hitch as for Fig. 8. Then, using second cord as knot bearer, make another double half hitch with first cord, Fig. 10. Four cords may also be used, Fig. 11. Work a

double half hitch first with fourth cord over two center cords, then with first cord, again over the two center cords.

Finishing Edges: Ends may be finished off by making a bar at end of macrame. Turn work over and pull each strand through back of bar, using crochet hook. Cut off strands, leaving about 1″ ends; tack ends to back to secure.

To finish edge with picots, after making bar, turn work over. Starting from left, draw first strand end through back of second knot; pull down tightly. Draw second strand through back of first knot; pull down to lie loosely over first strand, thus making a picot. Repeat with each pair of strands.

To make tassels or fringe, gather a number of strands together and tie together with an overhead knot close to bottom.

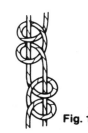

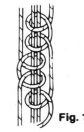

Fig. 10

Fig. 11

ALTERNATE HALF HITCHES 2-STRANDS

ALTERNATE HALF HITCHES 4-STRANDS

Terms Used in Macrame

A variety of different terms are used to describe macrame knots. Below is a list of terms used in this section, followed by some of the synonyms (in parentheses) found in other books on macrame.

Square Knot (flat knot, reef knot, Solomon's knot)
Half of a Square Knot (half knot, spiral or waved knot, macrame knot)
Half Hitch (simple knot, tatting knot, buttonhole loop, blanket stitch)
Double Half Hitch (double knot, clove hitch)
Overhand Knot (bead knot, thumb knot, simple knot, shell knot)
Mounting Knot and Reversed Double Half Hitch (lark's head)
Bars (cording)
Sennit (braid, chain, sinnet)
Mounting Cord (foundation cord, knot bearer, holding line, holding cord)
Knot Bearer (carrier strand, filler cord, leader)
Working Cord (knotting cord, warp)

How to Appliqué

Choose a fabric that is closely woven and firm enough so a clean edge results when the pieces are cut. Cut a pattern piece for each shape out of thin, stiff cardboard, and mark the right side of each piece. Press fabric smooth. Place cardboard pattern, wrong side up, on wrong side of fabric. Using sharp, hard pencils (light-colored pencil on dark fabric and dark pencil on light fabric), mark the outline on the fabric. When marking several pieces on the same fabric, leave at least ½″ between pieces. Mark a second outline ¼″ outside the design outline. Using matching

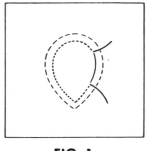

FIG. 1

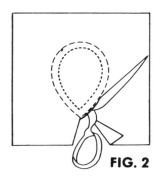

FIG. 2

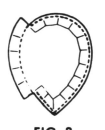

FIG. 3

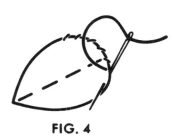

FIG. 4

thread and small stitches, machine-stitch all around design outline, as shown in Fig. 1. This makes edge easier to turn and neater in appearance. Cut out the appliqué on the outside line, as in Fig. 2. For a smooth edge, clip into seam allowance at curved edges and corners. Then turn seam allowance to back, just inside stitching as shown in Fig. 3, and press. Pin and baste the appliqué on the background, and slip-stitch in place with tiny stitches, as shown in Fig. 4. ◊

Basic How-To's

To Enlarge and Reduce Designs

There are various ways of enlarging or reducing designs so that all parts remain in proportion. The most commonly used are the "square" method, No. 1, and the diagonal method, No. 2. (Designs can also be enlarged or reduced by photostat, wherever such services are available.)

Method 1: If design is not already marked off in squares, make a tracing of original design. Mark off tracing with squares, $\frac{1}{8}''$ for small designs and $\frac{1}{4}''$, $\frac{1}{2}''$, or $1''$ for proportionately larger designs. On paper, mark the same number of squares, similarly placed, in the space to be occupied by the enlarged design. For instance, if you want to make the original design twice as high and twice as wide, make the squares twice as large. Copy design from smaller squares. Reverse procedure for reducing design to size needed.

Method 2: Make a tracing of original design. Draw a rectangle to fit around it. Draw a second rectangle of same proportions to fit desired size of design. Draw diagonals from corner to corner of each rectangle, as illustrated. In each rectangle, the point where diagonals meet is the center. Draw horizontal and vertical lines to divide each rectangle equally. Copy design from smaller divisions in corresponding larger divisions. Reverse procedure to reduce design. ◊

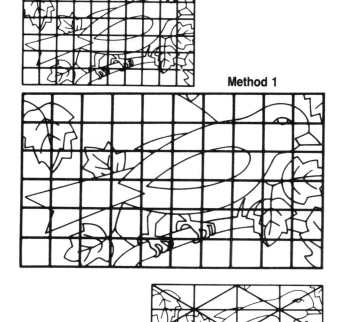

Method 1

Method 2

To Make a Pompon

Cut two cardboard disks desired size of pompon; cut out ¼" hole in center of both. Thread needle with two strands of yarn. Place disks together; cover with yarn, working through holes. Slip scissors between disks; cut all strands at outside edge. Draw strand of yarn down between disks and wind several times very tightly around yarn; knot, leaving ends for attaching pompon. Remove cardboard disks and fluff out pompon. ◇

To Make a Tassel

Wind yarn around cardboard cut to size of tassel desired, winding it 20 or more times around, depending on thickness of yarn and plumpness of tassel required. Tie strands tightly together around top as shown, leaving at least 3" ends on ties; clip other ends of strands. Wrap piece of yarn tightly around strands a few times, about ½" or 1" below top; then tie and knot. Trim the ends of the tassel. ◇

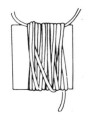 

TASSEL

To Make a Twisted Cord

Method requires two people. Tie one end of yarn around pencil. Loop yarn over center of second pencil, back to and around first, and back to second, making as many strands between pencils as needed for thickness of cord; knot end to pencil. Length of yarn between pencils should be three times length of cord desired. Each person holds yarn just below pencil with one hand and twists pencil with other hand, keeping yarn taut. When yarn begins to kink, catch center over doorknob or back of chair. Bring pencils together for one person to hold, while other grasps center of yarn, sliding hand down and releasing at short intervals, letting yarn twist to form cord. ◇

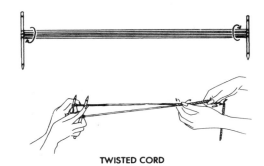

TWISTED CORD

STITCH DETAILS

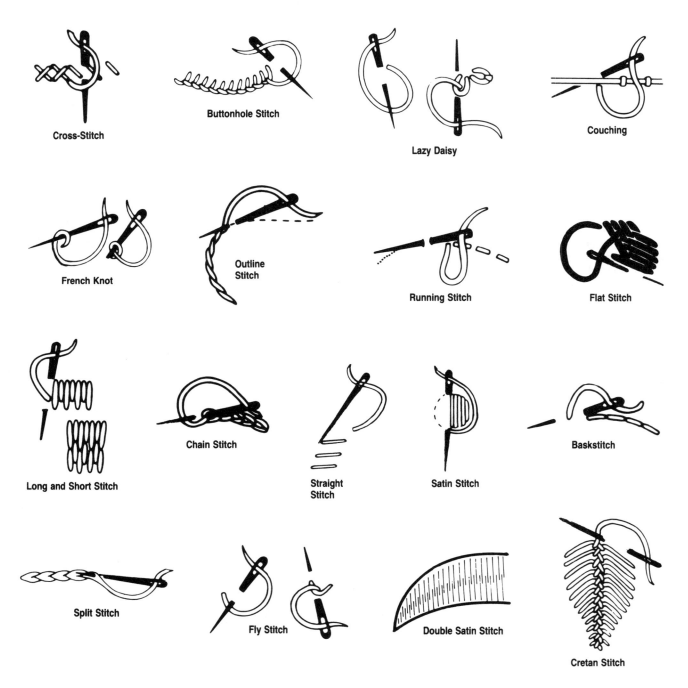

Cross-Stitch

Buttonhole Stitch

Lazy Daisy

Couching

French Knot

Outline Stitch

Running Stitch

Flat Stitch

Long and Short Stitch

Chain Stitch

Straight Stitch

Satin Stitch

Baskstitch

Split Stitch

Fly Stitch

Double Satin Stitch

Cretan Stitch

MACHINE EMBROIDERY

If you own a sewing machine, you can create beautiful embroideries in a fraction of the time it would take you by hand. The secret is in learning a special "free motion" technique, in which you move the fabric in any direction as the machine stitches. You needn't be a skilled seamstress or an expert at traditional embroidery to learn this exciting needle craft. All you need is a sewing machine in good running order, preferably one with the zigzag stitch built into most modern machines.

But whatever type of machine you have, explore its potential for "drawing" and "painting" with thread, while learning the few basics listed here. Then practice! In a short while, you will be ready for your first project.

MATERIALS TO USE

A firm, closely woven fabric will work best. Natural fabrics such as cotton will pucker less than synthetics, and if puckers do occur they are more easily ironed out. If working with a knit fabric or one that is too soft, reinforce it with a second layer, fusing Pellon® or basting organdy or strong tissue paper behind it.

Special cotton threads for machine embroidery are available in a wide range of colors. (Polyester is not recommended.) Thread size #50 will be suitable for most projects, although you might prefer size #30 for heavier fabrics. Experiment with various other threads, such as rayon imports; threads with a silky gloss will generally give the most attractive results.

TRANSFERRING DESIGNS TO FABRIC

If the pattern for your chosen design is shown actual size, just trace. If pattern is shown on squares, you must enlarge it to its actual size. Draw a grid on a sheet of paper with the same number of squares as our grid, but make each square of your grid the size directed (usually 1"). The grid can be easily drawn on graph paper. Then copy design onto your grid, square by square. (An easier procedure is to have the design enlarged by photostat, if such a service is available in your area.) Trace enlarged pattern or photostat. Transfer traced pattern to the fabric, using one of the following methods:

Carbon Paper: Place pattern on right side of fabric, with a piece of non-smudging dressmaker's carbon between. Carefully go over lines of design with a dry ball-point pen or a tracing wheel.

Colored Pencil: If embroidering on sheer fabric, lay fabric right side up over pattern; tape in place. Trace pattern through the fabric, using a sharp, waterproof pencil in a color to blend with thread or fabric. Do not use lead pencil, which may smear.

Transfer Pencil: Go over lines of tracing on wrong side with a sharp hot-iron transfer pencil. Tape pattern wrong side down onto right side of fabric. Follow manufacturer's directions for transferring with a hot iron.

Stitch Outlining: Pin traced design to right side of fabric, design side up. Stitch around outlines of design, either by hand, using small running stitch, or by machine with the free-motion technique (see below). Use thread in a color to blend with either fabric or embroidery. When outlining is completed, tear away paper, leaving stitches.

PREPARING MACHINE FOR FREE-MOTION EMBROIDERY

1. Consult your machine manual for any specific instructions.
2. Be sure your machine is in good running condition and is clean and well-oiled.
3. Remove presser foot. For some purposes, you may want to replace it with a darning spring or embroidery foot (for especially thick or heavy fabrics) or a buttonhole foot (for built-up satin-stitch lines).
4. Lower feed dogs (or cover feed dogs with a plate or raise throat, depending on machine).
5. Use a fine needle, usually size #11 or #70.
6. Thread machine, using desired color in needle and white or any color in bobbin, unless otherwise directed.
7. Loosen tension of needle thread slightly so that thread and fabric will not pucker. Tension of bobbin thread will probably not need adjusting. Before you begin your design, practice with the fabric and thread you will be using to find correct

tension. Top thread should lie firmly but not tightly on the fabric. If tension is too tight, thread may break; if too loose, thread will loop and snarl.

8. Set stitch-width dial as directed; set stitch-length dial at 0.

9. Secure fabric in 8″ or 9″ embroidery hoop, with adjustable side screw: Place outer ring flat; place fabric over it, design side up; set inner ring inside to form a well. (For hand embroidery, the rings are placed in the opposite position.) Tighten hoop; fabric must be held taut while you stitch to avoid puckering. If necessary, wrap small ring with twill tape to hold fabric. Push inner ring a bit lower than outer ring, so that fabric will glide smoothly over bed of machine. If marked design is very close to edge of fabric, you may need to baste on an extra piece temporarily, to hold fabric in hoop.

10. Tilt hoop and slide under needle, design side up.

11. Lower presser bar, to engage tension of needle thread.

STITCHING

To begin, hold top thread and turn wheel by hand until bobbin thread appears on right side of fabric. Hold both thread ends until a few stitches have been taken, then clip. As machine stitches over marked design, move hoop toward or away from your body, to the right or left in any direction desired, depending on design effect you wish to create. Keep the movement slow and even; a too rapid or jerky movement could cause thread to break. To end a thread, turn stitch-width dial to 0 with needle in up position, then sew three stitches in place; clip thread.

The free-motion technique can be used for a wide variety of effects, duplicating many hand-embroidery stitches. Use either straight stitch or zigzag stitch, both to make lines and to fill in solid areas.

Lines: For very thin lines, use straight stitch. Set stitch-width dial at 0 (neutral). Lower needle into fabric. Start stitching along lines of design, moving hoop slowly and evenly in any direction required (Fig. 1). For a stronger or more textured effect, stitch back over lines two or three times (Fig. 2).

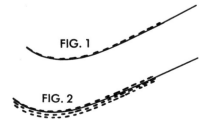

FIG. 1

FIG. 2

For heavier lines, use a wide or narrow zigzag stitch. To make a satin-stitch line, set stitch width at narrow (1 or 2). Move hoop very slowly as needle swings from side to side across the line, piling up stitches evenly and closely (Fig. 3). For contoured lines, do not rotate hoop as you go around a curve, but simply slide it sideways; the result will be a thick-and-thin curving line (Fig. 4).

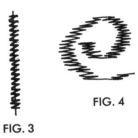

FIG. 4

FIG. 3

To make a line of outline stitching (also called side stitch in machine embroidery), set dial at any width, though wide (4-5) is most often used. Move hoop so that needle swings in a jogging pattern along, not across, line (Fig. 5). Move hoop a little faster than you would for satin stitch.

FIG. 5

Solid Areas: Solid-color shapes are usually filled with wide zigzag stitching. The stitch is the same as the outline stitch described above, though when used in this manner it resembles long and short stitch. Set the dial at 4-5 for large areas, narrowing it for smaller areas. Let the needle move freely in any direction desired; do not stitch in straight, even rows. For a naturalistic effect, you will want the stitching to follow the contour of the form you are making. To stitch a leaf, for example, turn the design so that you are stitching from base to tip. As you stitch, rotate the hoop slightly so that you are also curving outward from center of leaf toward its edges (Fig. 6). If shading a form with two or more colors, overlap edges of color areas in random fashion to blend. As you change colors, clip threads close.

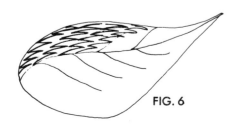

FIG. 6